CLASSIC
SERMON
OUTLINES

CLASSIC
SERMON
OUTLINES

*Over 100 sermon outlines
by three of the best known
preachers of all time*

Matthew Henry
George Whitefield
Alexander Maclaren

HENDRICKSON PUBLISHERS

Alexander Maclaren

CLASSIC
SERMON
OUTLINES

Over 100 sermon outlines
by three of the best known
preachers of all time

Matthew Henry
George Whitefield
Alexander Maclaren

HENDRICKSON PUBLISHERS

Classic Sermon Outlines

Copyright © 2001 by Hendrickson Publishers, Inc.
Published by Hendrickson Publishers, Inc.
P.O. Box 3473
Peabody, Massachusetts, 01961-3473

Maclaren's Sermon Outlines, first published in 1954 by Wm. B. Eerdmans
Publishing Co.
Matthew Henry's Sermon Outlines, first published in 1955 by Wm. B. Eerd-
mans Publishing Co.
Whitefield's Sermon Outlines, first published in 1956 by Wm. B. Eerdmans
Publishing Co.
Updated by Hendrickson Publishers in 2001.

Hendrickson Publishers' edition reprinted by arrangement with Wm. B.
Eerdmans Publishing Company.

Printed in the United States of America

ISBN 1-56563-654-6

Second printing — November 2002

Cover design by Richmond & Williams, Nashville, Tennessee
Interior design and typesetting by Darren Hurlburt, Communication Ink
Edited by Sharon Neal, Deneen Sedlack, and Shannon Goode

CONTENTS

Matthew Henry

Alexander Maclaren

Contents

George Whitefield

Matthew Henry

SERMON OUTLINES

Selected and Edited by
SHELDON B. QUINCER, D. D.

Matthew Henry

FOREWORD

Some of the greatest preachers the world has ever known were the godly ministers of the Word of past generations. Among these was Matthew Henry. While he has been known and loved for two centuries for his devotional commentary on the whole Bible, it has not been so generally known that he was a distinguished preacher.

He was born in Wales in 1662 and began his preaching ministry at the age of twenty-four. About two years later he was ordained and entered the active pastorate, serving the Chester Presbyterian Church. He served this congregation for twenty-five years. From Chester he accepted a call to London where he ended his active pastoral duties in 1714 when called to higher service in the heavenly kingdom.

The greatness of Matthew Henry's sermons consists in their Scriptural content, lucid presentation, practical application, and Christ-centeredness. Someone has described him: "Like the apostle Paul, whom he admired more than all mere mortals and whom he has signalized as 'the most active, zealous servant that ever our Master had,' he daily studied to know nothing 'save Jesus Christ and Him crucified.'"

These sermon outlines have been taken and edited from *The Miscellaneous Works of the Reverend Matthew Henry* (2 volumes) and from his devotional commentary, *An Exposition of the Old and New Testaments* (5 volumes).

Sheldon B. Quincer
Grand Rapids, Michigan, 1955

A MEMORIAL TO THE FIRE OF THE LORD

> *And he called the name of the place Taberah,*
> *because the fire of the Lord burnt among them.*
> —NUMBERS 11:3

WE HAVE here an account of the prudent and pious care which Moses took to preserve the memorial of a fire which happened in the camp of Israel by giving a new name of suitable signification to the place where it happened, which being left upon record here in the book of God is a monument of the fire further visible and more desirable than their pillar of stone; for wherever the books of Moses are read, there shall this be told for a memorial.

I. THE JUDGMENT OF GOD UPON ISRAEL.

A. *The Nature of the Judgment.*

It is called the fire of the Lord because it fell from heaven; it came immediately from the hand of God. Here it consumed the sinners to signify that their iniquity was such as should not be purged with sacrifice or offering forever, as another time it consumed the sacrificers when they offered strange fires.

B. The People of the Judgment.

The fire of the Lord burned among the people whom God favored, but they displeased Him when they sinned and His anger was kindled against them. Though the pillar of cloud and fire was over them to protect them while they kept themselves in the love of God, that should be no security to them when they rebelled against Him.

C. The Cause of the Judgment.

The people complained and it was that which provoked God to kindle His fire among them. Those who are always complaining about trifles must expect to have something given to them to complain about. Nothing is more displeasing to God than our being displeased at His method of settling matters.

II. THE MEMORIAL OF THE JUDGMENT OF GOD UPON ISRAEL.

A. The Purpose of the Memorial in Relation to Israel.

The fire of the Lord must not be forgotten; he therefore calls the place Taberah—a burning. And if posterity ask, "What burning?" it will be answered, "The burning of a part of the camp of the Israelites with the fire of the Lord for their discontent and murmuring."

B. The Purpose of the Memorial in Relation to Us.

By recording these things in His sacred writings God has more effectually preserved the memorial of them and transmitted it to us.

1. Personal rebukes. We must often call to mind the personal and private rebukes of Providence which we and our families have been under. We should remember what God has spoken not only by His Word, but also by His rod. We should remember them in order to renew our repentance for the sins that produced them.

2. Public judgments. We must call to mind public judgments upon the communities of which we are members; upon the land and nation and God's controversies with them; and upon the city and His voice that has cried to it. For as in the peace thereof we have peace, so in the trouble thereof we have trouble and must feel it.

III. THE LESSONS FROM THE JUDGMENT OF GOD UPON ISRAEL.

A. God Is Terrible in His Judgments.

See how terrible God is in His judgments and fear before Him. If the glory of His greatness be like fire to a people who are entering into covenant with Him, much more will the terror of His wrath be so to a people who have broken covenant with Him.

B. Sin Is a Mischievous Thing.

Sin provokes God to be our enemy and to fight against us. He never contends with a people, but it is sin that is the cause of the controversy. National sins bring national judgments. The sins of a city bring misery upon it. It was the wickedness of Sodom that made it combustible matter for the fire of God's wrath.

C. This World Is an Uncertain Thing.

This is seen in Job whom the rising sun found the richest of men and the setting sun left poor to a proverb. Our Savior speaks of the danger we are in of losing our treasures upon earth by the moth that corrupts or thieves that break through and steal (Matthew 6:19).

D. God Remembers Mercy in the Midst of Wrath.

When the fire of the Lord burned in the camp of Israel, Moses prayed and then the fire was quenched. The prophet Amos tells us that when in his time the Lord called to contend by fire he prayed, "O Lord God, cease I beseech Thee," and "the Lord repented for this: this shall not be, saith the Lord God" (Amos 7:4–6).

E. Man Is Dependent upon God for Safety.

"Except the Lord keep the city, the watchman waketh but in vain." It is therefore your great concern to make Him your friend and to keep yourselves in His love; to secure the favor of the Ruler of rulers from whom every man's judgment proceeds. He has put you into an easy way of doing this, not by costly sacrifices and offerings, but by faithful and earnest prayer, kept up in its life and not sunk into a formality.

F. The Great Day of the Lord Will Be a Dreadful Day.

See what a dreadful day the great day of the Lord will be when the world shall be on fire and the earth and all the works that are therein shall be burnt up. When the heavens being on fire shall be dissolved and the elements shall melt with fervent heat and all these things shall be dissolved (II Peter 3:11–12).

CONCLUSION

There is a fire yet more dreadful. The earth and the works that are therein will soon be burned up; but there is a lake of fire which burns eternally and shall never be quenched into which all the wicked and ungodly shall be cast by the irreversible sentence of the righteous Judge and in which they shall be tormented without end. Flee from wrath to come by fleeing from sin to Christ that you come not to the place of torment.

Matthew Henry

A TWOFOLD PRAYER

O let the wickedness of the wicked come to an end;
but establish the just.
—PSALM 7:9

WE ARE here taught to pray against all sin. And in praying against sin we pray for the sinners; for whatever works against the disease, works for the patient. We are also taught to pray for all saints. Let not those who are filthy be filthy still, but let those who are holy be holy still. Let the good be kept so and made better.

I. THE CONTENT OF THE PRAYER.

A. The Petition That God Will Bring the Wickedness of the Wicked to an End.

We must pray that God will bring our own wickedness and the wickedness of other people to an end.

1. Abandonment of wicked principles. It must be our heart's desire and prayer that wicked principles may be exploded and abandoned and that men may be set right in their judgments concerning good and evil, right and wrong, God and themselves, this world and the other.

2. Conversion of the wicked. Let us be humbly earnest with God in prayer that the eyes of the spiritually blind may be opened; and the ears of the deaf unstopped; that wandering sheep may be sought and saved and prodigal sons brought to themselves and then to the Father's house; that

God will translate those into the kingdom of His dear Son who have been long subjects in the kingdom of darkness.

3. Prevention and restraining of wicked practices. We must desire and pray that wicked practices may be prevented and restrained; that if the stream be not turned, yet it may be checked and may not become an over-flowing deluge. We should desire and pray that thus far, at least, the wickedness of the wicked come to an end, that it may not be committed openly and that the infection may not spread.

B. The Petition That God Will Establish the Just.

1. In integrity. Let us pray that the just may be established in their good principles and good resolutions and may faithfully adhere to them; that those who have clean hands may be stronger and stronger; though the stream be strong, that the righteous may never be carried down by it; that like Job in difficult and trying times they may hold forth their integrity.

2. In comfort and hope. In troublesome times good men are apt to be shaken in mind and to fear lest the cause and interest of Christianity should be sunk and run down. They are ready to give up all for gone. Therefore, we have need to pray for them that they may be established in the belief of the promise that the gates of hell shall never prevail against the church.

3. In the saints' undertaking to bring wickedness to an end. Pray that they may be established in their undertaking to do what they can to bring the wickedness of the wicked to an end. We ought to pray for civil rulers; for all ministers of the Word of God; for all who in their places are strong against sin that they may be established in their resolution not to draw back their hand from the battle against sin.

II. THE REASON FOR THE PRAYER.

A. A Holy Concern for the Honor of God.

All good people have a holy concern for the name and honor of God and the Lord Jesus and for the reputation of Christianity. Therefore, they cannot but desire the end of that which dishonors God. All the children of God having His glory as their highest end have it upon their hearts as their chief care, and it is dearer to them than any interests of their own.

1. It is the saints' highest end.

2. It is the saints' chief care.

B. A Tender Love for the Souls of Men.

The children of God have a tender love for the souls of men and a true desire of their welfare here and hereafter; and therefore they cannot but desire and pray for the ending of that which ruins souls.

1. The value of a soul. You know for what they were and in whose image they were made; for what they were bought and with what price they were bought; what service for God they are capable of doing; what happiness in God they are capable of enjoying.

2. The natural condition of the soul. It is alienated from its rightful Lord and sold for a mess of pottage, for the gratifications of a base lust, into the hands of a sworn enemy and made a prey to the roaring lion. Here is one made a cage of unclean and filthy birds who is capable of being made a temple of the Holy Spirit; a drudge of Satan who might have been a servant of God; an instrument of unrighteousness who might have been a vessel of honor.

C. A Great Value for the Grace of God.

1. The power of grace. All good people have a great value for the grace of God and are convinced of the sovereignty and power, the necessity and efficacy of that grace; and therefore, they pray for that grace, both for the reformation of sinners and for the establishment of the just. They know that nothing can be done without it and whatever good they wish to be effected, either upon saints or sinners, they depend upon that grace for it and its powerful influences.

2. The promise of grace. They know also that this grace is promised to the church, this clean water to cleanse it from all filthiness and from all of its idols. Yet God will be inquired of by His people, to do it for them; we must ask and then we shall receive.

CONCLUSION

Let us do what we can to bring the wickedness of the wicked to an end. Let our conduct in everything be such as becomes the Gospel of Christ, strict and conscientious. Let us do what we can to establish the just, to confirm the good in their goodness. Let those who fear the Lord speak often one to another for instruction, quickening, and encouragement.

Matthew Henry

A SONG OF COMFORT

> *The Lord is my Shepherd; I shall not want. He maketh me to lie down in green pastures: He leadeth me beside the still waters. He restoreth my soul: He leadeth me in the paths of righteousness for His name's sake. Yea, though I walk through the valley of the shadow of death, I will fear no evil: for Thou art with me; Thy rod and Thy staff they comfort me. Thou preparest a table before me in the presence of mine enemies: Thou anointest my head with oil, my cup runneth over. Surely goodness and mercy shall follow me all the days of my life, and I will dwell in the house of the Lord forever.*
>
> —PSALM 23

IT IS the duty of Christians to encourage themselves in the Lord their God; and we are here directed to take that encouragement both from the relation wherein He stands to us and from the expectation we have had of His goodness, according to that relation.

I. THE COMFORT OF PROVISION (Verse 1).

A. God's Care of Believers: "The Lord Is My Shepherd."

1. This is seen in that the Lord is called a shepherd. He is their Shepherd and they may call Him so. There was a time when David was a shepherd (Psalm 78:70–71); so he knew by experience the cares and tender affections of a good shepherd toward his flock.

2. This is seen in the shepherd's responsibilities. He that is the Shepherd of Isral is the Shepherd of every individual believer. He takes them into His fold and then takes care of them, protects them and provides for them with more care and constancy than a shepherd can that makes it his business to keep the flock.

B. Believer's Confidence in God: "I shall not want."

1. The confidence expressed. "If the Lord is my Shepherd, my Feeder, I may conclude I shall not want anything that is really necessary and good for me." Let not those fear starving that are at God's finding and have Him for their Feeder.

2. The truth implied. More is implied than is expressed. It is not only, "I shall not want," but, "I shall be supplied with whatever I need; and if I have not everything I desire, I may conclude it is either not fit for me or not good for me, or I shall have it in due time."

II. THE COMFORT OF GOD'S PRESENCE AND PROTECTION (Verses 2–4).

A. The Comforts of a Living Saint.

1. They are well pleased: "He maketh me to lie down in green pastures." God makes His saints to lie down; He gives them quiet and contentment in their own minds, whatever their lot is; their souls dwell at ease in Him and that makes every pasture green.

2. They are well guided: "He leadeth me beside the still waters." The Shepherd of Israel guides Joseph like a flock; and every believer is under the same guidance. He leads them by His providence, by His Word, by His Spirit. He disposes their affairs for the best, according to His counsel.

3. They are well helped: "He restoreth my soul." He brings us back when we wander. He recovers us when we are sick and revives us when we are faint "and so restores the soul that was ready to depart."

B. The Courage of a Dying Saint.

1. The supposition of imminent danger: "Though I walk through the valley of the shadow of death." Here is one word which sounds terrible—death.

But even in the supposition of distress there are four words which lessen the terror: shadow; valley; walk; through, that is, they will not be lost in this valley.

2. The triumph over danger: "I will fear no evil." A believer may meet death with a holy security and serenity of mind; (a) because there is no evil in it for the saint; (b) because he has God's gracious presence with him in his dying moments.

III. THE COMFORT OF GOD'S PERPETUAL MERCY (Verses 5–6).

A. God's Gracious Favors.

1. A sufficient supply: "Thou preparest a table before me." There has been provided for the children of God all things pertaining to life and godliness, all things requisite both for body and soul, time and eternity. David acknowledges that he had food sufficient.

2. A plentiful supply: "Thou anointest my head with oil, my cup runneth over." Plentiful provision is made for our bodies and for our souls; for the life that now is and for that which is to come. If Providence does not bestow upon us thus plentifully for our natural life, it is our own fault if it be not made up to us in spiritual blessings.

B. Continuance of God's Favors.

1. The personal assurance: "Surely goodness and mercy shall follow me." It is pardoning mercy, protecting mercy, sustaining mercy, supplying mercy.

2. The manner of conveyance of the favors: "follow me." It shall follow us as the water out of the rock followed the camp of Israel through the wilderness; it shall follow into all places and all conditions. It shall be always ready.

3. The constancy of the favors: "All the days of my life." They shall follow us even to the last; for whom God loves, He loves to the end. They shall be new every morning (Lamentations 3:22–23), like the manna that was given to the Israelites daily.

4. The certainty of the favors: "surely." It is as sure as the promise of the God of truth can make it; and we know whom we have believed.

13

5. The prospect of the perfection of joy: "I will dwell in the house of the Lord forever." Here is a prospect of the perfection of bliss in the future state. Some understand verse 5 to mean: "Goodness and mercy having followed me all the days of my life on this earth, when that is ended, I shall remove to a better world, to dwell in the house of the Lord forever, in our Father's house above where there are many mansions."

CONCLUSION

If God's goodness to us is like the morning light which shines more and more to the perfect day; let not ours to Him be like the morning cloud and the early dew that passes away. Those that would be satisfied with the fatness of God's house must keep close to the duties of it.

Matthew Henry

HOW TO SPEND THE DAY WITH GOD

On Thee do I wait all the day.
—PSALM 25:5

WHICH of us can truly say the words of the text? Which of us lives this life of communion with God, which is so much our business and blessedness? Yet, David's professions in the text show us what should be our practice.

I. A PATIENT EXPECTATION OF GOD'S MERCY.

A. Though We Must Wait Long.

It seems long while we are kept waiting, but it is no longer than God has appointed and we are sure His time is the best time and His favors are worth waiting for.

B. Though the Day Is Dark.

Though while we are kept waiting for what God will do we are kept in the dark concerning what He is doing and what is best for us to do, yet let us be content to wait in the dark.

C. Though the Day Is Stormy.

Even though the wind be contrary and drive us back, nay, though it be boisterous, yet we must wait and weather the storm by patience. Christ is in the ship.

II. A CONSTANT ATTENDANCE UPON GOD.

A. *The Meaning of Waiting upon God.*

1. It is a life of desire toward God. Our desire must be not only toward the good things that God gives, but toward God Himself, his favor and love, the manifestation of His name to us and the influences of His grace upon us.

2. It is a life of delight in God. Our delight in God must be such that we never wish for more than God. Believing Him to be the all-sufficient God we must be entirely satisfied in Him; let Him be mine and I have enough.

3. It is a life of dependence upon God. It is as the child who waits on his father, in whom he has confidence and on whom he casts his care. It is to expect all good to come to us from God.

4. It is a life of devotedness to God. To wait on God is entirely and unreservedly to refer ourselves to His wise and holy directions and disposals and cheerfully to acquiesce in them and comply with them.

B. *The Time of Waiting upon God.*

1. It is every day. We must wait on God every day; on the Lord's day and on weekdays; on idle days and on busy days; in days of prosperity and in days of adversity; in the day of youth and in the days of old age.

2. It is all the day. We must cast our daily cares upon God and manage our daily business for Him; receive our daily comforts from Him and resist our daily temptations and do our daily duties in His strength; and bear our daily afflictions with submission to His will.

III. PRACTICAL REMINDERS FOR WAITING UPON GOD.

A. *The Duty of Waiting upon God.*

1. In behalf of the family. When you meet with your families in the morning, wait upon God for a blessing upon them and render thanks for the mercies received. In the education of your children wait upon God to make their education successful.

2. In behalf of ourselves. Wait upon God in behalf of your business, in reading, at meal time, when visiting, in your charity, and when journeying; when alone as a guard against temptation.

B. The Motives for Waiting upon God.

1. The eye of God upon us. He sees all the motions of our hearts and sees with pleasure the motions of our hearts toward Him. This should lead us to set Him always before us.

2. The knowledge of God. "All things," even the thoughts and intents of the heart, "are naked and opened unto the eyes of Him with whom we have to do" (Hebrews 4:13). And we must give an account of ourselves to Him.

3. The graciousness of God. He continually waits to be gracious to us; He is always doing us good. He daily loads us with His benefits. His good providence waits on us all the day to preserve our going out and our coming in.

4. The ministry of holy angels. They are all appointed to be ministering spirits to minister for the good of them who shall be heirs of salvation (Hebrews 1:14) and more good offices they do us every day than we are aware.

5. It is heaven upon earth. This life of communion with God is a heaven upon earth. It is an advance installment of the blessedness of heaven and a preparative for it.

C. The Directions for Waiting upon God.

1. See God in creation. Look about you and see what a variety of wonders, what an abundance of comforts, with which you are surrounded and let them lead you to Him Who is the Giver of all good.

2. See the nothingness of a creature without God. The more we discern of the vanity and emptiness of the world and all our enjoyments in it and their utter insufficiency to make us happy, the closer we shall cleave to God and the more intimately we shall converse with Him.

3. Live by faith in the Lord Jesus. We cannot with any confidence wait upon God but in and through a Mediator. It is by His Son that God speaks to us and hears from us. All that passes between God and man must pass through that Daysman.

4. Be frequent and serious in pious ejaculations. It is not the length or language of prayer that God looks at, but the sincerity of the heart in it; and that shall be accepted, though the prayer be short and the groanings such as cannot be uttered.

5. Look upon every day as the last day. Although we cannot say that we ought to live as if we were sure this day would be our last, yet it is certain we ought to live as those who do not know but it may be so. If we thought more of death we would converse more with God.

CONCLUSION

If we continue waiting on God every day and all the day long, we shall grow more experienced and consequently more expert in communion with God. "Turn thou to thy God; keep mercy and judgment, and wait on thy God continually" (Hosea 12:6).

Matthew Henry

A THANKSGIVING SERMON

Thou crownest the year with thy goodness.
—PSALM 65:11

LET the feast of Thanksgiving be kept to the honor of that God who is the Alpha and Omega, the First and the Last; both the spring and center of all our glories. For of Him and through Him and to Him are all things. To Him must the vow of thanksgiving be performed for His mercies to the land of our nativity. And how can we sum up our acknowledgements of God's favors to our nation in more proper moods than those of the text?

I. COMMON PROVIDENCE CROWNS EVERY YEAR WITH GOD'S GOODNESS.

A. The Regular Succession of the Seasons.

Summer and winter crown the year; God made both, and both for the service of men. God's covenant with Noah and his sons (Genesis 8:22) by which the seasons of the year were resettled after the interruption of the deluge is the crown and glory of every year; and the constant and regular succession of summer and winter, seed time and harvest, in performance of that promise, is an encouragement to our faith in the covenant of grace, which is established as firmly as those ordinances of heaven.

19

B. The Fruits and the Products of the Earth.

The annual fruits and products of the earth, grass for the cattle and herbs for the service of men—with these the earth is every year enriched for use; as well as beautified and adorned for show. The harvest is the crown of every year and the great influence of God's goodness to an evil and unthankful world. And so kind and bountiful is the hand of Providence herein that we are supplied not only with food, but with a variety of pleasant things for ornament and delight.

II. SPECIAL PROVIDENCES CROWN SOME YEARS WITH GOD'S GOODNESS MORE THAN OTHERS.

A. Illustration from Jewish History.

Every year was crowned with God's goodness, but not to the extent of the sixth year when God made the earth to bring forth fruit for three years (Psalm 77:10). Every year was not a year of release, much less a year of jubilee. Sometimes the arm of Omnipotence is in a special manner made bare and He outdoes what He used to do that He may awaken a stupid and unthinking world to see the goings of our God in His sanctuary and that He may proclaim Himself glorious in holiness, fearful in praises, working wonders.

B. Practical Observation.

God's goodness must be recognized and acknowledged. Whatever has been or is our honor, our joy, our hope comes from God's hand and He must have the praise for it. We must take notice, not only of His wisdom and power in effecting things great and admirable in themselves, but His goodness and mercy in doing that which is happy and advantageous for us; and make that the theme of all of our songs. "For He is good: for His mercy endureth forever" (Psalm 136:1).

C. The Description of God's Goodness.

A crown signifies three things:

1. It dignifies and adorns. A crown denotes honor.

2. It surrounds and encloses. God has surrounded this year with His goodness, compassed and enclosed it on every side. So is translated the same word in Psalm 5:12: "With favor wilt thou *compass* (crown) him as with a shield."

3. *It finishes and completes.* God has crowned, that is, He has finished the year with His goodness. The happy issue of an affair we call the crown of it.

III. MAN'S RESPONSIBILITY TO GOD FOR HIS GOODNESS.

A. To Praise God.

Let us cast all the crowns of the blessings of the year at His feet by our humble, grateful acknowledgement of His infinite wisdom, power, and mercy. Let our closets and families witness to our constant pious adorations of the divine greatness and devout acknowledgements of the divine goodness to us and to our land; that every day may be with us a thanksgiving day and we may live a life of praise (Psalms 145:2; 119:164). Those who thus honor God no doubt He will yet further honor.

B. To Repent of Sin.

Let the goodness of God lead us to repentance and engage us all to reform our lives, to be more watchful of sin, and to abound more in the service of God and in everything that is virtuous and praiseworthy. Then, and then only, we offer praise so as to indeed glorify God when we order our conduct aright; and then shall we be sure to see His great salvation and be forever praising Him.

C. To Increase Our Goodness to One Another.

It is justly expected that they who obtain mercy should show mercy and so reflect the rays of the divine goodness upon all about them; being herein "followers of God as dear children" (Ephesians 5:1), "followers of Him that is good" (I Peter 3:13) in His goodness. Let God's goodness to us constrain us, as we have opportunity, to do good to all men; to do good with what we have in the world, as faithful stewards of the manifold grace of God; to do good with all the abilities God gives us.

D. To Support and Encourage Our Expectations for Next Year.

Has God crowned us with His goodness this year? Let us thence infer that if we approve ourselves faithful to God surely goodness and mercy shall still follow us. And our hopes ought to be the matter of our praises as well as our joys (Psalm 75:1). The wondrous works for which we are giving thanks this day are upon this account the more valuable in that they give us ground to hope that God's name is near, and in the accomplishments of His promise.

CONCLUSION

That comprehensive prayer, "Father glorify Thy name," has already obtained an answer from heaven—which true believers may apply to themselves—"I have both glorified it, and will glorify it again" (John 12:28). May the goodness and mercy of God so lavishly bestowed upon us as individuals and as a nation not only lead us to proclaim His praise orally, but to show forth our gratitude in lives surrendered to Him who is the giver of every good and perfect gift (James 1:17).

Matthew Henry

SERMON SIX

HOPE AND FEAR BALANCED

The Lord taketh pleasure in them that fear him,
in those that hope in his mercy.
—PSALM 147:11

THE favorites of God are those who fear Him and hope in His mercy. A holy fear of God must be a check upon our hope to keep us from presumption and a pious hope in God must be a check on our fear to keep us from sinking into despondency.

I. THERE MUST BE A BALANCED FEAR AND HOPE CONCERNING OUR SPIRITUAL LIFE.

A. We Must Have a Holy Dread of God and a Humble Delight in Him.

We should keep up a reverence of God's majesty with a fear of incurring His displeasure and at the same time a joy in His love and grace, and an entire complacency in His beauty and bounty and benignity.

1. Reverence for God's majesty.

2. Joy in God's love and grace.

B. We Must Tremble for Sin and Triumph in Christ.

We must be afraid of the curse and the terrors of sin, but rejoice in the covenant and the riches and graces of it.

23

1. Fear the curse and terrors of sin. We must look upon sin and be humbled and afraid of God's wrath.

2. Rejoice in the riches and graces of God's covenant. We must look upon Christ and be satisfied and hope in His mercy.

C. We Must Have a Jealousy of Ourselves and a Grateful Sense of God's Grace in Us.

1. The deceitfulness of the human heart. The heart of man is deceitful above all things. We have, therefore, reason to fear lest we should be mistaken and rejected as hypocrites.

2. The grace of God in us. Let not those who fear the Lord walk in darkness, but trust in the name of the Lord and stay themselves upon their God.

D. We Must Keep a Constant Caution over Our Ways and a Constant Confidence in the Grace of God.

1. Man's weakness. When we consider how weak we are we shall see cause enough to walk humbly with God. We have need to stand always on our guard.

2. Man's hope in God's mercy. In the midst of the fear we must hope in God's mercy, that He will take our part against our spiritual enemies and watch over us for good.

E. We Must Have a Holy Fear Lest We Come Short and a Good Hope That through Grace We Will Persevere.

1. Man's unworthiness. When we look upon the brightness of the crown set before us and our own meanness and unworthiness and the many difficulties, we may justly be afraid.

2. God's faithfulness. If it be the work of God's hands He will not forsake it, He will perfect it. "He is faithful that promised" (Hebrews 10:23).

II. THERE MUST BE A BALANCED HOPE AND FEAR CONCERNING OUR TEMPORAL LIFE.

A. *In Seasons of Prosperity.*

1. Recognize the sovereignty of the Divine Providence. We are in His hands as clay is in the hand of the potter to be formed, unformed, newly formed as He pleases.

2. Recognize the vanity of the world. There are no pleasures here below that are lasting, but they are all dying things. They are as flowers which soon fade.

3. Recognize that we are undeserving and ill-deserving. We shall see a great deal of reason not to be confident of our creature comforts when we consider that we are not worthy of them and much less worthy to have them secured to us.

4. Recognize that trouble and changes should be expected. Keep up a lively expectation of troubles and changes in this changeable, troublesome world. They are good for us, lest we grow proud and secure and in love with this world.

5. Recognize the approach of death. Though the comforts we enjoy should not be taken from us, though we were ever so sure they would not, yet we know not how soon we may be taken from them.

B. *In Seasons of Distress.*

1. Hope in God's power. No matter how imminent the danger, He can prevent it; no matter how great the straits, He can extricate us out of them.

2. Hope in God's providence. Hope in the usual method of providence, which sets prosperity and adversity one over against the other; and when the ebb is at the lowest makes the tide to turn.

3. Hope in God's pity and compassion. God is gracious and merciful. He does not afflict willingly, but when there is cause and when there is need; and therefore He will not always chide.

4. Hope in God's promise. God has promised that nothing shall harm His followers (I Peter 3:13); all things shall work together for good to them

(Romans 8:28), and shall not be able to separate them from God's love (Romans 8:39).

III. THERE MUST BE A BALANCED HOPE AND FEAR CONCERNING THE CHURCH IN RELATION TO PUBLIC AFFAIRS.

A. We Have Reason for a Holy Fear in Regard to Public Affairs.

1. Because we are a provoking people. God's name is dishonored, His day profaned, His good creatures abused by luxury and excess. Liberty to sin has been pleaded for a Christian liberty.

2. Because we are a divided people. It is not so much the difference of sentiment and practice; but that which does the mischief is the mismanagement of our differences and uncharitable censures one of another.

3. Because of the presence of evil. Let the people of God never expect, until they come to heaven, to be out of reach of evil, and therefore never expect to be perfectly quiet from the fear of it.

B. We Have Reason to Keep Up Good Hope in Regard to Public Affairs.

1. The Word of God. This is the foundation on which our hopes must be built and then they are fixed. See Revelation 11:15; Psalms 2:8; 98:3; Micah 4:3; Isaiah 11:1–9.

2. The work of God. The interest that lies so much upon our hearts, the progress of Christianity, is the work of His own hands which He will never forsake.

3. The wonders of God. When we are discouraged let us remember the works of the Lord; not only those of which our fathers have told us, but which we have seen in our days.

CONCLUSION

Be of good courage and hope in God; stay yourselves upon Him, strengthen yourselves in Him, look upwards with cheerfulness, and then look forward with satisfaction.

Matthew Henry

SERMON SEVEN

THE PLEASANTNESS
OF THE GODLY LIFE

Her ways are ways of pleasantness, and all her paths are peace.
—PROVERBS 3:17

TRUE religion and godliness is often in Scripture, and particularly in the book of Proverbs, represented and recommended to us under the name and character of wisdom. The text reveals that true piety has true pleasure in it.

I. THE CHARACTER OF THE PLEASANTNESS OF THE GODLY LIFE.

A. It Is Real and Not Counterfeit.

1. The counterfeit pleasures. Carnal worldlings pretend a great satisfaction in the enjoyments of the world and the gratification of sense; but "the end of that mirth is heaviness" and in that "laughter the heart is sorrowful."

2. The genuine pleasures. The pleasures of the godly life are solid, substantial pleasures and not painted; gold and not gilded over; these sons of pleasure "inherit substance." They have, like their Master, "meat to eat which the world knows not of."

B. It Is Rational and Not Brutish.

1. The pleasures of the soul. The pleasures of godliness are not those of the mere animal life which arise from the gratifications of the senses of the body and its appetites; no, they affect the soul. They are of a spiritual nature and satisfy.

2. The pleasures of sense. The brute creatures have the same pleasures of sense that we have; but what are those to man who is "taught more than the beasts of the earth and made wiser than the fowls of heaven"?

C. It Is Abiding and Not Transitory.

1. Perishing pleasures. The pleasures of sense are fading and perishing. As "the world passes away," so do the lusts of it. That which at first pleases and satisfies, after a while grows less attractive and becomes disgusting.

2. Permanent pleasures. The pleasures of godliness will abide; they wither not in winter, nor tarnish with time, nor does age wrinkle their beauty. Christ's joy which He gives to His own "no man takes from them."

II. THE PROOF OF THE PLEASANTNESS OF THE GODLY LIFE.

A. The Nature of True Godliness.

1. To know the true God and Jesus Christ. This is the first thing we have to do to get our understandings rightly informed concerning both the object and the medium of our religious or spiritual relations.

2. To cast all of our cares upon God. This is to commit all our ways and works to Him with an assurance that He will care for us. To be truly godly is to have our wills melted into the will of God in everything.

3. A life of communion with God. Good Christians have "fellowship with the Father and with His Son, Jesus Christ" and endeavor to keep up that holy converse. In reading and meditating upon Scriptures we hear God speaking to us. In prayer and praise we speak to God.

B. The Comfort and Privileges of Godliness.

1. The comforts purchased, promised, and provided. Christ purchased peace and pleasure for us. What He purchased has been promised to us and provision has been made for the application of that which has been purchased and promised: the Holy Spirit, the Scriptures, the ministry.

2. The privileges secured and procured. They are discharged from debts of sin; they have "the Spirit of God witnessing with their spirits that they are the children of God"; they have access to the throne of grace; they have a good conscience; they have the earnests and foretastes of glory.

C. The Experience of the Godly.

1. They find the rules and dictates of godliness agreeable and pleasant. They have found the rules and dictates of godliness very agreeable, both to right reason and to their true interest and therefore pleasant. They have found all of God's precepts to be right and reasonable and equitable.

2. They have found the exercise of devotion comfortable and pleasant. If there be a heaven upon earth it is in communion with God; in hearing from Him and in speaking to Him, in receiving the tokens of His favor and communications of His grace.

3. They find that pains and trouble are overcome by the pleasure of godliness. For this we may appeal to the martyrs and other sufferers for the name of Christ whose spiritual joys made their bonds for Christ easy and made their prisons their delectable orchards.

4. They find that the closer they keep to the ways of godliness the greater the pleasantness. The more godliness prevails the greater is the pleasure. What disquiet and discomfort wisdom's children have is the result of deviation from wisdom's ways or their slothfulness and trifling in these ways.

III. THE VINDICATION OF THE PLEASANTNESS OF THE GODLY LIFE.

A. The Misrepresentations of the Enemies of God.

1. The manner of misrepresentation. They suggest that Christ's yoke is heavy and His commandments grievous; to be godly is to bid adieu to all pleasure and delight and to turn tormentors to ourselves.

2. The answer. These enemies know not whereof they speak. Now in answer to these calumnies we have this to say that the matter is not so. Those who speak thus of godliness "speak evil of the things that they understand not."

B. The Misrepresentation of Proposed Friends of God.

1. The misrepresentation stated. Some are morose and sour in their profession—peevish and ill-humored. Others are melancholy and sorrowful in their profession, mourning under doubts and fears about their spiritual state.

2. The reply. (a) God is sometimes pleased for wise and holy ends, for a time, to suspend the communication of His comforts to His people. (b) It also may be the result of sin in the life. They run themselves into the dark and shut their eyes against the light.

C. Scriptural Difficulties.

1. Repentance. We must mourn for sin and reflect with regret upon our infirmities, but we must remember also that repentance is not caused by godliness; pleasure accompanies it; after repentance there is pleasure attending it.

2. Earnest labor. Agonizing is a part of godliness. In this there is comfort. We are enabled for it and encouraged in it.

3. Self-denial. The sensual pleasures we are to deny are comparatively despicable and really dangerous.

4. Tribulation. It is but light affliction at worst and as those afflictions abound for Christ so our "consolation also aboundeth by Christ."

CONCLUSION

Let us all then be persuaded to enter into and to walk in these paths of wisdom that are so very pleasant.

Matthew Henry

DESPISING THE SOUL

He that refuseth instruction despiseth his own soul.
—PROVERBS 15:32

IN THIS text Solomon in a few words gives such account of those whom he found he could do no good as they made their folly manifest before all men. They refuse instruction and thereby they despise their own souls.

I. THE MANNER OF DESPISING THE SOUL.

A. Some Despise the Soul in Opinion.

They advance notions that subtract from the honor of the soul.

1. Denial of the reality of the soul. Such believe that there is no substance but matter and shut out all incorporeal nature. To them sense and perception is the product of matter and motion.

2. Denial of the intelligence of the soul. Many, in order that they may not be charged with neglecting salvation or incurring condemnation of their own souls, choose to despise them as not capable of salvation or condemnation; and that they may not come under the imputation of acting unreasonably, ridicule reason.

3. Denial of the immortality of the soul. Those despise their own souls that deny the immortality of them; who, that they may justify themselves in living like beasts, expect no other but to die like beasts. "Let us eat and drink, tomorrow we shall die" and there is an end of us.

B. Some Despise the Soul in Practice.

1. They abuse the soul. The soul is abused when it is devoted to the service of Satan; when it is defiled with the pollutions of sin; when deceived by lies and falsehoods; when distracted and disquieted with inordinate cares or griefs about this world and its things; when it has an inordinate complacency and repose in the world.

2. They hazard the soul. The soul is hazarded when exposed to the wrath of God by wilful sin; when we build our lives upon the sand instead of the rock; when we give them as a pawn for the gains of this world.

3. They neglect the soul. They despise their soul who neglect to take care of its sin-wounds, who fail to get the wants of the soul supplied, who fail to guard their soul, who neglect the soul's eternal welfare.

4. They consider the body more important than the soul. Such employ the soul only to serve their bodies, whereas the body was made to serve the soul. They injure the soul to please the body. They endanger the soul to please the body.

II. THE FOLLY OF DESPISING THE SOUL.

A. This Is Seen When We Consider the Nature of the Soul.

1. It is of divine origin. The soul of man is of divine origin; it was not made of dust as the body was, but it was the breath of the Almighty. It had the image of God stamped upon it and is the masterpiece of God's workmanship on the earth.

2. It can know God. It is capable of knowing God and conversing with Him; it is capable of being sanctified by the spirit and grace of God; it is capable of being glorified with God, of seeing Him as He is.

3. It is capable of self-consciousness. Self-consciousness is in the nature of the soul. The soul is capable of reflecting upon itself and conversing with itself.

B. This Is Seen When We Consider the Nearness of the Soul.

1. It is man's possession. Our soul is our own, for we are entrusted with it as committed to our charge by God to be employed in His service now and fitted for a happiness hereafter.

2. It is the man himself. The soul is the man, and what is the man but a living soul? Abstract the soul as living and the body is a lump of clay; abstract the soul as rational and the man is as the beasts that perish.

C. This Is Seen When We Consider the Purchase of the Soul.

1. It was not purchased by silver and gold. As silver and gold would not satisfy the desires of a soul nor its capacities, so neither would they satisfy for the sins of the soul. We are "not redeemed with corruptible things."

2. It was purchased by the blood of Christ. Christ gave Himself, His own precious blood to be a ransom for our souls, a counterprice. He made His soul an offering for ours. Nothing less would buy them back out of the hands of Divine Justice—would save them from ruin and secure to them their blessedness.

D. This Is Seen When We Consider the Projects Concerning the Soul.

The Holy Spirit is striving with men's souls to sanctify and save them; the evil spirit goes about continually seeking to debauch and destroy them.

1. The projects of God. Think what projects the love of God has to save souls. He sent His Son to seek and save lost souls. He has given His Spirit to work upon our spirits and to witness to them. He has appointed ministers of the Gospel to "watch for your souls."

2. The projects of Satan. Think also what projects Satan has to ruin souls. What devices, what depths, what wiles he has in hunting for precious souls and how all the forces of the powers of darkness are kept continually in arms to war against the soul.

E. This Is Seen When We Consider the Perpetual Duration of the Soul.

1. The fact of its perpetual duration. The soul is an immortal spirit that will last and live forever. The spirit of a man is that candle of the Lord which will never be blown or burnt out.

2. The place of the perpetual duration of the soul. The soul will not only live and act when separated from the body, but it must be somewhere forever. There is everlasting happiness or everlasting misery designed for souls in the other world, according to their character in this and according as they are found at death.

CONCLUSION

Let us see and bewail our folly in having such low thoughts of our souls and learn to put due value upon them. Let us value other things as they have relation to our souls. Let us not despise the souls of others and in love do all we can for their salvation.

THE FOLLY OF DESPISING OUR OWN WAYS

> *But he that despiseth his ways shall die.*
> —PROVERBS 19:16

WE HAVE here fair warning to a careless world. O that it were taken! There are those by whom it is taken. David speaks of it with comfort that he had taken the warnings which God's commands gave and therefore hoped for the rewards they proposed (Psalm 19:11).

I. THE SINNER'S FALL AND RUIN: "HE SHALL DIE."

A. It Is a Spiritual Death.

1. The soul destitute of spiritual life. An impenitent soul lies under the wrath and curse of God which is its death. It is destitute of spiritual life and of its principles and powers. It is under the dominion of corruption which is as killing to the soul as the curse of God is a killing sentence.

2. The soul separated from communion with God. They shall die; that is, they shall be cut off from all communion with God, which is the life of the soul, and from all hope of His loving kindness, which is better than life. They shall die; that is, they shall be dead to God and to all good.

B. It Is an Eternal Death.

The eternal or second death is the sinfulness of man and the wrath of God immutably fixed. It is not the extinguishing of men's beings, but the extinguishing of their bliss.

1. It is real. Misery and torment in the next world will certainly be the portion of all who live and die ungodly lives (Romans 2:5–11).

2. It is fearful. The second death is inconceivably dreadful. Who knows what the power of God's anger is, either what He can inflict or what it is possible for a soul to suffer—or what a fearful thing it is for a sinner that has made himself obnoxious to God's justice?

3. It is near. There is but a step between the sinner and the second death and it may be a short step and soon taken. There is only one life between the sinner and hell and that is the sinner's own life which may shortly come to an end.

II. THE SINNER'S FAULT AND FOLLY: "DESPISETH HIS WAYS."

A. The Meaning of Despising Our Own Ways.

1. Unconcern about the end of our ways. This includes: (a) Failure to consider and direct our ways toward the God-purposed aim or end of our lives, namely, to show forth the praise of God and to live for Christ. (b) Failure to enquire what will be the last end in which our ways will terminate—heaven or hell.

2. Indifference to the rule of our ways. We despise our way if we set aside the rules which God has given us to obey: the Scriptures; and conscience in subordination to the Bible. We despise our way if we set up our rules of life in opposition to God's. Such are guided by personal desires and the cause and custom of this world.

3. Wavering in the course of our ways. It is certain those have not the concern they ought to have who have not resolution enough to persist in good purposes and to hold to them and have not sufficient constancy to proceed and persevere in the good practices wherein they have begun.

4. Failure to acknowledge and apply ourselves to God. This honor God has been pleased to put upon our ways, that He has undertaken to be our guide and guard in them, if we look up to Him as we ought (Psalms 37:23; 73:24; Isaiah 40:31). If therefore we do not have our eyes upon Him, if we make light of this privilege, as all those do who do not make use of it, we lose this honor.

5. *Careless of our past ways.* It is our concern to look back, because if we have done amiss there is a way provided to undo it by repentance. If we are unwilling that others should reprove us for wrong or to examine and correct ourselves we despise our own ways.

6. *Heedless and inconsiderate of the way before us.* If we think that God is neither pleased nor displeased with our thoughts, affections, words, or actions; if we do not care to avoid sin and do our duty as it ought to be done, we are careless of our way and despise it.

B. The Foolishness and Danger of Despising Our Own Ways.

1. *God observes our ways.* The God of heaven observes and takes particular notice of all our ways, even the ways of our hearts—their thoughts and intents are open before His eyes (Hebrews 4:13). He sees our ways as things that must be judged and which judgment must be given justly.

2. *Satan seeks to pervert our ways.* Satan is a subtle enemy that seeks to pervert our ways and to draw us into his service and interests. Satan's design is more than half accomplished when he has brought men to a state of indifference as to their actions and they let things go just as they will.

3. *Many persons watch us.* David prayed, "Lord, lead me in a plain path because of mine enemies"—because of them that observe me (Psalm 27:11). There are many who take notice of what we do and say: some watch us as a pattern; others, to reproach; still others, to rejoice when we walk in the truth.

4. *Man must give an account of all his ways.* As there is now an account kept of all sins in the book of God's omniscience and of the sinner's own conscience, so there must shortly be an account given of them all. They must all be reviewed. It is a folly for us to despise our own ways and make a light matter of them.

5. *Our ways most likely will determine our future life.* As you spend your time you are likely to spend your eternity. If the prevailing temper of your mind now is vain, carnal, selfish, sensual, earthly, and worldly, and you go

out of the world under the dominion of such a temper you are utterly unfit for heaven and so is heaven for you.

CONCLUSION

Are you in the broad way that leads to destruction, or in the narrow way that leads to life; among the many who walk in the way of their own hearts or among the few that walk in the way of God's commandments? Christ is the way—are you in the Christ?

Matthew Henry

SERMON TEN

A WORTHY TRIBUTE TO A GODLY MOTHER

Her children shall rise up, and call her blessed.
—PROVERBS 31:28

THIS is part of the just debt owing to the virtuous woman that answers the characters laid down in the foregoing verses; and part of the reward promised and secured to her by Him who in both worlds is and will be "the Rewarder of them that diligently seek and serve Him."

I. THE CHARACTER OF THE MOTHER DESERVING THE TRIBUTE.

A. *She Is Wise and Kind (Verse 26).*

1. The effects of her wisdom. Wisdom dictates her conversation. By opening the mouth with wisdom there is instilled in children's minds what they will afterwards employ. Such children will have reason to call their mother blessed for setting them an example for the good government of a tongue.

2. The description of her kindness. She is truly kind, that is, wisely so; she is tender to her children's comfort, but not indulgent of her children's follies. The mother who has this law in her tongue and in her heart and is always under its commands and regulations gains her children's love and is entitled to their good word.

B. She Is Industrious (Verse 27).

1. She is concerned for her family. She takes care of her family and all the affairs of it. She does not intermeddle in the concerns of other people's houses, she thinks it enough for her to look well to her own.

2. She is a good homemaker. Most of the characteristics given to her in the verses preceding the text fall under this head, where she is commended for her diligence and consideration in the management of her house and the affairs of it, which is her particular calling. It is to her praise that she looks well to the ways of her household, appointing them their portion of food and work.

C. She Is Virtuous (Verse 29).

1. The meaning of virtue. Virtue is vigor and boldness and resolution in that which is good; courage and spirit in doing our duty, in facing difficulties, giving reproofs, bearing reproaches, in proving opportunities, and pressing forward toward perfection. They are lively and cheerful, fervent in spirit, serving the Lord.

2. The excellency of virtue. Many daughters in their father's house, and in their single state, have done virtuously, but a good wife and mother, if she is virtuous, excels them all and does more good in her place than they can do in theirs. A man cannot have his house so well kept by good daughters as by a good wife and mother.

D. She Is Godly.

1. The importance of piety. It is the fear of God that crowns the character of this virtuous woman, without which, all the rest is of small account. She does not lack that "one thing needful." In all that she does she is guided and governed by the principles of conscience and a regard to God.

2. The description of piety. It is a holy awe and reverence of God that sets Him always before us, recognizing His authority and submitting ourselves to His precepts and His providence. It glorifies God as the greatest and best of beings and evidences it in a steady, uniform, and unhypocritical devotion.

II. KEEP THE CHILDREN'S DUTY IN RELATION TO A GODLY MOTHER.

A. Grateful Remembrance.

1. Of physical care. The tender and earnest care which God placed in the hearts of our mothers when we were in the helpless state of innocency, the pains they took with us when we were unable to do anything for ourselves, for all of this we can never make sufficient return.

2. Of spiritual nurture. As godly mothers we ought to do honor to their names and their memory should be doubly precious to us, remembering that under God we "owe unto them our own souls." Blessed are they of the Lord who taught us the knowledge of the Lord Jesus and followed it with constant and earnest prayers.

B. Fervent Thanksgiving.

1. For God's grace in them. The grace which led them on in their way and bore them as "upon eagles' wings," until He had brought them safely and comfortably to their journey's end—to that blessed state where they receive the end of their faith and hope, even the completion of the salvation of their souls.

2. For our benefit by the grace in them. Although they could not give us grace, yet God was pleased to make use of them as instruments in His hand in the beginning and carrying on of that good work. God enabled them to be guides to us and faithful monitors.

C. Acknowledge the Goodness of Their Way.

1. They were honorable. We must reckon that they were truly honorable and place more value on the fact that we are all children of saints rather than the children of nobles. This will quicken us to pursue honor in the same way in which "they attained a good report." Let us then have the same honor that our godly mothers had.

2. They were happy. They were happy in the enjoyment of themselves and of what God had given them in this world; happy in the quiet and repose of their own minds; and happy in the prospect of better things in the better country. The ways of God and godliness are good ways.

D. Follow in Their Steps of Virtue and Piety.

1. In compliance with their example. We ought to imitate them in everything that was praiseworthy. In compliance to the good example they set us, and in conformity to that, by which the instructions they gave us were both explained and enforced, and we were directed and encouraged in the way of duty.

2. In expectation of the bliss of heaven. Their serious piety was found unto praise and honor and glory in this world and will be much more so at the appearing of Jesus Christ. Let us therefore, having an eye to the same joy, run with patience the same race set before us. Let us proceed with holy vigor and persevere with an unshaken constancy.

CONCLUSION

It is, indeed, enough to make them truly and eternally happy that virtuous people are blessed of God; and "those whom He blesseth they are blessed indeed"; His pronouncing them happy makes them so. This is enough to engage us all to, and encourage us all in, the study and practice of virtue and piety.

Matthew Henry

SURRENDER TO GOD'S CALL

*Also I heard the voice of the Lord, saying Whom shall I send,
and who will go for us? Then said I, Here am I; send me.*

—ISAIAH 6:8

PERHAPS of all the Old Testament prophets, none had a more awful and solemn mission than the prophet Isaiah; who spoke so plainly and fully of Christ and the grace of the Gospel. If we look back to the preparation for his call (Isaiah 6:5–6) we shall see the prophet deeply touched by a humbling sense of his own sinfulness and a comfortable sense of his acceptance with God. The prophet being thus prepared has the work and trust committed to him.

I. THE COUNSEL OF GOD CONCERNING ISAIAH'S MISSION.

Although God does not need to be counseled by others nor to consult with Himself, yet sometimes the wisdom of God, though never at a loss, is expressed by a solemn consultation, to show that what God does is the result of an eternal counsel.

A. The Consultants.

1. God in His glory. It is God in His glory, the same that Isaiah saw in the first verse, "upon His throne, high and lifted up." Not that he saw God's essence, no man has seen that or can see it, but such a display of His glory in

43

vision, as He was pleased at this time to manifest Himself by, as to Moses and Israel at Mount Sinai.

2. God in three persons. This is plainly intimated in the plural number, *us.* It is one God who says, "Whom shall I send" and yet this One is three persons, the very same who said "Let *us* make man." To throw more light upon and to add greater weight, it is observable that the words which follow in the next two verses (Isaiah 6:9–10) are in the New Testament applied both to the Son (John 12:40) and to the Holy Spirit (Acts 28:25–26).

B. The Consultation.

1. The content of the consultation. "Whom shall I send and who will go for us." This refers to all the messages which Isaiah was entrusted to deliver in God's name. Not that God was in doubt as to whom to send. When He has a work to do, He will not want instruments to do it by, for He can find men fit or make them so. But it intimates that the business was such as required a well-accomplished messenger beyond those whom He had hitherto employed.

2. Observations of the consultation. Now we may gather three observations: (a) It is the unspeakable favor of God to us that He is pleased to communicate His mind to us and to make it known by men like ourselves. (b) It is a rare thing to find one who is fit to go for God, to carry His messages to the children of men. (c) None are allowed to go for God but those who are sent by Him.

II. THE CONSENT OF ISAIAH TO HIS GOD-GIVEN MISSION.

The errand on which Isaiah was to go was a very melancholy errand, yet he offered himself to the service. When we are called to act or speak for God we must go and leave the success to Him.

A. His Readiness.

1. A response without objections. Isaiah does not make objections as Moses did when he said, "O my Lord, I am not eloquent" (Exodus 4:10), or "Send by the hand of him whom Thou wilt send" (Exodus 4:13), anybody but me; but he responds, "Behold me; I present myself to Thee to be employed as Thou pleasest."

2. A voluntary response. He was a volunteer in the service; not pressed into it, but willing in this day of power. In this as in other things God loves a cheerful giver, a cheerful offerer. In all acts of obedience to the calls of God and assistance to the work of God we must be free and forward as those who know that we serve a good Master and His work is honorable and glorious.

B. His Resolution.

1. It is firm and fixed. The prophet gives not only a free consent; but he is firm and fixed in it; he does not hesitate or waver, but is ready both to swear by it and to perform it; and he will not be beaten off it no more than the people of Israel, when they said, "Nay, but we will serve the Lord" (Joshua 24:21); or Ruth, when she said, "Entreat me not to leave thee, or to turn from following after thee" (Ruth 1:16).

2. It is to abide by the service to the end, even through great difficulties. Here am I, not only ready to go, but resolved in the strength of divine grace to encounter the greatest difficulties and to abide by the service to the end. Send me and I will adhere to it whatever it cost me and will never draw back. And good reason have we thus to serve Christ for with such a steady and unshaken resolution did He undertake to save us. Those who thus set out with resolution may depend upon God to bear them out.

C. His Referring Himself to God.

His expressing himself thus, "Here am I, send me," intimates this: Lord, employ me as Thou thinkest fit; cut out what work thou pleasest for me. I will never prescribe, but ever subscribe. Here am I, ready to go to whom and on what errand Thou wilt, whatever objections may be made against it. Lord, I am at Thy service, entirely at Thy disposal. Let the will of God be done by me and done concerning me.

1. To have God's will done by him.

2. To have God's will done concerning him.

CONCLUSION

We must go forth in the strength of the Lord God or we shall go to no purpose. If we think to succeed in our strength, by our own wisdom or importunity, we only deceive ourselves. If, when God calls to you to appear and act for Him, you cheerfully say, "Here am I," you may be sure when you call to Him, He will also say, "Here am I." If you say, "Lord, send me," He will say, "Go, and I will be with thee."

Matthew Henry

CHRIST THE SUFFERING SUBSTITUTE

All we, like sheep, have gone astray; we have turned every one to his
own way; and the Lord hath laid on Him the iniquity of us all.
—ISAIAH 53:6

IT WAS a great mystery that so excellent a person should suffer such hard things; and it was natural to ask, "How did it come about? What evil did He do?" His enemies looked upon Him as suffering justly for His crimes; and though they could lay nothing to His charge they considered Him smitten of God. Because they hated Him and persecuted Him, they thought that God did likewise and that He was His enemy and fought against Him. They that saw Him hanging on the cross enquired not into the merits of His cause, but took it for granted that He was guilty of everything laid to His charge and that therefore vengeance suffered Him not to live. It is true, He was smitten of God, but not in the sense in which they meant it. It was for our good and in our stead.

I. MAN'S GUILT.

A. The Extent of It.

It is certain that we are all guilty before God; we have all sinned and have come short of the glory of God (Romans 3:23). "All we like sheep have gone astray," one as well as another; the whole race of mankind lies under the stain of original corruption and every individual stands charged with many actual transgressions. We have all gone astray from God our rightful Owner, alienated ourselves from Him, from the ends He designed us to move toward and the way He appointed us to move in.

B. The Nature of It.

We have gone astray like sheep which are apt to wander and are not apt, when they have gone astray, to find the way home again. That is our true character; we are bent to wander from God, but altogether unable of ourselves to return to Him. This is mentioned not only as our infelicity (that we go astray from the green pastures and expose ourselves to the beasts of prey), but as our iniquity. Sinners have their own iniquity, their beloved sin, which does most easily beset them; their own evil way of which they are particularly fond.

1. It is a wandering from God.

2. It is iniquity.

C. The Seriousness of It.

We affront God in going astray from Him, for we turn aside everyone to his own way and thereby set up ourselves and our own will in competition with God and His will; which is the malignity of sin. Instead of walking obediently in God's way we have turned wilfully and stubbornly to our own way, the way of our own heart, the way in which our own corrupt appetites and passions lead us. We have set up for ourselves to be our own masters, our own carvers, to do what we will and to have what we will.

1. We insult God.

2. We are wilfully disobedient to God.

II. GOD'S PROVISION.

A. The Appointment of Christ By the Will of the Father.

Our Lord Jesus was appointed to make satisfaction for our sins and to save us from the penal consequences of them by the will of His Father, for "the Lord hath laid on Him the iniquity of us all." God chose Him to be the Savior of poor sinners and would have Him to save them in this way, by bearing their sins and the punishment of them; not the same that we should have suffered, but that which was more than equivalent for the maintaining of the honor of the holiness and justice of God in the government of the world. Christ was delivered to death by the determinate counsel and foreknowledge of God (Acts 2:23). None but God had the power to lay our sins upon Christ because the sin was committed against Him and to Him the satisfaction was to be made and because Christ, His own Son, was sinless.

1. He was appointed to make satisfaction for sins.

2. He was appointed to save men from the penal consequences of sin.

B. The Transference of Our Sins upon Christ.

The way we are saved from the ruin of sin is by the laying of our sins on Christ as the sins of the Old Testament offerer were laid upon the sacrifice. Our sins were made to meet or fall upon Him. The laying of our sins upon Christ implies the taking of them off from us. We shall not fall under the curse of the law if we submit to the grace of the Gospel. They were laid upon Christ when He was made sin, a sin offering, for us and redeemed us from the curse of the law by being made a curse for us.

1. The fact of the transference of our sins upon Christ illustrated in the Old Testament.

2. The implication of the transference of our sins upon Christ.

C. The Extent of the Atonement.

It was the iniquity of us all that was laid on Christ; for in Him there is a sufficiency of merit for the salvation of all, which excludes none that do not exclude themselves. It intimates that this is the one only way of salvation. All that are justified are justified by having their sins laid on Jesus Christ and though they were ever so many, He is able to bear the weight of them all.

1. It is sufficient for all.

2. It is efficient only to those who believe.

CONCLUSION

God laid upon Christ our iniquity; but did He consent to it? Yes, He did. Therefore, when He was seized He requested those into whose hands He surrendered Himself that His surrender should be His disciples' discharge: "If ye seek me, let those go their way" (John 18:8). By His own voluntary will He made Himself responsible for our debt. Because He did the Father's will and made atonement for the sin of man, He rolled away the reproach of His death and stamped immortal honor upon His sufferings notwithstanding the disgrace and ignominy of them.

Matthew Henry

A GRACIOUS INVITATION

Ho, everyone that thirsteth, come ye to the waters, and he that hath no money; come ye, buy and eat; yea, come, buy wine and milk without money, and without price.

—ISAIAH 55:1

WE ARE invited to come and take the benefit of that provision which the grace of God has made for souls, of that which is "the heritage of the servants of the Lord" (Isaiah 54:17) and not only their heritage hereafter, but their cup now.

I. THE PERSONS INVITED.

A. The Extent of the Invitation.

1. The fact. Jews and Gentiles. "Ho (take notice of it; he that hath ears to hear, let him hear), every one." Not the Jews only, to whom first the word of salvation was sent, but the Gentiles, the poor and the maimed, the lame and the blind, are called to this marriage supper, whoever can be picked up out of the highways and the hedges.

2. The intimation. Christ is sufficient for all. It intimates that in Christ there is enough for all and enough for each; that ministers are to make a general offer of life and salvation to all; that in Gospel times the invitation should be more largely made than it had been, and should be sent to the Gentiles.

B. The Qualification for Acceptance of the Invitation.

1. Desire is necessary. They must thirst. All are welcome to Gospel grace only upon these terms, that Gospel grace is welcome to them. Those who are satisfied with the world and its enjoyments; those who depend upon the merit of their own works for righteousness; these do not thirst, they have no sense of need and therefore they will not condescend to behold Christ. Those who thirst are invited to waters as those who labor and are heavy laden are invited to Christ for rest.

2. Desire must precede the gift of grace. Where God gives grace, He first gives to thirst after it; and where He has given to thirst after it, He will give it.

II. THE RESPONSIBILITY OF THE PERSONS INVITED.

A. They Are to Come to the Waters.

1. It is the place of supply. Come to the waterside, to the ports, and queys, and wharfs, on the navigable rivers into which goods are imported, thither come and buy, for that is the marketplace of foreign commodities; and to us they would have been forever foreign, if Christ had not brought in an everlasting righteousness.

2. It is a picture of coming to Christ our Savior. Come to Christ for He is the Fountain opened, He is the smitten Rock. Come to the healing waters, come to the living waters; "whosoever will let him take of the water of life" (Revelation 22:17). Our Savior referred to it when He said, "If any man thirst, let him come unto me and drink" (John 7:37).

B. They Are to Come and Partake.

1. They are to come and buy. Come and buy, and we can assure you that you shall have a good bargain of which you will never repent nor lose by it. Come and buy; make it your own by an application of the grace of the Gospel to yourselves; make it your own upon Christ's terms and stand not hesitating about the terms or deliberating whether you shall agree to them.

2. They are to come and eat. Make it still more your own, as that which we eat is more our own than that which we only buy. We must buy the truth, not that we may lay it by to be looked at, but that we may feed and feast upon it and that the spiritual life may be nourished and strengthened by it. When we have bought what we need let us not deny ourselves the comfortable use of it.

III. THE PROVISION OF THE INVITATION.

A. The Substance of the Provision.

1. The substance stated. "Come and buy wine and milk," which will not only quench the thirst, but nourish the body and revive the spirits. The world comes short of our expectations; we promise ourselves, at least, water in it, but we are disappointed of that. But Christ outdoes our expectations; we come to the waters and would be glad of them, but we find there wine and milk.

2. The truth taught. We must come to Christ to have milk for babes, to nourish and cherish them that are but lately born again; and with Him strong men shall find that which will be a cordial to them; they shall have wine to make glad their hearts. We must part with our poison that we may procure this wine and milk.

B. The Communication of the Provision.

1. The freeness of the offer. "Buy wine and milk without money, and without price." A strange way of buying, not only without ready money (that is common enough), but without any money or the promise of any; yet it seems not so strange to those who have observed Christ's counsel to the Laodicean Church that was wretchedly poor, "and knowest not that thou art wretched, and miserable, and poor, and blind, and naked: I counsel thee to buy of me gold tried in the fire, that thou mayest be rich" (Revelation 3:17–18).

2. The implications of the freeness of the offer. Our buying without money intimates: (a) that the gifts offered are invaluable. (b) He makes these proposals, not because He has occasion to sell, but because He has a disposition to give. (c) The things offered are already bought and payment made. Christ paid the price of purchase. (d) We are welcome to the benefits of the promise, though we are utterly unworthy of them and unable to purchase them.

CONCLUSION

We ourselves are not of any value, nor anything that we have or can do, and we must own it, that if Christ and heaven be ours we must see ourselves forever indebted to free grace. "For by grace are ye saved through faith; and that not of yourselves: it is the gift of God: not of works, lest any man should boast" (Ephesians 2:8, 9).

Matthew Henry

THE YEAR OF
THE REDEEMED

The year of my redeemed is come.
—ISAIAH 63:4

THERE will come a year of redemption for those who suffer in the cause of Christ. God will not and men shall not contend forever; nor shall the rod of the wicked rest always upon the lot of the righteous, although it may rest long there.

I. THE DESCRIPTION OF THE YEAR OF THE REDEEMED.

A. *The Year of Recompence for the Controversy of Zion (Isaiah 34:8).*

1. For the sons of Zion. God espouses the cause of the sons of Zion who have been abused by their enemies and trodden down and broken to pieces as earthen pitchers.

2. For the worship of Zion. Jehovah's controversy is for the songs of Zion, which their persecutors have profaned by their insolence and contempt of the Jews and their religion when they upbraided them in their captivity with the songs of Zion (Psalm 137:3, 8).

3. For the powers of the king of Zion, which the enemies have usurped. The offices of our Lord have been invaded by corrupt ecclesiasticism. Shall not the crown of the exalted Redeemer be supported against these usurpations?

4. For the pleasant things of the palaces of Zion, which have been laid waste. God keeps an account of the mischief done at any time and will bring it all into the reckoning when the year of recompenses comes.

B. The Year of Release for God's Captives.

1. Release from oppressed consciences. The compliance to tyranny while the soul remains unbended is a grievous affliction; the freeing of the oppressed from this force will be a most glorious deliverance.

2. Release of oppressed confessors. Humanity obliges us much and Christianity much more, to pity the distressed state of those who are in bonds and banishment for the Word of God and for the testimony of Jesus Christ. Then shall be the time when the house of the prisoners shall be opened and every man's chains fall from his hands.

C. The Year of the Revival of Primitive Christianity.

1. Prominence of godliness among men. The year of the revival of primitive Christianity in the power of it will be the year of the redeemed. This we long to see, the dominance of serious godliness in the lives of all who are called Christians.

2. Worldwide spread of the Gospel. When the bounds of Christianity will be enlarged by the conversion of nations to the faith of Christ; when the kingdoms of this world become the kingdoms of the Lord and His Christ and the Redeemer's throne set up where Satan's seat is, then will the year of the Redeemed come.

3. Suppression of sin. Mistakes shall be rectified, corruptions purged out. Every plant that is not of our heavenly Father's planting shall be rooted up and the plants that are of His planting shall be fruitful and flourishing. Vice and profanity shall be suppressed and all iniquity shall stop her mouth.

4. Unity among God's people. Divisions shall be healed and the unity of the Spirit kept in the bond of peace. All shall agree to love one another although they cannot agree in everything to think with one another.

5. Outpouring of the Holy Spirit. The Spirit shall be poured out from on high so that truth will triumph over error, devotion over profaneness, virtue over all immoralities, justice and truth over treachery and all unrighteousness.

II. THE GROUND FOR THE CERTAINTY OF THE COMING OF THE YEAR OF THE REDEEMED.

A. *The Justice and Righteousness of God.*

1. The fact of God's justice and righteousness. Though clouds and darkness are round about God so that we know not the way that He takes, yet judgment and justice are the habitation of His throne; and so will it appear when the mystery of God shall be finished and the heavens shall declare His righteousness.

2. The encouragement of God's justice and righteousness. Look up with an eye of faith to heaven above and see the Lord God Omnipotent upon a throne, high and lifted up; the throne of glory, the throne of government which He has prepared and established in the heavens.

3. The certainty of God's just and righteous acts. They are mistaken who think that God has forsaken the earth; who say in their hearts: "God hath forgotten" and "will not require it" (Psalm 10:11, 13). The day is coming when it shall be evident and every man will own it. "Verily there is a reward for the righteous; verily there is a God that judgeth the earth" (Psalm 58:11).

B. *The Performance of God's Promises to His People in All Ages.*

1. This is evidenced in the history of the Jewish nation. God came to deliver Israel from Egyptian bondage. In the times of the judges first one enemy and then another oppressed them, but in due time God raised up deliverers. The Babylonian captivity came to an end.

2. This is evidenced in the history of the Christian church. The Christian church has been often afflicted. Many have been the troubles of the followers of Christ, but the Lord has delivered them out of them all.

III. THE ENCOURAGEMENT TO HOPE FOR THE APPROACHING OF THE YEAR OF THE REDEEMED.

A. *The Measure of Iniquity Is Increasing.*

The measure of the iniquity of the church's enemies fills swiftly. The powers with which we are contesting seem to grow more and more false and treacherous, cruel, and barbarous; which cannot but ripen their vintage for the great winepress of the wrath of God (Revelation 14:19).

B. The Present Shaping of Affairs Presents a Hopeful Prospect.

As for God, His work is perfect; when He begins He will make an end. What we have received from God emboldens us to expect more.

IV. THE CHRISTIAN'S DUTY IN REFERENCE TO THE YEAR OF THE REDEEMED.

A. It Is His Duty to Engage in Earnest Prayer.

When Daniel understood by books that the seventy years of Jerusalem's desolations were expiring, he set his face to seek the Lord by prayer and supplication, with fasting. When we see mercies coming toward us let us meet them by our prayers.

B. It Is His Duty to Be Obedient to the Laws of Love and Holiness.

Let us prepare ourselves by bringing every thought into obedience to the two royal laws of holiness and love. When we expect God to do wonders among us, it concerns us to sanctify ourselves.

C. It Is His Duty to Patiently Wait for the Year of the Redeemed.

If the days of our brethren's afflictions should be prolonged and their deliverance be deferred, yet let us not be weary, nor faint in our minds. The year of the redeemed will come at the time infinite Wisdom has appointed.

CONCLUSION

Let us give all diligence to make our eternal redemption sure and then we shall be happy, though we live not to see the glories of the year of the redeemed on earth.

Matthew Henry

A GLORIOUS DESCRIPTION OF GOD

God is jealous, and the Lord revengeth; the Lord revengeth, and is furious: the Lord will take vengeance on His adversaries, and He reserveth wrath for His enemies. The Lord is slow to anger, and great in power, and will not at all acquit.
—NAHUM 1:2–3

NINEVEH knows not God, that God which contends with her, and therefore is here told what a God He is. It is good for us all to mix faith with that which is here said concerning Him, which speaks a great deal of terror to the wicked and comfort to good people. This glorious description of the Sovereign of the world, like the pillar of cloud and fire, has a bright side toward Israel and a dark side toward the Egyptians.

I. HE IS A GOD OF INFLEXIBLE JUSTICE.

A. He Resents the Insults and Indignities of Men.

1. The breadth of His jealousy. He resents the affronts and indignities done Him by those who deny His being or any of His perfections, that set up other gods in competition with Him, that destroy His laws, or ridicule His Word. He is jealous for His own honor in the matters of His worship and will not endure a rival; He is jealous for the comfort of His worshippers; He is jealous for His land and will not have that injured.

2. The nature of His fury. God is a revenger and He is furious; He has fury (so the word is), not as man has it, in whom it is an ungoverned passion, but He has it in such a way as becomes the righteous God. He has anger, but He has it at command and under government. He is always Lord of His anger.

B. He Reckons with the Men Who Insult Him.

1. The certainty of it. We are not only told that God is a Revenger, but that He will take vengeance. Whoever are His adversaries and enemies among men, He will make them feel His resentments; and though the sentence against His enemies is not executed speedily, yet He reserves wrath for them and reserves them for it in the day of wrath.

2. An illustration of it. This revelation of the wrath of God against His enemies is applied to Nineveh (verse 8). The army of the Chaldeans shall overrun the country of the Assyrians and lay it all to waste. "Darkness shall pursue His enemies," terror and trouble shall follow them whithersoever they go. If they think to flee from the darkness they will fall into that which is before them.

II. HE IS A GOD OF IRRESISTIBLE POWER.

A. The Power of God Asserted and Proved.

1. The testimony of the atmospheric heaven. If we look up into the regions of the air we shall find proofs of God's power. He has "His way in the whirlwind and in the storm" (verse 3). Wherever there is a whirlwind and a storm God has the command of it, the control of it, makes His way through it, goes His way in it, and serves His own purpose by it.

2. The testimony of the deep. If we cast our eye upon the great deeps we find that the sea is His; He made it and when He pleases He rebukes it and makes it dry. He gave proofs of His power when He divided the Red Sea and the Jordan River (Exodus 14:21–22; Joshua 3:13; 4:10, 11, 19).

3. The testimony of the earth. If we look around us on this earth we find proof of His power. His power is often seen in earthquakes which shake the mountains and melt the hills. When He pleases "the earth is burnt at His presence by the scorching heat of the sun" (verse 5).

B. *The Power of God in Relation to His Anger.*

1. God is a consuming fire. If God is an almighty God we may thence infer, "Who can stand before His indignation?" (verse 6). See God here as "a consuming fire" (Hebrews 12:29), terrible and mighty. Here is His indignation against sin, His fury poured out, not like water, but like fire, like the fire and brimstone rained upon Sodom (Psalm 11:6).

2. Sinners are an unequal match for the wrath of God. "Who can abide in the fierceness of His anger?" (verse 6). As it is irresistible, so it is intolerable. Some of the effects of God's displeasure in this world a man may bear up under, but the fierceness of His anger, when it fastens immediately upon the soul, who can bear it?

III. HE IS A GOD OF INFINITE MERCY.

A. *This Is Seen in That He Is Slow to Anger.*

He is not easily provoked, but ready to show mercy to those who have offended Him and to receive them into favor upon their repentance.

1. He is not easily provoked.

2. He is ready to show mercy.

B. *This Is Seen in That He Cares for His Own.*

1. God is good to those who trust Him. When the tokens of His rage against the wicked are abroad, He takes care for the safety and comfort of His own people (verse 7). The Lord is good to those who are good and to them He will be "a stronghold in the day of trouble."

2. God's power is employed for the protection and satisfaction of His children. The same almighty power that is exerted for the terror and destruction of the wicked is engaged and shall be employed for the protection and satisfaction of His own people. He is able both to save and to destroy. In the day of public trouble, when God's judgments are in the earth, He will be a place of defence to those that by faith put themselves under His protection, those that trust in Him in the way of their duty, that live a life of dependence upon Him and devotedness to Him.

CONCLUSION

Let each one take his portion from this passage of Scripture. Let sinners read it and tremble; let saints read it and triumph. The wrath of God is here revealed from heaven against His enemies, His favor and mercy are here assured to His faithful, loyal subjects and in both is revealed His almighty power, making His wrath very terrible and His favor very desirable.

Matthew Henry

SERMON SIXTEEN

GOD'S GRACIOUS NOTICE OF HIS SAINTS

*Then they that feared the Lord spoke often one to another; and
the Lord hearkened, and heard it, and a book of remembrance
was written before Him for them that feared the Lord, and that
thought upon His name. And they shall be mine, saith the Lord
of Hosts, in that day when I make up my jewels; and I will spare
them, as a man spareth his own son that serveth him.*

—MALACHI 3:16–17

HERE IS the gracious notice God takes of the pious talk of the
saints and the gracious recompence of it. Even in this corrupt and de-
generate age, when there was so great a decay, nay, so great a contempt
of serious godliness, there were some that retained their integrity and
zeal for God.

I. THE MANNER IN WHICH THE SAINTS DISTINGUISHED THEMSELVES.

A. They Feared the Lord.

1. They reverenced God. This fear of the Lord is the beginning of wisdom (Psalm 111:10) and the root of all godliness. They reverenced the majesty of God, submitted to His authority, and had a dread of His wrath in all
that they thought and said.

2. They complied with God. They humbly complied with God and never spoke any strong words against Him as was commonly done in Malachi's day (verse 13). In every age there has been a remnant that feared the Lord, though sometimes but a little remnant.

B. They Thought upon the Lord's Name.

1. They meditated upon God. They seriously considered and frequently meditated upon the discoveries God has made of Himself in His Word and by His providences; and their meditation of Him was sweet to them and influenced them.

2. They desired to honor God. They consulted the honor of God and aimed at that as their ultimate end in all they did. Those that know the name of God should often think of and dwell upon it in their thoughts. It is a copious, curious subject and frequent thoughts of it will contribute much to our communion with God and the stirring up of our devout affections to Him.

C. They Spoke Often of God.

1. The nature of their conversation. They spoke often one to another concerning the God they feared and that name of His of which they thought so much; for out of the abundance of the heart the mouth will speak; and a good man out of the good treasure of these will bring forth good things (Luke 6:45).

2. The purpose of their conversation. They that feared the Lord kept together as those that were company for each other. They spoke kindly and endearingly one to another for the preserving and promoting of mutual love, that they might not wax cold when iniquity did abound. They spoke knowingly and edifyingly to one another for the increasing and improving of faith and holiness.

II. THE MANNER IN WHICH GOD DIGNIFIED THE SAINTS.

A. He Took Note of Their Conversation.

1. The Lord was present with them. He took notice of their pious discourses and was graciously present at their conferences. When the two disciples, going to Emmaus, were discoursing concerning Christ, He hearkened and heard and joined Himself to them and made a third (Luke 24:15).

2. The Lord takes cognizance of all conversation. God says that He hearkened and heard what bad men would say and that they spoke not right (Jeremiah 8:6); here He hearkened and heard what good men say and they spoke aright. God observes all the gracious words proceeding out of the mouths of His people, even in the most private conference, and He will reward openly.

B. He Kept an Account of Them.

1. The explanation. "A book of remembrance was written before Him." Not that God needs to be reminded of things by books and writings, but it is an expression intimating that their pious affections and performances are kept in remembrance as punctually and particularly as if they were written in a book; as if journals were kept of all their conferences.

2. The reason. God remembers the services of His people in order that He may say, "Well done, enter thou into the joy of thy Lord" (Matthew 25:21). Never was any good word spoken of God or for God, from an honest heart, but it was registered in order that it might be recompensed in the resurrection of the just and in no wise lose its reward.

C. He Promises to Them a Future Share in His Glory.

1. The saints are God's jewels. They are highly esteemed by Him and are dear to Him. They are comely with a comeliness that He puts upon them and He is pleased to glory in them. He looks upon them as His own proper goods, His choice goods, His treasure laid up in His cabinet. The rest of the world is but lumber in comparison with them.

2. The gathering up of God's jewels. There is a day coming when God will make up His jewels. They shall be gathered up out of the dirt and gathered together from all places. All the saints will then be gathered to Christ, and none but saints, and saints made perfect. Then God's jewels will be made up as stones into a crown, as stars into a constellation.

3. God's public confession of His saints. Those who now own God for theirs, He will then own for His. He will publicly confess them before angels and men. "They shall be mine." Their relation to God shall be acknowledged. He will separate them from those that are not His and give them their portion with those who are His.

D. He Promises to Them a Present Share in His Grace.

1. The assurance of grace. God had promised to own them as His and to take them to be with Him. But it might be a discouragement to them to think that they had offended God, and He might justly disown them and cast them off. As to that, He says, "I will spare them," I will not deal with them as they deserve. The word usually signifies to spare with commiseration and compassion, as a father pitieth his children.

2. The saints' duty in relation to God. It is our duty to serve God with the disposition of children; we must be sons. We must be His servants. God will not have His children trained up in idleness. They must do Him service from the principle of love.

3. The fatherly tenderness and compassion of God. If we serve God with the disposition of children, He will spare us with the tenderness and compassion of a father. Even God's children that serve Him stand in need of sparing mercy, that mercy which has kept us from being consumed and which keeps us out of hell.

CONCLUSION

When iniquity was bold and barefaced, the people of God took courage and stirred up themselves: when godliness was reproached and misrepresented, its friends did all they could to support it; when seducers were busy to deceive, they that feared the Lord were industrious to strengthen one another. Let us follow in the train of this godly remnant.

Matthew Henry

SERMON SEVENTEEN

FORGIVENESS OF SIN AS A DEBT

And forgive us our debts.
—MATTHEW 6:12

And forgive us our sins.
—LUKE 11:4

FROM this petition in the Lord's prayer, thus differently expressed by the two evangelists, we may observe that sin is a debt to God and the pardon of sin is the forgiveness of this debt.

I. SIN IS A DEBT TO GOD.

A. The Manner in Which Men Become Debtors to God.

1. As the servant is indebted to his master. Our Savior represents our case like that of a servant to a king who at the time of reckoning was found to be in debt to the king (Matthew 25:24–30).

2. As the tenant is in debt to his landlord. As a tenant who is behind in his rent or has damaged the landlord's property.

3. As the borrower is indebted to the lender. God has bestowed many mercies upon us, that is, He has been lending to us as the case has required.

66

4. *As the trespasser is indebted to the trespassed.* We have broken through the fences and bounds which God by His commands has set for us; therefore we are trespassers in debt to God.

5. *As the debt of a covenant breaker.* We have by solemn promise engaged ourselves to be the Lord's and to obey Him, but we have broken our covenant with God, so we are in debt to Him.

6. *As the debt of a malefactor to the law and to the government* when he is found guilty of treason or felony and consequently the law is to have its course against him.

7. *As the debt of an heir-at-law upon his ancestor's account,* that is, of a son who is liable to his father's debts after his death as far as his inheritance will go. By Adam's disobedience, we were all made sinners.

8. *As the debt of a surety upon account of the principle.* The guilt we have contracted by partaking of other men's sins, by being partners with them in sin.

B. *The Nature of the Debt of Sin.*

1. *It is an old debt.* The foundation of this debt was laid in Adam's sin and consequently we were born in debt.

2. *It is a just debt.* No matter how high the penalty is with which we are loaded it is less than our iniquities deserve.

3. *It is a great debt.* Until we return to God in repentance we continue to add to our debt, treasuring up unto ourselves guilt and wrath against the day of wrath.

C. *The Nature of the Debtors.*

1. *Careless and unconcerned.* Bad debtors are oftentimes careless and unconcerned about their debts. Thus sinners deal with their convictions, diverting them with the business of the world or drowning them in pleasures.

2. *Wasteful.* Sinners make waste of their time and opportunity and of the noble powers and faculties with which they are endued.

3. Indifferent toward creditors. Sinners take no pleasure in hearing from God, in speaking to Him, or in having anything to do with Him.

4. Fearful. Sinners carry about them a misgiving conscience which often reproaches them and fills them with secret terrors and bitterness.

5. Dilatory and deceitful. Bad debtors are apt to promise payment, but break their word. It is so with sinners.

D. The Danger of Debt.

1. An account is kept of all of our debts. If the debtor keeps not an account of his debts, yet the creditor does; they are all kept on record with God.

2. Man is insolvent. We are utterly insolvent and have not the wherewithal to pay our debts.

3. No earthly friend to help. Sinful men have no prospect of help from their fellowmen because they are in the same helpless condition and as deep in debt.

4. Payment demanded. The debts we owe to God are ever and immediately demanded and the right is kept up by a continual claim.

5. Death will arrest us for the debts. Death is our discharge from other debts, but it lays us more open than ever to the debts against God. After death the judgment (Hebrews 9:27).

6. The approach of the day of reckoning. As sure as we see *this* day, we shall see *that* day when every man must give an account of himself unto God.

7. Hell is the destination of debtors. It is a pit of weeping and wailing and gnashing of teeth out of which there is no redemption.

II. THE FORGIVENESS OF DEBTS.

A. The Things Included in the Forgiveness of Sin as a Debt.

1. God stays the process and does not allow the law to have its course. Judgment is given against us, but execution is not taken out upon the judgment.

2. God cancels the bond. He pardons sin thoroughly and fully, so as to remember it no more against the sinner.

3. God acquits the sinner. This acquittal is delivered by the Spirit into the believer's hand, speaking peace to him, filling him with comfort, arising from a sense of his justification and its tokens and pledges.

4. God admits us to communion with Himself. He condescends to deal with us again and to admit us into covenant and communion with Himself.

B. The Ground of Hope for the Forgiveness of Sin as a Debt.

1. The goodness of God. We may ground our expectations upon the goodness of His nature (Psalm 86:5).

2. The mediation of Christ. God forgives our debt because Jesus Christ by the blood of His cross has made satisfaction for it.

C. The Requirement for the Forgiveness of Sin as a Debt.

1. Confess the debt. This confession of debt must be specific and accompanied with godly sorrow.

2. Acknowledge the judgment of all we have to Christ. Our own selves we must give unto the Lord, and for us to live must be Christ.

3. Honor Christ. We must disclaim all dependence upon our sufficiency and rest upon Christ only as a complete and all-sufficient Savior.

4. Study what we shall render to Christ. Take all occasions to speak of that great love wherewith He loved us.

5. Engage ourselves for the future, that we will render to God the things that are His and be careful not to run into debt again.

6. Forgiveness of others. God will have His children to be like Him, merciful and good.

CONCLUSION

Oh that the love of Christ may constrain us to love Him and live for Him who loved us and died for us.

Matthew Henry

LAYING UP TREASURE

Lay not up for yourselves treasures upon earth: but lay up for yourselves treasures in heaven: for where your treasure is, there will your heart be also.
—MATTHEW 6:19–21

WORLDLY mindedness is as common and as fatal a symptom of hypocrisy as any other. For by no sin can Satan have a surer and faster hold of the soul, under the cloak of a visible and passable profession of Christianity than by this. Therefore, Christ proceeds to warn us against coveting the wealth of the world.

I. GOOD CAUTION.

A. The Meaning of Treasure.

A treasure is an abundance of something that is in itself, at least in our opinion, precious and valuable and likely to stand us in good stead hereafter. It is that something which the soul will have, which it looks upon as the best thing, which it has a complacency and confidence in above all other things.

B. The Prohibition against Laying Up Earthly Treasures.

"Lay not up for yourselves treasures upon earth." A good caution against making the things that are seen and that are temporal our best things and placing our happiness in them. Christ's disciples had left all to follow Him, let them still keep in the same good mind.

C. The Explanation of the Prohibition against Laying Up Earthly Treasure.

1. Earthly treasures should not be considered the best things. We must not count these things the best things, not the most valuable in themselves, nor the most serviceable to us. We must not call them glory, as Laban's sons did (Genesis 31:1), but see and own that they have no glory in comparison with the glory that excelleth (II Corinthians 3:10).

2. Abundance of earthly treasures should not be coveted. We must not covet an abundance of these things nor be still grasping at more and more of them, and adding to them, as men do that which is their treasure, as never knowing when we have enough.

3. Earthly treasures should not be trusted in for security. We must not confide in earthly treasures for futurity, to be our security and supply in time to come. We must not say to the gold, "Thou art my hope."

4. Earthly treasures should not content us. We must not content ourselves with them as all we need or desire. We must be content with a little for our passage through life, but not with all for our portion. These things must not be made our consolation, our good things. Let us consider that we are laying up, not for posterity in this world, but for ourselves in the other world.

II. GOOD COUNSEL.

A. The Substance of the Counsel.

"Lay up for yourselves treasures in heaven." This good counsel is an entreaty to make the joys and glories of the other world, those things not seen that are eternal, our best things and to place our happiness in them.

B. The Implications of the Counsel.

1. The certainty of the heavenly treasures. There are treasures in heaven as sure as there are on this earth; and those in heaven are the only true treasures, the riches and glories and pleasures that are at God's right hand, which those who are sanctified truly arrive at when they come to be perfectly sanctified in heaven.

2. The wisdom of laying up heavenly treasures. It is our wisdom to lay up our treasure in those heavenly treasures; to give all diligence to make sure our title to eternal life through Jesus Christ and to depend upon that as our happiness and look upon all things here below with a holy contempt, as not worthy to be compared with it. Let us not burden ourselves with the cash of this world, but lay up in store good securities.

3. The security of the heavenly treasures. It is a great encouragement to us to lay up treasure in heaven in knowing that there it is safe. It will not decay of itself, no moth or rust will corrupt it; nor can we be by force or fraud deprived of it; thieves do not break through and steal. It is a happiness above and beyond the changes and chances of time. It is an inheritance that is incorruptible (I Peter 1:4).

III. GOOD REASONS.

A. Against Laying Up Earthly Treasures.

1. Because they are liable to loss and decay by internal corruption. That which is treasure upon earth moth and rust will corrupt. If the treasure be laid up in fine clothes, the moth eats them and they are spoiled. Gold and silver tarnishes and grows less with using. Worldly riches have in themselves a principle of corruption and decay; they wither of themselves and make themselves wings.

2. Because they are liable to loss and decay by external violence. "Thieves break through and steal." Every hand of violence will be aiming at the house where the treasure of this world is laid up; nor can anything be laid up so safe, but we may be spoiled of it. It is folly to make that our treasure of which we may so easily be robbed.

B. In Favor of Laying Up Heavenly Treasures.

1. Because it affects our thoughts. "Where your treasure is," on earth or in heaven, "there will your heart be." We are therefore concerned to be right and wise in the choice of our treasure, because the temper of our minds will be accordingly, either carnal or spiritual, earthly or heavenly. Where the treasure is, there is the love and affection (Colossians 3:2).

2. Because it affects our lives. The way the desires and pursuits go, toward that place the aims and intents are levelled, and all is done with that in view. Where a treasure is, there our cares and fears are, lest we come short of it; about that we are more solicitous; there our hope and trust is; there our joys and delights will be.

CONCLUSION

If we know and consider ourselves what we are, what we are made for, how long our continuance, and that our souls are ourselves, we shall see it a foolish thing to lay up treasure on earth. Acceptance with God is treasure in heaven which can neither be corrupted nor stolen. If we have thus laid up treasure with Him, with Him our hearts will be.

Matthew Henry

SERMON NINETEEN

A THREEFOLD INVITATION

> *Come unto me all ye that labor and are heavy laden, and I will give you rest. Take my yoke upon you, and learn of me; for I am meek and lowly in heart: and ye shall find rest unto your soul: for my yoke is easy, and my burden is light.*
> —MATTHEW 11:28–30

HERE is an offer that is made to us and an invitation to accept it. After so solemn a preface (verses 25–27) we may well expect something very great; and it is so, a faithful saying and well worthy of all acceptance; words whereby we may be saved. We are here invited to Christ as our priest, prince, and prophet; to be saved, to be ruled, to be taught by Him.

I. AN INVITATION TO REST (Verse 28).

A. The Character of the Persons Invited.

1. The description. "All that labor and are heavy laden." All those and only those are invited to rest in Christ who are sensible to sin as a burden and groan under it, who are not only convinced of the evil of sin, but are contrite in soul for it; that are really sick of their sins, weary of the service of the world and of the flesh.

2. The illustrations. Ephraim who bemoaned his sins (Jeremiah 31:18–20); the prodigal and the publican who confessed their condition

(Luke 15:17; 18:13); Peter's hearers who were pricked in their hearts (Acts 2:37); and the Philippian jailor who trembled (Acts 16:29–30). This is a necessary preparation for pardon and peace. The Comforter must first convince (John 16:8) and then He will deal.

B. The Substance of the Invitation.

1. The call given. "Come unto me." We must accept Him as our Physician and Advocate; freely willing to be saved by Him, in His own way, and upon His own terms. Come and cast thy burden upon Him. This is the Gospel call, "The Spirit and the bride say, come. And let him that heareth say, come. And let him that is athirst come. And whosoever will, let him take the water of life freely" (Revelation 22:17).

2. The blessing promised. "I will give you rest." Jesus Christ will give assured rest to those weary souls who by a living faith come to Him for it; rest from the terror of sin, in a well-grounded peace of conscience; rest from the power of sin, in a regular order of the soul and its due government of itself; a rest in God and a complacency of soul in His love.

II. AN INVITATION TO SUBMISSION (Verse 29).

A. The Significance of the Yoke.

1. It is Christ's yoke. We must come to Jesus Christ as our ruler and submit ourselves to Him. To call those who are weary and heavy laden to take a yoke upon them looks like adding affliction to the afflicted; but the pertinency of it lies in the word "my." "You are under a yoke which makes you weary, shake that off and try mine, which will make you easy."

2. It suggests service and submission. Servants and subjects are said to be under the yoke (I Timothy 6:1; I Kings 12:10). To take Christ's yoke upon us is to put ourselves into the relation of servants and subjects to Him and then to conduct ourselves accordingly, in a conscientious obedience to all His commands and a cheerful submission to all His disposals. It is to obey the Gospel of Christ.

B. The Nature of the Yoke and Burden.

1. It is an easy yoke. The yoke of Christ's commands is an easy yoke; it is not only easy, but gracious. It is sweet and pleasant. There is nothing in it to gall the yielding neck, nothing to hurt us, but on the contrary, much to refresh us. It is a yoke that is lined with love. His commands are so reasonable and profitable.

2. It is a light burden. The afflictions from Christ which befall us as men and, especially, afflictions for Christ which befall us as Christians constitute the burden of Christ. This burden in itself is not joyous, but grievous; yet as it is Christ's, it is light. Paul knew as much of it as any man and he calls it a light affliction. God's presence, Christ's sympathy, and especially the Spirit's aids and comforts make suffering for Christ light and easy.

III. AN INVITATION TO LEARN (Verses 29–30).

A. The Conditions to be Met in Order to Learn.

1. We must will to learn. We must come to Jesus Christ as our Teacher and set ourselves to learn of Him. Christ has erected a great school and has invited us to be His scholars. We must enter ourselves and associate with His scholars.

2. We must heed His teaching. We must daily heed the instructions He gives by His Word and Spirit. We must converse much with what He said and have it ready to use upon all occasions. We must conform to what He did and follow His steps (I Peter 2:21).

B. The Reasons Given for Learning.

1. Christ is worthy to teach. "I am meek and lowly in heart" and therefore fit to teach you. He is meek and can have compassion on the ignorant. Many able teachers are hot and hasty, which is a discouragement to those who are dull and slow; but Christ knows how to bear with such and to open their understandings. He is lowly in heart. He condescends to teach poor scholars and novices. He teaches the first principles and stoops to the most humble capacities.

2. The effect of Christ's teaching. Rest for the soul is the most desirable rest. The only sure way of finding this rest is to sit at Christ's feet and hear His word. The way of duty is the way of rest. The understanding finds rest in the knowledge of God and Jesus Christ. The effections find rest in the love of God and Jesus Christ. This rest is to be had with Christ for all those who learn of Him.

CONCLUSION

This is the sum and substance of the Gospel, the call and offer. We are told, in a few words, what the Lord Jesus requires of us and it agrees with what God said of Him once and again: "This is my beloved Son, in whom I am well pleased; hear ye Him."

Matthew Henry

SERMON TWENTY

THE ANGEL'S RESURRECTION MESSAGE

And the angel answered and said unto the women, Fear not ye: for I know that ye seek Jesus, which was crucified. He is not here: for He is risen, as He said. Come, see the place where the Lord lay: and go quickly, and tell His disciples that He is risen from the dead.
—MATTHEW 28:5–7

WE MAY THINK that it would have been better if a competent number of witnesses would have been present to see the resurrection of the Lord Jesus; but let us not prescribe to God, who ordered that the witnesses of His resurrection should see Him risen, but not see Him rise.

I. THE ENCOURAGEMENT AGAINST FEARS (Verse 5).

A. The Circumstances.

To come near to graves and tombs, especially in silence and solitude, has something in it that is frightful. Much more was it to these women, to find an angel at the sepulchre.

1. The solitude of the sepulchre.

2. The presence of an angel.

B. The Reassurance.

1. The expression of the reassurance. The keepers shook and became as dead men (verse 4), but fear not ye. Let the sinners in Zion be afraid (Isaiah 33:14), for there is cause for it; but fear not ye faithful seed of Abraham. Why should the daughters of Sarah, that do well, be afraid with any amazement (I Peter 3:6)?

2. The reason for the reassurance. "Fear not ye. Let not the news I have to tell you be any surprise to you; for ye were told before that your Master would rise. Let it be no terror to you, for His resurrection will be your consolation. Fear not ye, for I know that ye seek Jesus. I know you are friends to the cause."

II. THE ASSURANCE OF THE RESURRECTION OF CHRIST (Verse 6).

A. The Fact of the Resurrection.

1. The statement. "He is not here, for He is risen." He is not dead, but alive again; we cannot as yet show you Him, hereafter you will see Him. To be told, "He is not here," would have been no welcome news to those who sought Him, if it had not been added, "He is risen."

2. The warning. We must not hearken to those who say "Lo, here is Christ or Lo, He is there," for He is not here, He is not there, He is risen. In all of our inquiries after Christ, we must remember that He is risen and we must seek Him as one who is risen.

B. The Proof of His Resurrection.

1. The evidence of the empty tomb. "Come and see where the Lord lay. You see that He is not here and remembering what He said you may be satisfied that He is risen. Come see the place and you will see that He is not there, you will see that He could not be stolen from there and therefore must conclude that He is risen."

2. The comfort of the empty tomb. It may have a good influence upon us if we come and with an eye of faith see the place where the Lord lay. See the marks He has left there of His love in condescending so low for us. When we look into the grave where we expect to lie, to take off the terror of it, let us look into the grave where the Lord lay.

C. The Importance of His Resurrection.

1. It is the fulfilment of the Word of Christ. The angel, when he said, "He is not here, He is risen," reveals to us that he preaches no other Gospel than what He had already received, for he refers himself to the Word of Christ as sufficient to bear him out. "He is risen as He said."

2. It is the proper object of faith. This he vouches as the proper object of faith: "He said that He would rise and you know that He is the Truth itself and therefore have reason to expect that He should rise. Why should you be backward to believe that which He told you would be?"

III. THE RESPONSIBILITY IN VIEW OF THE RESURRECTION OF CHRIST (Verse 7).

A. The News of the Resurrection Must Be Proclaimed.

1. To encourage the disciples. "Tell His disciples" in order that they may be comforted; that they may encourage themselves under their present sorrows. It was a dismal time with them, between grief and fear; what cheerful news would this be to them now, to hear that their Master is risen!

2. To revivify the disciples. This news was told to them in order that they may enquire further into themselves. This message was sent to them to awaken them from that strange stupidity which had seized them and to raise their expectations. This was to set them on seeking Him and to prepare them for His appearance to them.

B. The News of the Resurrection Must Be Proclaimed by Its Witnesses.

1. The vessels chosen for the proclamation of the resurrection. The women were sent to tell the news of the resurrection to the disciples. Still God chooses the weak things of the world to confound the mighty (I Corinthians 1:27) and puts the treasure not only in earthen vessels (II Corinthians 4:7), but here into the weaker vessels (I Peter 3:7).

2. The honor of the proclamation of the resurrection. This was an honor placed upon them and a recompense for their constant affectionate adherence to Him at the cross and in the grave, and a rebuke to the disciples who forsook Him.

C. The Required Obedience to the Command Must Be Immediate.

1. The reason for the immediacy. They were bid to go quickly upon this errand. Why, what haste was there? Would not the news be welcome at any time? Yes, but the disciples were now overwhelmed with grief and Christ would have this information hastened to them. When Daniel was humbling himself before God for sin, the angel Gabriel was caused to fly swiftly with a message of comfort (Daniel 9:21).

2. The required readiness. We must always be ready: (a) to obey the commands of God; (b) to do good to our brethren and to carry comfort to them, as those that felt from their afflictions: "Say not, Go and come again, and tomorrow I will give," but now quickly.

CONCLUSION

In the preceding two chapters of Matthew (26 and 27) we see the Captain of our salvation engaged with the powers of darkness and our Champion fell before them. The powers of darkness seem to ride as masters, but then the Lord arose. The Prince of Peace comes out of the grave a Conqueror, yea, more than a conqueror. He lives!

Matthew Henry

A SERMON ON DISPUTES

What was it that ye disputed among yourselves by the way?
—MARK 9:33

OUR Lord Jesus is here calling His disciples to an account about a warm debate they happened to have among themselves, as they traveled along, upon a question often started, but not yet determined. Which of them should be the greatest?

I. ALL BELIEVERS MUST EXPECT TO BE CALLED TO AN ACCOUNT BY OUR LORD.

A. The Present Life Determines the Future.

Believers are travelers, under the conduct of our great Master, toward the better country; and according as our steps are, while we are in the way, our rest will be when we are at our journey's end.

B. The Present Works and Words Will Be Reviewed in the Future.

Every work and every word will be brought into judgment, will be weighed in a just and unerring balance, will be produced in evidence for us or against us.

C. The Judge Will Be the Lord Jesus Christ.

1. The fact stated. The account must be given to our Lord Jesus. To Him the Father has committed all judgment (John 5:22; II Corinthians 5:9–10).

2. The lessons implied. Therefore we should judge ourselves and prove our own work. It is also a good reason why we should not judge one another or be severe in our censures of one another.

II. ALL BELIEVERS MUST GIVE AN ACCOUNT OF THEIR CONVERSATIONS AMONG THEMSELVES.

A. Christ Takes Note of Our Conversation.

For "every idle word that men shall speak, they shall give account thereof in the day of judgment. For by thy words thou shalt be justified and by thy words thou shalt be condemned" (Matthew 12:36, 37).

B. Christ Takes Note of Our Edifying Conversation.

There is not a good word coming from a good heart and directed to a good end, but is heard in secret and shall be rewarded openly (Malachi 3:16).

C. Christ Takes Note of Our Corrupt Conversation.

If any corrupt communication proceeds out of our mouths, Christ observes it and is displeased and we shall hear of it again.

III. ALL BELIEVERS WILL ESPECIALLY BE CALLED TO GIVE AN ACCOUNT OF THEIR DISPUTES.

A. An Explanation of Disputes.

1. The meaning. Disputing supposes some variance and strife, and a mutual contradiction and opposition arising from it.

2. The classification. (a) There are disputes that are of use among Christians; for example, for the conviction of unbelievers, the confirmation of those in danger of being led astray. (b) There are also disputes which cannot be vindicated and of which we are ashamed.

B. The Occasions of Disputes.

1. Differences of opinion. Disputes commonly arise from differences of opinion, either in religion and divine things; or in philosophy, politics, or other parts of learning; or in the conduct of human life.

2. Separate and interfering interests in this world. Neighbors and relatives quarrel about their rights and properties, their estates and trades, their honors and powers and pleasures. These disputes, as they are the most common, so they are the most scandalous.

3. Passion and clashing tempers. Some indulge themselves in a crossness of temper that makes them continually uneasy to all about them. They love to thwart and disagree and to dispute everything, though ever so plain or trifling.

C. Proper Conduct in Disputes.

1. Be on the side of truth and right. As far as we are able to make a judgment, let us see to it that we have the truth and right on our side and not be confident and further than we see just cause to be so.

2. If doubtful, remember you may be wrong. In matters of doubtful disputation, while contending for that which we take to be right, let us think it possible that we may be in the wrong.

3. Have full control of yourself. Let us carefully suppress all inward tumults, whatever provocation may be given us; and let our minds be calm and sedate in whatever argument we are engaged.

4. Observe proper charity. Let us in all of our disputes keep ourselves under the commanding power and influence of holy love; for that victory is dearly purchased, that is obtained at the expense of Christian charity.

5. Remember the account that must be given to our Lord. Often think of the account we must shortly give to our great Master of all of our disputes with our fellow servants by the way.

IV. ALL BELIEVERS WILL BE MOST STRICTLY RECKONED WITH FOR THEIR DISPUTES ABOUT SUPREMACY.

A. The Disciples' Subject of Dispute.

It was about precedency and superiority—"Who should be the greatest?"

B. The Lord's Attitude toward the Disciples' Dispute.

He is displeased with them because it is an indication that they aimed at being great in the world.

C. The Reasons for Our Lord's Displeasure Concerning the Disciples' Dispute.

1. It was the result of a mistaken notion of Christ's kingdom. The disciples had imbibed the notion that our Lord Jesus, though He appeared meanly at first, would soon reign over a temporal kingdom.

2. It was contrary to His laws of humility and love. It is against the law of humility to covet to be great in this world and against the law of love to strive who shall be greatest.

3. It was contrary to the example set by the Lord Jesus. The same mind should have been in them that was in Him who "made Himself of no reputation (emptied Himself)" and who washed the disciples' feet (Philippians 2:7; John 13:4–5).

4. It would render them unfit for their appointed service. It was very absurd for the disciples to strive who should be greatest when they were all to labor and suffer reproach and poverty and ignominy.

5. It was a corrupt temper that would be the bane of the church. It would be the reproach of its ministry, an obstruction to its enlargement, the disturbance of its peace and the original of all the breaches that would be made upon its order and unity.

CONCLUSION

Let us never argue about who shall be greatest in this world for it is despicable and dangerous; but let all our strife be who shall be best. Especially let us strive to excel ourselves and to do more good than we have done (Philippians 3:13, 14).

Matthew Henry

SERMON TWENTY-TWO

CHRIST'S DISCOURSE ON REGENERATION

> *Except a man be born again, he cannot see the kingdom of God.*
> *Except a man be born of water and of the Spirit, he cannot enter*
> *into the kingdom of God. The wind bloweth where it listeth, and*
> *thou hearest the sound thereof, but cannot tell whence it cometh,*
> *and wither it goeth: so is everyone that is born of the Spirit.*
> —JOHN 3:3, 5, 8

NOT MANY mighty and noble are called, yet some are, and here was one. This was a man of the Pharisees, bred to learning, a scholar. The principles of the Pharisees and peculiarities of their sect were directly contrary to the spirit of Christianity; yet there were some in whom even those high thoughts were cast down and brought into obedience to Christ. It was in response to Nicodemus's visit that the Lord Jesus discourses on the new birth.

I. THE NATURE OF REGENERATION.

A. It Is a New Life.

Birth is the beginning of life; to be born again is to begin anew, as those that have hitherto lived either much amiss or to little purpose. We must not think to patch up the old building, but begin from the foundation.

B. It Is a New Nature.

1. We must be born anew. We must have a new nature, new principles, new affections, new aims. We must be born anew. By our first birth we were corrupt, shapen in sin and iniquity; we must therefore undergo a second birth, our souls must be fashioned and enlivened anew.

2. We must be born from above. This new birth has its rise from heaven: "Which were born, not of blood, nor of the will of the flesh, nor of the will of man, but of God" (John 1:13). Its tendency is to heaven; it is to be born to a divine and heavenly life, a life of communion with God and the upper world, and in order to do this, it is to partake of a divine nature and bear the image of the heavenly.

II. THE NECESSITY FOR REGENERATION.

A. This Is Seen in That Christ Declared It.

Christ has said it and as He himself never did nor ever will abrogate it, so all the world cannot gainsay it. He who is the great Lawgiver and the great Mediator of the new covenant and the great Physician of souls, who knows man's case and what is necessary to his cure, has said: "Ye must be born again."

B. This Is Seen in That We Cannot Understand the Nature of the Kingdom of God without Regeneration.

Such is the nature of the things pertaining to the kingdom of God (in which Nicodemus desired to be instructed) that the soul must be newly modelled and moulded; the natural man must become a spiritual man before he is capable of receiving and understanding them. "But the natural man receiveth not the things of the Spirit of God: for they are foolishness unto him: neither can he know them, because they are spiritually discerned" (I Corinthians 2:14).

C. This Is Seen in That We Cannot Receive the Comfort of the Kingdom of God without Regeneration.

We cannot without the new birth, receive the comfort of it; cannot expect any benefit by Christ and His Gospel which is absolutely necessary to our happiness here and hereafter. Considering what we are by nature, how corrupt and sinful; what God is, in whom alone we can be happy; and what heaven is, to which the perfection of our happiness is reserved; it will appear in the nature of the thing that we must be born again; because it is impossible that we should be happy, if we are not holy.

1. Because of what we are.

2. Because of what God is.

3. Because of what heaven is.

III. THE METHOD OF REGENERATION.

A. The Method Stated.

1. What it is not. It is not wrought by any wisdom or power of our own. "Not of works, lest any man should boast" (Ephesians 2:9). "Not by works of righteousness which we have done" (Titus 3:5).

2. What it is. To be born again is to be born of the Spirit. It is wrought by the power and influence of the blessed Spirit of Grace. It is the sanctification of the Spirit (I Peter 1:2) and renewing of the Holy Spirit (Titus 3:5). The word He works by is His inspiration and the heart to be wrought on He has access to. Those who are regenerated by the Spirit are made spiritual and refined from the dross and dregs of sensuality.

B. The Method Illustrated.

1. It is compared to water. To be born again is to be born of water and of the Spirit, that is, of the Spirit working like water. That which is intended here is to show that the Spirit, in sanctifying a soul (1) cleanses and purifies it as water; takes away its filth by which it was unfit for the kingdom of God. It is the washing of regeneration (Titus 3:5); (2) cools and refreshes the soul as water does the hunted hart and the weary traveller.

2. It is compared to wind. The Holy Spirit's work in regeneration compared to wind indicates: (1) The Spirit works arbitrarily and as a free agent. The wind blows where it will and is not subject to our command, but is directed of God. The Spirit dispenses His influences on whom and in what measure and degree He pleases. (2) He works powerfully and with evident effects. (3) He works mysteriously and in secret, hidden ways. The manner and methods of the Spirit's working are a mystery.

CONCLUSION

"Ye must be born again." Christ shows that it is necessary in the nature of the thing, for we are not fit to enter into the kingdom of God until we are born again. "That which is born of the flesh is flesh." Here is our malady and the causes of it, which are such as speak plainly that there is no remedy but the new birth.

Matthew Henry

FAITH IN CHRIST INFERRED FROM FAITH IN GOD

Ye believe in God, believe also in me.
—JOHN 14:1

THAT which is here intended as a comfort in time of trouble will not be so unless it be our practice, for it is our duty at all times not only to believe in God, but to believe also in Jesus Christ.

I. THE OBJECTS OF FAITH.

A. God the Father Almighty and Christ the Father's Only Begotten Son.

We cannot believe in God as the Father without believing in Him who is the Son of the Father, the only begotten of the Father and therefore of the same nature with Him.

B. God the Eternal Mind and Christ the Eternal Word and Wisdom.

God is an infinite Spirit and He has told us that the Redeemer is the Word. As the thought is one with the mind that thinks it and yet may be considered as distinct from it, so Christ was and is one with the Father and yet distinct from the Eternal Wisdom.

C. God the Creator and Governor of the World and Christ the Power of God.

Nothing appears more evident by the light of the Gospel than the fact that God made the worlds by His Son and by Him all things consist (hold together).

D. God Our Owner by the Right of Creation, Christ Our Owner by the Right of Redemption.

As to God we owe our being because He made us; so to Christ we owe our well-being, our recovery from that deplorable state into which we were plunged by sin.

E. God Our Judge and Christ Our Advocate.

We are conscious that we are sinners and that from God our judgment must proceed. Whenever we think of giving an account to God we must remember the Lord Jesus as the only mediator between us and God.

F. God Our End and Christ Our Way.

We know that God who made us is He for whom we are made and He is alone able to make us happy. The Gospel tells us that Christ is the true and living way to the Father (John 14:6).

II. THE ACTS OF FAITH.

A. Acquaintance with God and with Christ.

We think we are concerned to know God; we are, but that will not be life eternal to us, unless withal we know Jesus Christ whom the Father has sent to acquaint us with Him.

B. Adoration of God and Christ.

Those who believe in God as Sovereign Lord will see themselves obliged to give Him the glory due to His name and to pay their homage to Him. And thus we must express our faith in Christ as the restored blind man: "Lord, I believe; and he worshipped Him" (John 9:38).

C. Reverence of God and Christ.

If we believe in the majesty of God we shall tremble at His presence and be afraid of falling under His displeasure, much more of remaining under it. Let us also believe in Christ and thus express it.

D. Study to do the Will of God and Christ.

All who believe in God study to do His will and we must also study to do the will of Christ and in the temper of our minds and tenor of our lives to comply with it.

E. Delight Ourselves in God and Christ.

Since, through faith, we rejoice in God, so believing we must rejoice also in Christ; for in Him dwell not only the awful, but all the amiable perfections of the divine nature. It is in Christ Jesus that we rejoice and in God through Him.

F. Dependence and Confidence in God and Christ.

We rely upon God to direct us, to support and strengthen us, to pity us; and now let us thus believe also in Jesus Christ and make Him our hope.

III. THE NECESSARY CONNECTION BETWEEN FAITH IN GOD AND IN CHRIST.

A. If We Believe in God, We Must Believe in Christ Who Is One with the Father.

Christ has told us, "I and My Father are one" (John 10:30). We come to the knowledge of God by the knowledge of Jesus Christ and whoever believes in the Father, as far as the Son is revealed to him to be one with the Father, will believe also in Him.

B. If We Believe in God, We Must Believe in Christ Who Has Been Commissioned, Sent, and Testified to by God.

We do not believe in God unless we believe what He has said concerning His Son and rest upon it (Luke 10:16; Matthew 3:17; John 5:30).

C. If We Believe in God, We Must Honor Him by Believing in Christ.

If we confess that Jesus Christ is Lord, it is to the glory of God the Father (Philippians 2:11).

D. If We Believe That God Spoke by Moses and the Prophets, We Must Believe in Christ of Whom They Bear Testimony.

All the prophets bear witness to Christ and in all the ceremonies of Mosaic institution He was typified. Our Lord insisted that one of the strongest proofs of His divine mission was the Old Testament Scriptures.

E. If We Rightly Apprehend How Matters Stand between God and Man Since the Fall, We Will Believe the Gospel Record of a Mediator between God and Man.

1. Man in a great measure has lost the knowledge of God. We cannot but perceive that man has in a great measure lost the knowledge of God and therefore he should gladly believe in Christ who has revealed God to us.

2. There is an infinite distance between God and man. The light of nature shows us the glory of a God above us; whence we all are tempted to infer that we cannot have communion with Him. Shall we not therefore welcome the tidings of a Mediator between God and man?

3. There is a quarrel between God and man because of sin. The God who made us is not only above us, but against us; and therefore we should gladly believe in Him by whom that quarrel is taken up, in whom God was reconciling the world to Himself (II Corinthians 5:19).

4. Man is corrupt and sinful. We find by daily experience that our minds are alienated from God and there is in them a strong bias toward the world and the flesh; that we are not of ourselves inclinable to or sufficient for anything that is good.

5. Man's spirit is immortal. If we believe that God is the Father of our spirits we cannot but perceive that they are immortal and we are made for another world and therefore we will gladly believe in One who will be our guide to that world.

CONCLUSION

Let that be the language of our settled judgments, which a learned and religious man took for his motto: "Christ is a Christian's all." Let a martyr's testimony be the language of our pious affections: "None but Christ, none but Christ."

Matthew Henry

SERMON TWENTY-FOUR

WONDERFUL LOVE

As the Father hath loved me, so have I loved you:
continue ye in my love.
—JOHN 15:9

IT IS generally agreed that Christ's discourse in this and the next chapter was at the close of His Last Supper, the night in which He was betrayed. Now that He was about to leave the disciples, they would be tempted to grow strange to one another and therefore He presses it upon them to love one another.

I. THE FATHER'S LOVE FOR CHRIST.

A. The Fact of the Father's Love for His Son.

"As the Father hath loved me." He loved Him as Mediator: "This is my beloved Son" (Matthew 3:17; 17:5). He was the Son of His love. He loved Him and gave all things into His hands (John 13:3).

B. The Son's Abiding in His Father's Love.

1. He continuously loved the Father. He continually loved His Father and was beloved of Him. Even when He was made sin and a curse for us and it pleased the Lord to bruise Him, yet He abode in the Father's love.

2. He cheerfully suffered because He loved the Father. Because He continued to love His Father, He went cheerfully through His sufferings, and therefore His Father continued to love Him.

C. The Requisite for Christ to Abide in His Father's Love.

1. Obedience was required. He abode in His Father's love because He kept His Father's law: "I have kept my Father's commandments, and abide in His love" (verse 10).

2. Obedience manifested His love. Hereby He showed that He continued to love His Father, that He went on and went through with His undertaking. Therefore the Father continued to love Him. His soul delighted in Him because He did not fail, nor was discouraged (Isaiah 42:1, 4).

II. THE SON'S LOVE FOR HIS DISCIPLES.

A. The Pattern of His Love.

1. The love as a Son. "As the Father hath loved me, so have I loved you." A strange expression of the condescending grace of Christ! As the Father loved Him who was most worthy, He loved them who were most unworthy. The Father loved Him as His Son and He loves them as His children.

2. The love that gave all things. "The Father gave all things into His hands," so with Himself. He freely gives us all things. The Father loved Him as Mediator, as head of the Church, and the great trustee of divine grace and favor, which He had not for Himself only, but for the benefit of those for whom He was intrusted; and He says, "I have been a faithful trustee. As the Father has committed His love to Me, so I transmit it to you."

B. The Proofs and Products of His Love.

1. Christ's voluntary death. Christ loved His disciples, for He laid down His life for them. Others have laid down their lives, content that their lives should be taken from them; but Christ gave up His life, was not merely passive, but made it His own act and deed.

2. Christ's covenant of friendship. The followers of Christ are the friends of Christ. He is graciously pleased to call and count them so. They that do the duty of His servants are admitted and advanced to the dignity of His friends (verses 14–15). He is afflicted in their afflictions and takes pleasure in their prosperity.

3. His communication of His mind to the disciples. "All things that I have heard of My Father I have made known unto you" (verse 15). As to the secret will of God, there are many things which we must be content not to know; but as to the revealed will of God, Jesus Christ has faithfully handed to us what He received of the Father.

4. His choosing men to represent Him on the earth. Christ loved His disciples, for He chose and ordained them to be the prime instruments of His glory and honor in the world (verse 16). It is fitting that Christ should have the choosing of His own ministers; still He does it by His providence and Spirit.

III. THE DISCIPLES' LOVE FOR CHRIST.

A. It Is to Be a Continuous Love.

"Continue in your love to me and in mine to you."

1. They are to continue to love Him. All that love Christ should continue in their love to Him, that is, be always loving Him and taking all occasions to show it, and to love to the end.

2. They are to continue in His love. We must place our happiness in the continuance of Christ's love to us and make it our business to give continued proofs of our love to Christ, that nothing may tempt us to withdraw from Him or provoke Him to withdraw from us.

B. It Is to Be a Joyous Love.

1. Abiding joy. The words "that my joy might remain in you" (verse 11) are so placed in the original that they may mean: (a) "My joy in you may remain." If they bring forth fruit and continue in His love He will continue to rejoice in them. (b) "Your joy in me may remain." It is the will of Christ that His disciples should constantly rejoice in Him (Philippians 4:4).

2. Fullness of joy. Not only that you might be full of joy, but that your joy in Christ and in His love may rise higher and higher until it comes to perfection, when "ye enter into the joy of your Lord."

C. It Is to Be an Obedient Love.

1. The promise. "Ye shall abide in my love" (verse 10), as in a dwelling place, at home in Christ's love; as in a resting place, at ease in Christ's love; as in a stronghold, safe in God's love. "Ye shall abide in my love," you shall have grace and strength to persevere in loving Christ.

2. The condition of the promise. "If ye keep my commandments" (verse 10). The disciples were to keep Christ's commandments, not only by constant conformity to themselves, but by a faithful delivery of them to others; they were to keep them as trustees in whose hands the great deposit was lodged. They were to teach all things that Christ had commanded (Matthew 28:20).

CONCLUSION

The surest evidence of our love to Christ is obedience to the laws of Christ. Such are loved by the Father and the Son. Both of these loves are the crown and comfort, the grace and glory which shall be to all them that love the Lord Jesus Christ in sincerity.

Matthew Henry

THE BENEFITS OF JUSTIFICATION

Therefore being justified by faith, we have peace with God . . .
we have access by faith . . . rejoice in the glory of God . . .
we glory in tribulations.
—ROMANS 5:1–5

THE PRECIOUS benefits and privileges which flow from justification are such as should quicken us all to give diligence to make it sure to ourselves that we are justified and then to take the comfort it renders to us and to do the duty it calls from us. The fruits of this tree of life are exceedingly precious.

I. WE HAVE PEACE WITH GOD (Verse 1).

A. The Condition of Man Reveals His Need for Peace.

It is sin that breeds the quarrel between us and God, creates not only a strangeness, but an enmity. The holy, righteous God cannot in honor be at peace with a sinner while he continues under the guilt of sin. Justification takes away the guilt and so makes way for peace. And such are the benignity and good will of God to man that immediately upon the removal of the obstacle the peace is made.

B. The Character of the Peace of the Justified Man.

There is more in this peace than barely a cessation of enmity, there is friendship and loving kindness, for God is either the worst enemy or the best friend. Abraham being justified by faith was called the friend of God (James 2:23), which was his honor, but not his peculiar honor; Christ has called His disciples friends (John 15:13–15). Surely a man needs no more to make him happy than to have God as his friend.

C. The Channel by Which Peace Is Brought to Man.

This peace is through our Lord Jesus Christ; through Him as our great Peacemaker, the Mediator between God and man (I Timothy 2:5), that blessed Daysman that has laid His hand upon us both. "He is our peace" (Ephesians 2:14), not only the Maker, but the matter and maintenance of our peace (Colossians 1:20).

II. WE HAVE ACCESS TO GOD (Verse 2).

A. The Saints' Happy State.

It is a state of grace, God's loving kindness to us and our conformity to God. Now "unto this grace we have access"— an introduction. This implies that we were not born in this state; but we are brought into it. "By whom we have access by faith"; by Christ as the author and principal agent; by faith as the means of this access. Not by Christ in consideration of any merit of ours; but in consideration of our believing dependence upon Him.

B. The Saints' Happy Standing.

"Wherein we stand": a posture that denotes our discharge from guilt. It denotes also our progress. While we stand we are going; we must not lie down, as if we had already attained, but stand as those that are pressing forward. The phrase denotes, further, our perseverance. We stand firm and safe, upheld by God's power. It denotes our confirmation in God's favor.

III. WE REJOICE IN THE HOPE OF THE GLORY OF GOD (Verse 2).

A. The Persons Who May Hope for the Future Glory of God.

Besides the happiness in hand there is a happiness in the hope of the glory which God will put upon His saints in heaven. Only those who have access by faith into the grace of God now may hope for the glory of God hereafter. There is no good hope of glory but what is founded in grace;

grace is glory begun, the pledge and assurance of glory. He "will give grace and glory" (Psalm 84:11).

B. The Future Hope of Glory Is Sufficient for Present Joy.

Those who hope for the glory of God hereafter have enough to rejoice in now. It is the duty of those who hope for heaven to rejoice in those hopes.

IV. WE GLORY IN TRIBULATIONS FOR GOD (Verse 3).

One would think that the peace, grace, glory, and the joy in the hope of it were more than we could pretend to have and yet it is not only so, there are more instances of our happiness; we glory in tribulations, especially tribulation for righteousness' sake. Why?

A. Tribulation Produces Patience.

Tribulation worketh patience, not in or of itself, but the powerful grace of God working in and with the tribulation. It proves and by proving improves patience; as parts and gifts increase by exercise. That which works patience is a matter of joy; for patience does us more good than tribulations can do us hurt. Tribulation in itself works impatience; but as it is sanctified to the saints it works patience.

B. Patience Produces Experience.

It works an experience of God which gives songs in the night. The patient sufferers have the greatest experience of the divine consolations which abound as afflictions abound. It is by tribulation that we make an experiment of our own sincerity and therefore such tribulations are called trials. It works an approbation, as he is approved that has passed the test. Job's tribulation wrought patience and that patience produced an approbation (Job 2:3).

C. Experience Produces Hope.

He who, being thus tried, comes forth as gold will thereby be encouraged to hope. This experiment or approbation is not so much the ground as the evidence of our hope and a special friend to it. Experience of God is a prop to our hope; He who has delivered, does and will deliver. Experience of ourselves helps to evidence our sincerity.

D. Hope Makes Not Ashamed.

It is a hope that will not deceive us. Nothing confounds more than disappointment. Everlasting shame and confusion will be caused by the perishing of the expectation of the wicked, but "the hope of the righteous shall be gladness" (Proverbs 10:28; see Psalms 22:5; 71:1). Or, it makes us unashamed of our sufferings. Because we have hopes of glory we are not ashamed of these sufferings.

CONCLUSION

This hope will not disappoint us because it is sealed with the Holy Spirit as the Spirit of love. The love is shed abroad as sweet ointment perfuming the soul; as rain watering it and making it fruitful. The ground of all our comfort and holiness, and preservance in both is laid in the shedding abroad of the love of God in our hearts. It is that which constrains us (II Corinthians 5:14).

Matthew Henry

THE HOLY SPIRIT AND PRAYER

Likewise the Spirit also helpeth our infirmities: for we know not what we should pray for as we ought: but the Spirit itself maketh intercession for us with groanings which cannot be uttered. And He that searcheth the hearts knoweth what is the mind of the Spirit, because He maketh intercession for the saints according to the will of God.
—ROMANS 8:26–27

THE APOSTLE, having fully explained the doctrine of justification and pressed the necessity of sanctification, in this chapter applies himself to the consolation of the Lord's people. It is the will of God that His people should be a comforted people. And we have here such a display of the unspeakable privileges of true believers as may furnish us with an abundant matter for joy and peace in believing, that by all of these immutable things, in which it is impossible for God to lie, we might have a strong consolation. One of these privileges is prayer. While we are in this world, hoping and waiting for what we see not, we must be praying. Hope supposes desire and that desire offered up to God is prayer.

I. THE NEED FOR THE AID OF THE HOLY SPIRIT IN PRAYER.

A. We Do Not Know What to Pray for as We Ought.

We are not competent judges of our own condition. We are shortsighted and very much biased in favor of the flesh and apt to separate the end from the way. "Ye know not what ye ask" (Matthew 20:22). We are like foolish children that are ready to cry for fruit before it is ripe (Luke 9:54–56).

1. Because we are shortsighted.

2. Because we are biased in favor of the flesh.

B. We Do Not Know How to Pray as We Ought.

1. Hindrances in prayer. As to the manner, we know not how to pray as we ought. It is not enough that we do that which is good, but we must do it well; seek in a due order; and here we are often at a loss— graces are weak, affections cold, thoughts wandering. It is not always easy for one to find it in his heart to pray (II Samuel 7:27).

2. Hindrances to prayer affect all believers. The Apostle speaks of the matter of not knowing how to pray in the first person: "We know not." He puts himself among the rest. Folly, weakness, and distraction in prayer are that of which all the saints complain. If so great a saint as Paul knew not how to pray, what reason have we to go forth about that duty in our own strength?

II. THE HOLY SPIRIT'S AID IN PRAYER.

A. He Helps Our Infirmities.

1. The explanation. He helps our praying infirmities which most easily beset us in that duty. The Spirit in the Word of God helps—many rules and promises are there for our help. The Spirit in the heart helps—dwelling in us, working in us, as the Spirit of grace and supplication; for this end the Holy Spirit was poured out.

2. The requirement. He helps us as we help one that would lift up a burden, by lifting at the other end; He helps with us, with us doing our endeavor, putting forth the strength we have. We must not sit still and expect that the Spirit will do all. We cannot without God and He will not without us.

B. How He Helps Our Infirmities.

1. By dictating our requests. The Spirit dictates our requests, indites our petitions, draws up our plea for us. He as an enlightening Spirit teaches us what to pray for; as a sanctifying Spirit He works and excites praying graces; as a comforting Spirit He silences our fears and helps us over all of our discouragements. He is the spring of all our desires and breathings toward God.

2. With unutterable groanings. The strength and fervency of those desires which the Holy Spirit works are hereby intimated. There may be praying in the Spirit where there is not a word spoken; as Moses (Exodus 14:15) and Hannah (I Samuel 1:13) prayed. It is not the rhetoric and eloquence, but the faith and fervency of our prayers that the Spirit works, as an intercessor, in us.

3. According to God's will. The Spirit in the heart never contradicts the Spirit in the Word. Those desires that are contrary to the will of God do not come from the Spirit. The Spirit interceding in us evermore melts our wills into the will of God. "Not as I will but as Thou wilt."

III. THE SUCCESS OF THE HOLY SPIRIT'S AID IN PRAYER.

A. God Knows Our Need.

This is assured because He searches the heart.

1. This Divine heart searching is a disturbing truth to the hypocrite. To the hypocrite, whose religion lies in his tongue, nothing is more dreadful than the fact that God searches the heart and sees through all of his disguises.

2. This Divine heart searching is a comforting truth to the believer. To a sincere Christian, who makes heart work of his duty, nothing is more comfortable than the fact that God searches the heart, for then He will hear and answer those desires which we lack words to express. He knows "what we have need of before we ask" (Matthew 6:8).

B. God Knows the Mind of the Spirit.

He knows what is the mind of His own Spirit in us. As He always hears the Son interceding for us (John 11:42), so He always hears the Spirit interceding in us, because His intercession is according to the will of God.

1. He hears the intercession of Christ for us.

2. He hears the intercession of the Spirit in us.

CONCLUSION

What could have been done more for the comfort of the Lord's people? Christ has said, "Whatever you ask the Father according to His will, He will give it you." But how shall we learn to ask according to His will? The Spirit will teach us that. There it is, that the children of God never seek in vain.

Matthew Henry

THE CHRISTIAN'S RESPONSIBILITY TO GOD

*I beseech you therefore, brethren, by the mercies of God,
that ye present your bodies o living sacrifice, holy, acceptable
unto God, which is your reasonable service. And be not conformed
to this world: but be ye transformed by the renewing of your
mind, that ye may prove what is that good, and acceptable,
and perfect will of God.*
—ROMANS 12:1–2

THE APOSTLE having confirmed the fundamental doctrines of Christianity now stresses Christian duties. Christianity is practical. It tends to the right ordering of the life. It is designed not only to inform our judgments, but to transform our lives. The text reminds us of our duty to God.

I. THE PRESENTATION OF THE BODY TO GOD.

A. The Nature of the Presentation.

1. A voluntary sacrifice. Presenting of them denotes a voluntary act done by virtue of that absolute despotic power which the will has over the body and all the members of it. It must be a free will offering. This is to glorify God with our bodies (I Corinthians 6:20).

2. A living sacrifice. A body sincerely devoted to God is a living sacrifice, a living sacrifice inspired with the spiritual life of the soul. It is Christ living in the soul by faith that makes the body a living sacrifice (Galatians 2:20). Holy love kindles the sacrifices, puts life into the duties.

3. A holy sacrifice. There must be real holiness which stands in an entire rectitude of heart and life, by which we are conformed in both to the nature and will of God. Our bodies must not be made the instruments of sin and uncleanness, but set apart for God and put to holy uses.

B. The Arguments Favoring the Presentation.

1. The mercies of God. God is a merciful God, therefore let us present our bodies to Him. He will be sure to use them kindly and knows how to consider the frames of them for He is of infinite compassion. We receive from Him every day the fruits of His mercy (Lamentations 3:22).

2. The acceptability of it to God. The great end to which we should labor is to be accepted of the Lord (II Corinthians 5:9), to have Him well pleased with our persons and performances. Now these living sacrifices are acceptable to God; while the sacrifices of the wicked, although fat and costly, are an abomination to the Lord.

3. The reasonableness of the presentation. God does not impose upon us anything hard or unreasonable, but that which is altogether agreeable to the principles of right reason. God deals with us as with rational creatures and will have us so to deal with Him. Thus must the body be presented to God.

II. RENEWAL OF THE MIND.

A. The Meaning of Renewal of the Mind.

See to it that there be a saving change wrought in you and that it be carried on. Conversion and sanctification are the renewing of the mind; a change not of substance, but of the qualities of the soul.

1. Conversion. It is the receiving of new dispositions, inclinations, sympathies, and antipathies; the understanding enlightened, the conscience softened, the thoughts rectified and the will bowed to the will of God; the affections made spiritual and heavenly: so that the man is not what he was (II Corinthians 5:17).

2. Sanctification. The progress of sanctification, dying to sin more and more and living to righteousness more and more, is the carrying on of this renewing work until it is perfected in glory.

B. The Manner of the Renewal of the Mind.

1. It is the work of God. We cannot work such a change ourselves; we could as soon make a new world as to make a new heart by any power of our own; it is God's work. It is God that turns us and then we are turned.

2. It is our duty to seek God's grace to bring this about. "Be ye transformed," that is, use the means which God has appointed and ordained for it. Lay your souls under the changing, transforming influences of the blessed Spirit; seek unto God for grace in the use of all the means of grace. Although the new man is created of God, yet we must put it on (Ephesians 4:24).

C. The Obstacle to the Renewing of the Mind.

1. The obstacle named. The great enemy to this renewing which we must avoid is conformity to this world. All the disciples and followers of the Lord Jesus must be nonconformists to this world. Do not fashion yourselves according to the world.

2. The obstacle explained. We must not conform to the things of the world; they are mutable and the fashion of them is passing away. Do not conform to the lusts of the flesh or the lusts of the eye. We must not conform to the men of the world, of that which lies in wickedness, that is, we must not follow the multitude to do evil.

D. The Effect of the Renewal of the Mind.

It is the proving of the good, acceptable, and perfect revealed will of God concerning what He requires of us. This reminds us of three things.

1. The will of God is good, acceptable, and perfect. It is good in itself; it is good for us. It is acceptable, it is pleasing to God. It is perfect, to which nothing can be added. The revealed will of God is a sufficient rule of faith and practice.

2. The will of God should be proved. It concerns the Christian to know the will of God; to know it with judgment and approbation; to know it experimentally; to know the excellency of the will of God by the experience of a conformity to it.

3. The transformed mind is the best able to prove the will of God. The promise is, "If any man will do His will, he shall know of the doctrine" (John 7:17). An honest, humble heart that has spiritual senses exercised and is delivered into the mold of the Word, loves it and practices it.

CONCLUSION

Our duty to God, as Christians, is to yield to Him and transform our minds by His grace. Thus to be godly is to surrender ourselves to God. This is a prerequisite to fruitful service.

Matthew Henry

SERMON TWENTY-EIGHT

THE TREASURE IN EARTHEN VESSELS

*But we have this treasure in earthen vessels, that the excellency
of the power may be of God and not of us.*
—II CORINTHIANS 4:7

THE heavens indeed declare the glory of God, but they do not show us how we may glorify God, much less how we may be glorified with Him. Here, therefore, where natural reason and natural religion leave us at a loss, the Gospel of Christ takes us up and shows us the glory of God shining in the face of Christ, where it shines clearer and stronger and brighter and with more satisfaction than it does in the face of the whole creation; for it declares Christ reconciling the world to Himself.

I. THE GOSPEL OF CHRIST IS THE TREASURE.

A. The Gospel Is a Treasure because it Consists of an Abundance of That Which Is of Inestimable Value.

There are treasures of wisdom and knowledge in the truths which the Gospel reveals to us, about which the understanding finds the best employment. There are treasures of comfort and joy in the offers which the Gospel makes to us and the blessings it assures to all believers, in which not only the necessities of the soul are well provided for, but its desires abundantly satisfied and its true and lasting happiness inviolably secured. There is a treasure of grace and strength in the Spirit and His operations in us.

B. The Gospel Is a Treasure because There Is No End to It.

It is deposited in good hands whence we may draw from it, but cannot be deprived of it. It is deposited in the wisdom and counsel of God, in Christ, in the Scriptures. It is a treasure that will not only suit the present exigences of the soul, but will last as long as it lasts. It is the word of the Lord which endures forever, when all the glory of man is withered as the grass. It is a treasure which glorified saints will be living plentifully and pleasantly upon to eternity.

C. The Gospel Is a Treasure because It Is of Universal Use.

It is not only valuable in itself, but every way suitable and serviceable to us. It is a treasure of food for all those who hunger and thirst after righteousness. It is a treasure of arms and ammunition for our spiritual warfare. It furnishes us with the answers to every temptation and with the whole armor of God. It is a treasure in the heart of every true believer. If the Gospel of Christ has the innermost and uppermost place in our lives we are rich toward God.

II. CHRISTIANS ARE THE EARTHEN VESSELS.

A. They Are Only Vessels.

They can give only what they have received. God is the fountain of light and life and living waters and all their springs are in Him. It is the commandment which is the lamp and the law is the light; the believers are but as candlesticks in which this light is set up and by which it is held forth. A man can receive nothing which he can depend upon himself or recommend to others with any assurance, unless it be given him from above.

B. They Are Earthen Vessels.

Believers are compared to earthen vessels because: (1) They are made of the same mold as other people; (2) oftentimes in respect to their outward condition they are of small account, men of low degree; (3) they are subject to many infirmities; (4) not all of the same constitution—some are weak and others are strong; (5) they are what God, the Potter, makes them; (6) they are vessels of service; (7) oftentimes despised and trampled upon by men; (8) they are frail and mortal and dying and on that account earthen vessels.

III. GOD PLACES THE TREASURE IN EARTHEN VESSELS TO MAGNIFY HIS POWER.

A. Divine Power Was Given to the Apostles to Strengthen Them for Their Work.

To preach down Judaism and paganism and preach up the kingdom of the crucified Jesus was a service that required a far greater strength, both of judgment and resolution, than the apostles had of themselves. If they had not been full of power by the Spirit of the Lord they could never have spoken as they did with that wisdom which all their adversaries were not able to gainsay or resist. Also, they could never have made such vigorous attacks upon the devil's kingdom, nor have gathered such a harvest of souls to Jesus Christ.

B. Divine Power Was Given to the Apostles to Support Them in Their Hardships.

God chose the service of such men as were despised in order that He might magnify His own power in keeping the spirit which He had made from failing before Him. One would wonder how the apostles kept up their spirits. It was not by any power of their own, but underneath them were the everlasting arms and when they were pressed out of measure, above strength, so that they despaired of life, yet they did not faint because they were borne up by the power of God who raises the dead.

C. Divine Power Was Given to the Apostles to Give Them Success.

The world was to be enlightened with the lights and enriched with the treasure that was lodged in the earthen vessels. It is not what the apostles have wrought, but what God has wrought by them. The Gospel of Christ is the power of God to salvation. The wonderful achievements of the Gospel! The trophies of its victory over the powers of darkness! The numerous instances of its convincing and sanctifying power! Many sinful hearts have by it been made to tremble and many gracious souls to triumph.

CONCLUSION

Thank God for the Gospel treasure though it is in earthen vessels. Thank God that it is in such vessels that it may be the nearer to you and the more within your reach. Give all diligence to make sure your interest in this treasure. What will it avail us that we have the Gospel in our land if we have it not in our hearts? What will it avail us that we have the sound of it about us and not the savor of it within us?

Matthew Henry

THE PROMISES OF GOD

Having therefore these promises, dearly beloved, let us cleanse
ourselves from all filthiness of the flesh and spirit, perfecting
holiness in the fear of God.
—II CORINTHIANS 7:1

WE WILL consider the promises of God under four heads, namely, the Christian's possession of the promises, the content of the promises, the blessed fruits of the promises, and the Christian's obligation or duty because of the promises.

I. THE POSSESSION OF GOD'S PROMISES.

A. The Privilege of the Possession of the Promises.

It is the unspeakable privilege of all believers to have as a certain possession the precious promises of God.

B. The Explanation of the Possession of the Promises.

We have the promises as tokens of God's favor toward us; as fruits of Christ's purchase; as declarations of God's good will toward men; as a foundation of our faith and hope; as the directions and encouragements of our desires in prayer; as the means by which the grace of God works for our holiness and comfort, as the pledge and assurance of future blessedness.

II. THE CONTENT OF GOD'S PROMISES.

A. Promises of Spiritual Blessings.

God has promised that all of our sins shall be pardoned (Isaiah 43:25); that He will answer our prayers (John 14:13); that He will silence our fears (Isaiah 41:13); that He will proportion our trials to our strength (I Corinthians 10:13); that He will perfect the work of grace in us (Philippians 1:6); that He will never desert us (Hebrews 13:5); that He will give us victory over our spiritual enemies (Romans 16:20).

B. Promises of Physical Blessings.

He has also promised to protect us from all evil (Psalm 121:7, 8); to feed us with food convenient for us (Psalm 37:3); to raise up our bodies to life again (John 6:40).

III. THE FRUITS OF GOD'S PROMISES.

A. Strength.

The promises furnish us with a strength sufficient against sin and for duty.

B. Victory.

These promises speak the language of Caleb and Joshua who said, "We are well able to overcome the people," when they were about to enter into Canaan while the other spies discouraged the tribes of Israel. Thus we may say through the strength of divine grace we shall be enabled to overcome all of our spiritual enemies, namely, the world, the flesh, and the devil.

C. Faithfulness.

God is faithful to the promises which He has made to us. Therefore, we must not be false to those promises which we have made to Him.

D. Obedience.

In having these promises we have great honor put upon us and we ought to carry it as becomes us. God has promised to be to us a faithful God, a loving and tender Father. Let us not wander out of the way of duty.

E. Reward.

The promises secure to us an abundant reward for our obedience. "Therefore, my beloved brethren, be ye steadfast, unmovable, always abounding in the work of the Lord, forasmuch as ye know that your labor is not in vain in the Lord" (I Corinthians 15:58).

IV. THE CHRISTIAN'S DUTY IN VIEW OF GOD'S PROMISES.

A. To Be Cleansed from All Filthiness of the Flesh and Spirit.

1. The Reason. Look upon sin as filthiness. It is odious to God, contrary to that purity of nature which appears in His promises. Look upon sin as that which unfits us for communion with God. Sin in Scripture is called and compared to a wound, to a plague, to leprosy.

2. The manner. Let us cleanse ourselves from this filthiness by receiving the Lord Jesus Christ; for it is He who is made to us both righteousness and sanctification. Let us mortify the habits of sin and purge out the old leaven, both in the head and in the heart. Let us watch against all occasions of sin. Keep at a distance from everything which has the appearance of evil. Let us resolve for the future to have no more to do with sin.

3. The extent. (a) We must cleanse ourselves from all filthiness of the flesh—slothfulness and the love of ease, sensuality and the love of pleasure, from gratifying the desires of the body with forbidden fruit. (b) We must cleanse ourselves from all filthiness of the spirit—pride, covetousness, love of the world, fraud, deceit, injustice, sinful anger, malice, hatred, and desire of revenge.

B. To Perfect Holiness in the Fear of God.

1. The necessity for holiness. We cannot perfect holiness unless we begin it. This means that we must be devoted to God, conformed to His likeness and to His will, employed in the worship of God, engaged in the interests of God's work amongst men. To be holy is to be on the Lord's side and to espouse His cause, to be His witnesses, to be courageous and valiant for the truth, to contend earnestly for it.

2. The necessity of sincerity in holiness. We must be sincere in our holiness, that is perfecting holiness. For sincerity is our Gospel perfection, as a good man said. By this is understood that (a) the whole man must be sanctified. The understanding must be enlightened, the will brought into obedience to the will of God, both to the will of His precepts to do them and to do the will of His providences to submit to them. (b) The whole work of God must be regarded and respected (Psalm 119:6, 80, 128).

3. *The necessity of progress in holiness.* (a) The habits of grace must grow more confirmed and rooted, our resolutions against sin more settled and our resolutions for God and duty more steady. (b) The actings of grace must grow more vigorous and lively. (c) We must be more watchful and on our guard. (d) We must be actuated and animated by the fear of God resulting in faithfulness in family and private devotions, a reverent regard for the majesty and authority of God, and fear of God's wrath and displeasure.

CONCLUSION

Apply the promises to yourselves, live upon them, take them to be your heritage forever. Both you that are young and you that are old treasure up the promises. Apply the precepts to yourselves and live up to them and be holy in all manner of conduct. Keep a conscience always void of offence both toward God and toward man.

CHRISTIAN UNITY

Endeavoring to keep the unity of the Spirit in the bond of peace.
—EPHESIANS 4:3

THE FORMER part of this epistle (chapters 1–3) consists of several important doctrinal truths. The latter part (chapters 4–6) contains the most weighty and serious exhortations that can be given. The former part informs the minds of men in the great doctrines of the Gospel and the latter is designed for the direction of their lives. The text exhorts to mutual unity and concord.

I. THE MEANS OF CHRISTIAN UNITY.

A. The Statement of the Means (Verse 2).

1. Lowliness and meekness. By lowliness we are to understand humility, and entertaining mean thoughts of ourselves, which is opposed to pride. By meekness is meant that excellent disposition of soul which makes men unwilling to provoke others and not easily to be provoked or offended with their infirmities. It is opposed to angry resentments and peevishness.

2. Long-suffering and loving forbearance. Long-suffering implies a patient bearing of injuries without seeking revenge. Forbearing one another in love signifies bearing their infirmities out of a principle of love; and so as not to cease to love them on the account of these.

B. The Importance of the Means.

1. These are necessary because of the perversity of human nature. The best Christians have need to bear one with another and to make the best one of another; to provoke one another's graces (Hebrews 10:24), and not their passions. We find much in ourselves which is hard to forgive ourselves; and therefore, we must not think it much if we find that in others which we think hard to forgive them; and yet we must forgive them as we forgive ourselves.

2. These are necessary for the practice of unity. The first step toward unity is humility; without this there will be no meekness, no patience, no forbearance; and without these, no unity. Pride and passion break the peace and make all the mischief. Humility and meekness restore the peace and keep it. Only by pride comes contention (Proverbs 13:10); only by humility comes love. The more lowly mindedness, the more like-mindedness. We do not walk worthy of the vocation wherewith we are called if we are not meek and lowly of heart.

II. THE NATURE OF CHRISTIAN UNITY.

A. It Is a Spiritual Unity.

1. The seat of Christian unity. The seat of Christian unity is in the heart or spirit; it does not lie in one set of thoughts or in one form and mode of worship, but in one heart and one soul.

2. The producer of Christian unity. This unity of heart and affection is of the Spirit of God; it is wrought by Him and is one of the fruits of the Spirit. This we should endeavor to keep. We must do our utmost. If others quarrel with us, we must take all possible care not to quarrel with them. If others will despise and hate us, we must not despise and hate them.

B. It Is a Peaceful Unity.

1. The bond of peace unites persons. Peace is a bond which unites persons and makes them live friendly one with another. A peaceable disposition and conduct bind Christians together; whereas discord and quarrel disband and disunite their hearts and affections.

2. The bond of peace strengthens society. The bond of peace is the strength of society. Not that it can be imagined that all good people should be in everything of the same sentiments and the same judgment; but the bond of peace unites them all together so that they will not be unnecessarily obstinate one to another. As in a bundle of rods, they may be of different lengths and different strength; but when they are tied together by one band, they are much stronger than any, even than the thickest and strongest were of themselves.

III. THE MOTIVES FOR THE PROMOTION OF CHRISTIAN UNITY.

A. The Consideration of the Various Unities.

1. The enumeration of the unities. One body and one Spirit; one hope (verse 4). One Lord; one faith; one baptism (verse 5). One God and Father of all (verse 6).

2. The significance of the various unities. There should be one heart because there is one body and one Spirit. Two hearts in one body would be monstrous. The one body is animated by one Spirit, the Holy Spirit. All Christians are called to the same hope and therefore should be of one heart. All Christians have the same Lord to whom they are subject and were saved by the same faith. All were baptized by the same baptism in the name of the Father, Son, and Holy Spirit. One God owns all of the true members of the church for His children.

B. The Consideration of the Various Gifts.

1. The freely bestowed gifts. "But unto every one of us (Christians) is given grace, according to the measure of the gift of Christ" (verse 7). Every Christian has received some gift of grace, in some kind or degree or other, for the mutual help of one another. All of the members of Christ owe all the gifts and graces that they have to Him: and this is a good reason why we should love one another because to "every one of us is given grace." All to whom Christ has given grace and upon whom He bestowed His gifts ought to love one another.

2. The design of the bestowal of the gifts. The gifts of Christ were intended for the good of His church and in order to advance His cause and interest among men. All these being designed for one common end, is a good reason why all Christians should agree in brotherly love; and not envy one another's gifts. All of the gifts are for the restoration, strengthening, and confirmation of the saints so that they might contribute to the good of the whole.

CONCLUSION

Christians ought to accommodate themselves to the Gospel by which they are called and to the glory to which they are called. We are called Christians; we must answer that name, and live like Christians. We are called to God's kingdom and glory; that kingdom and glory, therefore, we must mind and walk as becomes the heirs of them. Therefore, we should put forth every effort "to keep the unity of the Spirit in the bond of peace."

Matthew Henry

THE INSTRUCTION OF YOUTH

*Hold fast the form of sound words which thou hast heard of me
in faith and love which is in Christ Jesus.*
—II TIMOTHY 1:13

TIMOTHY was blessed with two advantages in his childhood and youth; he was brought up under the tutoring of a godly mother and grandmother (II Timothy 1:5; 3:15) and under the instruction of a faithful ministry (II Timothy 1:13).

I. THE ADVANTAGE TO YOUTH TO LEARN GOD'S WORD.

A. The Words of the Gospel Are Sound Words.

1. This implies that they are valuable and valid. They are what they seem to be. You may trust them as you may that which is sound and will never be made ashamed of your confidence in them. They are unchangeable and inviolable.

2. This implies that there is virtue to be drawn from them. The word translated sound is sometimes rendered healthful or healing. These words when mixed with faith restore the soul and heals its maladies.

B. The Words of the Gospel When Simply Systematized Are Helpful.

It is good to have forms of the sound words drawn up for the use of learners. These should not take the place of the Scriptures, but a help to the further study of them.

1. By this the main principles of Christianity are brought together. Catechisms and confessions of faith pick up from the several parts of Holy Writ those passages which contain the essentials of religion, the foundations and main pillars upon which Christianity is built.

2. By this the truths of God are arranged and put in order. These forms of sound words show us the order that is in God's Word, the harmony of divine truths, how one thing tends to another, and all center in Christ.

3. By this the truths of God are brought down to the understanding of youth. To those who are young, the Scriptures need to be explained; to them we must give the sense and cause them to understand the reading and this is done in part by these forms of sound words.

C. The Words of the Gospel When Well Taught and Learned Bring Blessing.

1. The time spent in learning God's Word is well employed. If the time is spent in good exercises, in conversing with the Word of God, in reviewing and repeating to ourselves the things of God it is better than keeping a man from wasting an estate.

2. It gives ability to better understand and profit by the Word preached. Those who have not been taught do most need instruction by the preaching of the Word, yet those who have been well taught do most desire it because they understand it.

3. It gives a good foundation for the work of grace in the soul. Ordinarily Christ enlightens the understanding by the use of means and gives a knowledge of divine things by the instructions of parents and ministers and afterwards by His Spirit and grace brings them home to the mind and conscience resulting in salvation.

4. It arms against the assaults and insinuations of seducers. Those who are well instructed in the Scriptures and understand the evidence of divine truths are aware of the fallacies with which others are beguiled and know how to detect and escape them.

5. It prepares one to do good to others. Your being well instructed in the forms of sound words will qualify you to be useful in your generation for the glory of God and the edification of others.

6. It assists the spiritual progress of the believer. Timothy, by the help of these forms of sound words, was nourished up in faith and good doctrine (I Timothy 4:6). They who have pure hearts and clean hands hereby shall become stronger.

II. THE CHARGE TO HOLD FAST TO GOD'S WORD.

A. To Hold Fast in Remembrance.

1. It will be of good use. It will be of good use to you to retain the words you learn; and in order to do that frequently review them and repeat them over to yourselves.

2. It will be ready for use. The remembrance of them will be of use to us daily; both to fortify us against every evil word and work and to furnish us for every good word and work.

B. To Hold Fast in Faith.

1. Assent to the words as faithful sayings. You must set your seal that God is true and every word of His is so, even that which you cannot comprehend as the eternity of God or the immensity of His perfections.

2. Grow to a full assurance of the truth. Know not only what it is we believe; but why we believe it; and be ready always to give a reason of the hope that is in us (I Peter 3:15).

3. Faithful application of the truth. You must make faithful application of these sound and healing words to yourselves; else they will not answer the end or be healing to you any more than uneaten food.

C. To Hold Fast in Love.

1. Delight in them. Take delight in them and in the knowledge of them. That which we love we will hold fast and not easily part with it. That which is not thus delighted in will not be long held fast.

2. Be affected by them. Lay them to heart as things that concern you to the last degree. Be affected with love to the Word of God and then you will conceive a high value and veneration for Christ.

3. Be influenced by them. As faith works by love, so love works by keeping God's commandments (I John 5:3). We then hold fast the sayings of Christ when we govern ourselves by them.

D. To Hold Fast in Christ Jesus.

We must hold fast the sound words of the Gospel in that faith and love which has:

1. Christ as the author. It is that faith and love which is wrought in us, not by our own strength or resolutions, but by the Spirit and grace of Christ.

2. Christ as the object. It is Christ that we must embrace and hold fast. It is by faith in Christ and love to Christ that we must hold fast what we have received.

3. Christ as the end. It must be that faith and love which has an eye to Christ; which has this always in view, to glorify Christ and to be glorified with Christ.

CONCLUSION

Let us close with a few words of exhortation. Let us bless God that our lot is cast in a land of light. Let parents faithfully instruct their children in the form of sound words. Let the ministers of Christ look upon themselves as under a charge to feed Christ's lambs.

THE FAITH OF ABRAHAM

By faith Abraham obeyed. By faith he sojourned in the land of promise; for he looked for a city whose builder and maker is God. By faith Abraham offered up Isaac: accounting that God was able to raise him from the dead.
—HEBREWS 11:8–10, 17–19

THE WRITER having, in the close of the foregoing chapter, recommended the grace of faith and a life of faith as the best preservative against apostasy; he now enlarges upon this excellent grace. In doing this he writes more about the achievements of Abraham's faith than any of the other patriarchs.

I. THE GROUND OF ABRAHAM'S FAITH (Verse 8).

A. The Call of God.

1. The nature of the call. In Acts 7:2, Stephen relates the manner in which Abraham was called. This was an effectual call by which he was converted from the idolatry of his father's house. It was the call of God and therefore a sufficient ground for faith and rule of obedience.

2. The lessons from the call. (a) The grace of God is free in taking of the worst of men and making them the best. (b) God must come to us before we come to him. (c) In converting sinners God works a glorious work. (d) This call is to leave sin and sinful company.

B. The Promise of God.

1. The substance of the promise. God promised Abraham that the place he was called to he would afterward receive for an inheritance.

2. The observations concerning the promise. God calls His people to an inheritance: by His effectual call He makes them children and so heirs. This inheritance is not immediately possessed by them, they must wait for it. However, the promise is sure and shall have its seasonable accomplishment. The faith of parents often procures blessings for their posterity.

II. THE EXERCISE OF ABRAHAM'S FAITH (Verses 8, 9, 17).

A. An Implicit Obedience to the Call of God.

1. He went out, not knowing where he went. He placed himself in the hand of God to send him wherever He pleased. He subscribed to God's wisdom as best to direct; and submitted to His will as best to determine everything that concerned him. Implicit faith and obedience are due to God and to Him only.

2. He sojourned in the land as a stranger. This was in exercise of his faith. Abraham lived in Canaan as a sojourner, a stranger, and dwelt in tents with Isaac and Jacob. He lived there in an ambulatory moving condition, living in daily readiness for his removal. Thus should we all live in this world.

B. An Implicit Obedience to the Command of God.

1. It was a test of faith. Genesis 22:1 tells us: "God in this tempted Abraham"; not to sin, for so God tempts no man (James 1:13), but tried his faith and obedience. God had before this tried the faith of Abraham; but this trial was greater than all. Read the account of it in Genesis 22.

2. It was a test faithfully met. Abraham obeyed; he offered up Isaac. He intentionally gave him up by his submissive soul to God and was ready to do it actually according to the command of God. He went as far in it as to the very critical moment when God prevented him.

III. THE SUPPORTS OF ABRAHAM'S FAITH (Verses 10, 19).

A. The Hope of Heaven.

1. The description of heaven. It is a city; a regularly established, defended, and supplied society. It is a city with foundations: the unchangeable purposes and almighty power of God; the merits and mediation of the Lord Jesus; the promises of the everlasting covenant. It is a city which God planned and made.

2. The influence of heaven. He looked for it; he believed there was such a state; he waited for it. As he did so it was a support to him under all the trials of his sojourning; it helped him to bear patiently all the inconveniences of it and actively to discharge all the duties of it.

B. *The Power of God.*

1. He believed God could raise the dead. His faith was supported by the sense he had of the mighty power of God, who was able to raise the dead; he reasoned thus with himself and so he resolved all his doubts.

2. He believed God could raise his son from the dead. It does not appear that Abraham had any expectation of being prevented from offering up his son; but he knew that God was able to raise him from the dead; and he believed that God would do so since such great things depended on his son which must fail if Isaac had not a further life.

IV. THE REWARD OF ABRAHAM'S FAITH (Verse 19).

A. *He Received His Son.*

He had parted with him to God and God gave him back again. The best way to enjoy our comforts with comfort is to resign them up to God; He will then return them, if not in kind yet in kindness.

1. Abraham had given his son to God.

2. God gave him back to Abraham.

B. *He Received His Son from the Dead in a Figure.*

1. Abraham considered Isaac as dead. He received him from the dead, for he gave him up for dead. He was as a dead child to Abraham and the return was to him no less than a resurrection.

2. This was a figure of the death and resurrection of Christ. It was a figure or parable of the sacrifice and resurrection of Christ, of whom Isaac was a type. It was a figure and pledge of the glorious resurrection of all true believers whose life is not lost but hid with Christ in God (Colossians 3:3).

CONCLUSION

Because the Gospel is the end and perfection of the Old Testament, which had no excellency except in its reference to Christ and the Gospel, it was expected that the faith of the New Testament saints should be as much more perfect than the faith of the Old Testament saints. Thus it should be with us.

Matthew Henry

SERMON THIRTY-THREE

GOD, THE FATHER AND FOUNTAIN OF ALL GOOD

Every good gift and every perfect gift is from above, and cometh down from the Father of lights, with whom is no variableness, neither shadow of turning. Of His own will begat He us with the Word of Truth, that we should be a kind of firstfruits of His creatures.
—JAMES 1:17–18

AFTER the inscription and salutation (James 1:1), Christians are taught how to conduct themselves when under the cross. Several graces and duties are recommended; and those who endure their trials and afflictions as the apostle here directs, are pronounced blessed, and are assured of a glorious reward (verses 2–12). But those sins which bring sufferings, or the weaknesses and faults men are chargeable with under them, are by no means to be imputed to God; who cannot be the author of sin, but is the author of all good.

I. GOD IS THE FATHER OF LIGHTS.

A. He Is the Creator of Visible Light.

The visible light of the sun and of the heavenly bodies is from God. He said "Let there be light, and there was light" (Genesis 1:3). Thus God is at once represented as the Creator of the sun.

B. He Is Compared with Light.

"As the sun is the same in its nature and influences, though the earth and clouds often interposing make it seem to us as varying, by its rising and setting, and by its different appearances or entire withdrawal; when the change is not in it: so God is unchangeable and our changes and shadows are not from any mutability or shadowy alterations in Him, but from ourselves" (Baxter). "The Father of lights, with whom there is no variableness, neither shadow of turning." What the sun is in nature, God is in grace, providence, and glory; aye, and infinitely more.

II. GOD IS THE GIVER OF EVERY GOOD GIFT.

A. The Light That God Gives to Men.

As the Father of lights, God gives the light of reason. "The inspiration of the Almighty giveth understanding" (Job 32:8). He gives also the light of learning. Solomon's wisdom in the knowledge of nature, in the acts of government, and in all of his improvements is ascribed to God. The light of divine revelation is more immediately from above. The light of faith, purity, and all manner of consolation is from Him. So that we have nothing good except what we receive from God.

B. The Acknowledgement That Men Should Recognize.

We must own God as the author of all the powers and perfections that are in man and the giver of all the benefits which we have in and by those powers and perfections; but none of their darkness, their imperfections, or their ill actions are to be charged on the Father of lights; from Him proceeds every good and perfect gift, both pertaining to this life and that which is to come.

III. GOD IS THE SOURCE OF REGENERATION AND ITS CONSEQUENCES.

A. A True Christian is a Regenerated Person.

As every good gift is from God, so particularly our regeneration and all the holy, happy consequences which flow from it must be ascribed to Him. "Of His own will He begat us with the Word of Truth." A true Christian is a creature begotten anew. He becomes as different a person from what he was before the renewing influences of divine grace as if he were formed over again and born afresh, as is true of every true Christian.

B. The Source of Regeneration.

The source of this good work is declared in the text. It is God's own will, not by our skill or power, not from any good foreseen in us or done by us, but purely from the good will and grace of God.

C. The Means Whereby Regeneration is Effected.

The means whereby this is effected is pointed out: "the Word of Truth," that is, the Gospel; as St. Paul expresses it more plainly, "I have begotten you in Jesus Christ through the Gospel" (I Corinthians 4:15). This Gospel is indeed a word of truth; or else it could never produce such real, such lasting, such great and noble effects. We may rely upon it and venture our immortal souls upon it. And we shall find it a means of our sanctification as it is a word of truth (John 17:17).

D. The End and Design of Regeneration.

The end and design of God's giving renewing grace is here laid down; "that we should be a kind of firstfruits of His creatures"; that we should be God's portion and treasure and a more peculiar property to Him, as the firstfruits were; and that we should become holy to the Lord, as the firstfruits were consecrated to Him. Christ is the Firstfruits of Christians, Christians are the firstfruits of creatures.

CONCLUSION

Thus we see that God is the Father and fountain of all good. We should take particular care not to err in our conceptions of God. Do not wander from the Word of God and accounts of Him you have there. Do not stray into erroneous opinions and go off from the standard of truth; the things which you have received from the Lord Jesus and by the direction of His Spirit. The truth, as it is in Jesus, stands thus: that God is not and cannot be the author and patronizer of anything that is evil; but must be acknowledged as the Cause and Spring of everything that is good. "Every good gift and every perfect gift is from above, and cometh down from the Father of lights, with whom is no variableness, neither shadow of turning."

Matthew Henry

SERMON THIRTY-FOUR

THE FRAILTY AND HOPE OF MAN

All flesh is as grass, and all the glory of man as the flower of grass.
The grass withereth, and the flower thereof falleth away: but the
Word of the Lord endureth forever.

—I PETER 1:24, 25

IN THE PLACE from which Peter quotes the text (Isaiah 40:6–8) it is a voice of one crying in the wilderness, who, that he might prepare the way of the Lord in the desert, is ordered to proclaim these words. I need not tell you that John the Baptist was that voice. It is his modest testimony concerning himself. These words set before us the vanity of the natural man and the enduring character of the holy Word of God: "All flesh is as grass; the Word of the Lord endureth forever."

I. THE LAMENTATION: THE VANITY OF MAN.

A. Man Is Weak and Low.

1. He is as lowly as the grass. Mankind is indeed as numerous as the grass of the field, which multiplies, replenishes, and covers the earth; but like grass is of the earth, earthy, mean, and of small account. Alas! The kingdoms of men which make so great a noise, so great a figure in this world, are as but so many fields of grass compared with the holy and blessed inhabitants of the upper regions.

134

2. He is as weak as the grass. Proud men think themselves like the strong and stately cedars, oaks, or pines, but they soon find themselves as grass, as grass of the field, liable to be nipped with every frost, trampled by every foot, continually insulted by common calamities of human life, which we can no more resist or guard ourselves against than the grass can secure itself from the fatal blast, when the wind passeth over it and it is gone.

B. Man Is Withering and Fading.

1. Therefore let us consider ourselves as grass. Be not proud or presumptuous, be not confident of a long continuance here. We must expect to wither and should prepare accordingly and lay up our portion and happiness in none of the delights and accommodations of this life, but in something suited to the nature of an immortal soul. We may wither suddenly and know not how soon; therefore we must never adjourn to another day the necessary preparations for our removal. Let us not indulge the body too much nor bestow too much time, care, and pains upon it to the neglect of the soul.

2. Therefore let us consider others as grass. Let us see others also to be as grass and cease from men, because mankind is no more than thus to be accounted. If all flesh is grass, then let us not trust in the arm of flesh, for it will soon be a withered arm and unable to support and protect us. They who make it their arm will be like the heath in the desert, destitute and dejected. Grass is too short, too slender to lean upon.

II. THE CONSOLATION: THE ETERNAL WORD OF GOD.

A. The Bible Is Everlasting Truth.

1. It saves. Though man and his glory are fading and withering, yet God and His Word are everliving and everlasting. Nothing can make man a solid, substantial being except the new birth; being born again of the incorruptible seed which is the Word of God. This will transform him into a most excellent creature, whose glory will not fade like a flower, but shine like an angel. This word is daily set before us in the preaching of the Gospel.

2. It preserves. The only way to render this perishing creature incorruptible is to receive the Word of God, for that remains everlasting truth and if received will preserve him to everlasting life and abide with him forever.

B. The Bible Is an Everlasting Rule of Faith and Practice.

You profess to make the Scripture the commanding rule of your worship and you say that you cannot admit any religious rites but what are there appointed; but you contradict yourselves and give the lie to your profession if you do not make the Scriptures the commanding rule of your conduct also. Govern your thoughts, words, and actions by the Word of God and not by the will of the flesh or the course of this world. As Christianity is found in our Bibles, so our Bibles should be found in our hearts and lives.

1. It is the rule of our worship.

2. It should be the rule of our life.

C. The Bible Is an Everlasting Fountain of Comfort.

1. It refreshes and encourages. There is in the Word of the Lord an everlasting fountain of comfort and consolation for us to be refreshed and encouraged thereby and to draw water from it with joy. Study your Bibles. Let God's Word be your delight and your counsellor, make it familiar to you and when you go it shall lead you, when you sleep it shall keep you, when you wake it shall talk with you. Take God's statutes as your heritage forever and let them be the rejoicing of your hearts.

2. It is the foundation of our hopes. God's Word is an everlasting foundation on which to build our hopes. The foundation of God stands sure (II Timothy 2:19). This never-failing Word is the firm and immoveable rock upon which the church is built, therefore the gates of hell shall not prevail against it.

CONCLUSION

Man in his utmost glory is still a withering, fading, dying creature. In his entrance into the world, in his life, and in his fall he is like grass. Take him in all of his glory; his wit, beauty, strength, vigor, wealth, honor; these are but as the flower of grass which soon withers and dies away. Divine revelation will ride out the storm of all opposition and triumph over the powers of darkness. It will not only keep its ground, but gain its point. It goes forth conquering and to conquer.

Matthew Henry

MEEKNESS AND QUIETNESS OF SPIRIT

Even the ornament of a meek and quiet spirit,
which is in the sight of God of great price.
—I PETER 3:4

THE APOSTLE Peter endeavors to wean the Christians from the vanity of outward ornaments and to bring them into love with the better ornaments, those of the mind, the graces of the blessed Spirit, called "the hidden man of the heart"; one of which is meekness and quietness of spirit.

I. THE NATURE OF MEEKNESS AND QUIETNESS OF SPIRIT.

Meekness and quietness seem to import much the same thing, but the latter having something of metaphor in it illustrates the former.

A. The Explanation of the Character of Meekness.

1. In relation to God. It is the easy and quiet submission of the soul to the word and providence of God, to His whole will.

2. In relation to man. This Holy Spirit wrought fruit teaches us to prudently govern our own anger and teaches and enables us patiently to bear the anger of others.

B. The Character of Quietness.

1. What it is. Quietness is the evenness, the composure, and the rest of the soul, which speaks both of the nature and the excellency of the grace of meekness. The greatest comfort and happiness of man is sometimes set forth by quietness.

2. How it illustrates meekness. (a) We must be quiet as the air is quiet from the winds. (b) As the sea is quiet from the waves, so is the uneasiness of man quieted. (c) Quiet as the land is quiet from war so is the quietness of soul. (d) So is the quiet satisfaction of a weaned child.

II. THE EXCELLENCY OF MEEKNESS AND QUIETNESS OF SPIRIT.

A. The Power of a Meek and Quiet Spirit.

1. It gives victory. No triumphant chariot is so easy, safe, and glorious as that in which a meek and quiet soul rides over all the provocations of an injurious world. Meekness is a victory over ourselves and the rebellious lusts in our bosoms.

2. It gives beauty. The beauty of a thing consists in the symmetry, harmony, and agreeableness of all parts. What is meekness, but the soul's agreement with itself? Next to the beauty of holiness, which is the soul's agreement with God, is the beauty of meekness.

3. It is an ornament. The text speaks of it as an adorning much more excellent and valuable than gold, pearls, or the most costly array. It is an adorning of the soul which recommends us to God. It is an adorning of God's making and accepting.

4. It gives true courage. True courage is such a presence of mind as enables a man rather to suffer than to sin; to choose affliction rather than iniquity; to pass by an affront although he may lose by it, and be hissed at for a fool rather than engage in a sinful quarrel.

5. It produces conformity to the best patterns. To be meek is to be like the greatest saints. It is to be like the greatest angels. It is to be like God Himself who is slow to anger and in whom there is no fury.

B. The Pleasure of a Meek and Quiet Spirit.

1. The meek and quiet Christian enjoys himself. Calm are the thoughts, serene are the affections, rational are the prospects, and even and composed are the resolves of a meek and quiet soul. They are free from the pains and tortures of an angry man.

2. The meek and quiet Christian enjoys his friends. Man was intended to be a social creature and a Christian much more so. But the angry man is unfit to be so; he takes fire at every provocation. Meekness is the bond of Christian communion.

3. The meek and quiet Christian enjoys God. This is the quintessence of all happiness and that without which all our other enjoyments are sapless and insipid. "The meek also shall increase their joy in the Lord" (Isaiah 29:19).

4. The meek and quiet Christian's enemies cannot disturb these enjoyments. His enjoyment is not only sweet, but safe and secure. As far as he acts under the law of meekness it is above the reach of the assaults of those who wish ill to it.

C. The Profitableness of a Meek and Quiet Spirit.

1. It is the condition of a promise. The meek are blessed for they shall inherit the earth (Matthew 5:5). It is not always the largest proportion of this world's goods that falls to the meek man's share, but whether he has more or less, he has it by the best title and he knows how to make a right and good use of it.

2. It has a direct tendency to present benefit and advantage. (a) Meekness has a good influence upon our health. Inordinate passions injure the body. (b) It has a good influence upon the preservation and increase of wealth. (c) It has a good influence upon our safety.

D. The Preparative Value of a Meek and Quiet Spirit.

1. It prepares for any duty. It puts and keeps the soul in a frame for all religious exercises. We are fishers of men, but we seldom fish in troubled waters. Prayer is another duty for which meekness prepares us, as well as for the proper observance of the Lord's day and the Lord's Supper.

2. It prepares for any relation to which God may call us. Relations are various—superiors, inferiors, equals; he that is of a meek and quiet spirit is cut out for any of them. There are various duties and graces to be exercised; but meekness is the golden thread that must run through all.

3. It prepares for any condition. Whether the outward condition be prosperous or adverse, whether the world smile or frown upon us, a meek and quiet spirit is neither lifted up with the one nor cast down with the other, but always in the same poise.

4. It prepares for persecution. If tribulation and affliction arise because of the Word the meek and quiet spirit is armed for it, so as to preserve its peace and purity, that we may neither torment ourselves with a base fear nor pollute ourselves with a base compliance.

CONCLUSION

The ornament I have been recommending to you is confessedly excellent and lovely; will you put it on and wear it, that by this all men may know that you are Christ's disciples?

Alexander Maclaren

SERMON OUTLINES

Selected and Edited by
SHELDON B. QUINCER, D. D.

Alexander Maclaren

FOREWORD

Alexander Maclaren was born in Glasgow, Scotland, and educated in England where he spent most of his long life. He served two churches, namely, Portland Chapel, Southampton, for ten years and Union Chapel, Manchester, for over a period of forty-five years.

Pre-eminently a preacher, Dr. Maclaren well deserves to be known as "the Prince of Bible Expositors." In recognition of his pulpit attainments the University of Edinburgh bestowed upon him the degree of Doctor of Divinity. His sermons are considered models in structure and content.

In addition to his _Expositions of Holy Scripture_ (published in eleven volumes by the Wm. B. Eerdmans Publishing Co.), for which he is best known, more than twenty other volumes of his sermons have been published, which are now out of print and difficult to obtain. In the compilation of this volume, the editor has limited his selection of sermons from these lesser known and more or less hard to secure works.

The reader will recognize as he reads this volume that an effort has been made to include a wide variety of sermons both as to subjects and texts. The subject matter includes doctrinal, devotional, evangelistic, and biographical material. As to texts, only a few times has more than one text been taken from one book of the Scriptures. An effort has been made to select texts from as many sections of the Bible as possible. There are texts from thirty-one books—thirteen from the Old Testament and eighteen from the New Testament.

The purpose in preparing this volume for publication is not that the sermons may be preached verbatim, but to aid the young preacher or the layman who is untrained in the science of sermonizing and sometimes called upon to bring a Bible message, in the better preparation of his sermons or messages; thereby making him a more effective messenger of the

Word of Truth. With this end in view the sermons have been outlined in more detail than usually found in the original volumes. They have also been abridged. That which has been considered the best of the content of the sermons has been retained to make the outlines intelligible and suggestive. It should also be stated that on the first page of each sermon outline the volume from which it was taken is indicated.

It is the earnest prayer of the editor that *Maclaren's Sermon Outlines* will be used to the glory of our Lord and Savior Jesus Christ and to the blessing of all who read and use them.

Sheldon B. Quincer
Grand Rapids, Michigan
March, 1954

Alexander Maclaren

SERMON ONE

JOSEPH'S FAITH

> _Joseph took an oath of the children of Israel saying God will surely visit you, and ye shall carry up my bones from thence._
> —GENESIS 50:25

THIS is the one act of Joseph's life which the author of the Epistle to the Hebrews selects as the sign that he, too, lived by faith. "By faith Joseph, when he died, made mention of the departing of the children of Israel; and gave commandment concerning his bones" (Hebrews 11:22). It was at once a proof of how entirely he believed God's promise, and of how earnestly he longed for its fulfillment. It was a sign, too, of how little he felt himself at home in Egypt, though to outward appearance he had become completely one of its people.

I. FAITH IS ALWAYS THE SAME, THOUGH KNOWLEDGE VARIES.

A. The Difference Between Creed and Faith.

The one may vary, does vary, within very wide limits; the other remains the same. The things believed have been growing from the beginning—the attitude of mind and will by which they have been grasped has been the same from the beginning and will be the same to the end. The contents of faith, that on which it relies, the treasure it grasps, changes; the essence of faith, the act of reliance, the grasp which holds the treasure, does not change.

1. Creed varies.

2. Essence of faith never changes.

B. The Patriarchal Creed and Faith.

1. Although the Patriarchal creed was imperfect, yet they had a clear knowledge of God. They knew his inspiring, guiding presence; they knew the forgiveness of sins; they knew, though they very dimly understood, the promise, "In thy seed shall all the families of the earth be blessed" (Genesis 28:14).

2. In Patriarchal times as well as now faith was necessary to salvation. Joseph and his ancestors were joined to God by the very same bond which unites us to Him. There has never been but one path of life: "They *trusted* God and were lightened, and their faces were not ashamed."

C. The Relation of Creed to Faith.

1. Creed does not save. Brethren, what makes a Christian is not the theology you have in your heads, but the faith and love you have in your hearts.

2. Creed is necessary to saving faith. There can be no saving faith in an unseen person except through the medium of thoughts concerning Him, which thoughts put into words are a creed. "Christ" is a mere name, empty of all significance till it be filled with definite statements of who and what Christ is.

II. FAITH HAS ITS NOBLEST OFFICE IN DETACHING FROM THE PRESENT.

A. Detachment from Worldly Surroundings.

Joseph's dying words open a window into his soul and betray how little he had felt that he belonged to the order of things in the midst of which he had been content to live. We may be sure that, living, the hope of the inheritance must have burned in his heart as a hidden light and made him an alien everywhere but on its blessed soil.

1. Joseph's detachment from worldly surroundings did not make him discontented with his earthly environment and responsibilities.

2. *Joseph's detachment from worldly surroundings is revealed in his dying words.*

B. Requirements for Detachment from Worldly Surroundings.

1. *Thoughts must be directed by faith in God.* If the unseen is ever to rule in men's lives it must be through their thoughts. It must become intelligible, clear, real. Such certitude is given by faith alone.

2. *Desires must be directed by faith in God.* If the unseen is ever to rule in men's lives it must become not only an object to certain knowledge, but also for ardent wishes. It must cease to be doubtful and must seem infinitely desirable.

C. Benefits of Living a Life Detached from the World.

1. *Discipline.* A man that is living for remote objects is, insofar, a better man than one who is living for the present. He will become thereby the subject of a mental and moral discipline that will do him good.

2. *Change of character.* Whatever makes a man live in the past and in the future raises him; but high above all others stand those to whom the past is an apocalypse of God, with Calvary for its center, and all the future is fellowship with Christ, and joy in the heavens.

3. *Change of center of interest.* This change of the center of interest from earth to heaven is the uniform effect of faith. "Abraham," says the New Testament, "dwelt in tabernacles, for he looked for a city" (Hebrews 11:8–10).

III. FAITH MAKES MEN ENERGETIC IN THE DUTIES OF THE PRESENT.

A. Joseph Was Faithful in His Duties in the World.

1. *The world's sneer that Christianity makes a man indifferent to activity in this present life.*

2. *Joseph's life contradicts the world's sneer.* Joseph was a true Hebrew all his days. But that did not make him run away from Pharaoh's service. He lived by hope and that made him the better worker in the passing

moment and kept him tugging away all his life at the oar, administering the affairs of a kingdom.

B. Duties of the Present Life Become Greater to the Persons Realizing the Reality of Heaven.

1. The things of the present life are made less in their power to absorb or trouble.

2. The things of the present life are made greater in importance as preparations for what is beyond.

C. Faith Energizes Man for Work.

1. The reason: Faith will energize us for any sort of work, seeing that it raises all to one level and brings all under one sanction and shows all as co-operating to one end.

2. The illustration: The muster roll of the heroes of faith in the Epistle to the Hebrews (Ch. 11) marks the variety of grades of human life represented there, all fitted for their tasks and delivered from the snare that was in their calling by that faith which raised them above the world and therefore fitted them to come down on the world with stronger strokes of duty.

3. The secret: Trust Christ, live with Him and by hope of the inheritance.

CONCLUSION

Let us see that our clearer revelation bears fruit in a faith in the great Divine promises as calm and firm as this dying Patriarch had. Then the same power will work not only the same detachment and energy in life, but the same calmness and solemn light of hope in death.

Alexander Maclaren

MOSES AND HOBAB

And Moses said unto Hobab. Leave us not, I pray thee; foras-
much as thou knowest how we are to encamp in the wilderness,
and thou mayest be to us instead of eyes.
—NUMBERS 10:29, 31

THE FUGITIVES whom Moses led reached Sinai in three months after leaving Egypt. They remained there for at least nine months. Some time before the encampment broke up, a relative of Moses by marriage, Hobab by name, had come into camp on a visit. He was a Midianite by race, one of the wandering tribes from the south-east of the Arabian Peninsula. He knew every foot of the ground. So Moses, who had no doubt forgotten much of the little desert skill he had learned in keeping Jethro's flock, prays Hobab to remain with them and give them the benefit of his practical knowledge.

I. A SENSE OF THE UNKNOWN WILDERNESS BEFORE US.

A. General Complexion of the Future May Be Roughly Estimated.

We know very early in life that the thread of our days is a mingled strand and the prevailing tone a sober, neutral tint. The main characteristics of what we shall meet we well enough know.

B. The Particular Events of the Future Are Hidden.

It is strange and impressive when we come to think how Providence, working with the same uniform materials in all human lives, can yet, like some skillful artist, produce endless novelty and surprises in each life. The solemn ignorance of the next moment is sometimes stimulating and joyous. But to all there come times when their ignorance is saddening.

C. The Aspect of Life Represented as a Wilderness.

There are dangers and barren places and a great solitude in spite of love and companionship, and many marching and lurking foes, and grim rocks, and fierce suns, and parched wells, and shadeless sand wastes enough in every life to make us quail often and look grave always when we think of what may be before us.

II. AN ILLUSTRATION OF THE WEAKNESS THAT CLINGS TO HUMAN GUIDES.

A. The True Meaning of the Text.

The true lesson of the incident considered in connection with the following section is that for men who have God to guide them it argues weakness of this faith and courage to be much solicitous of any Hobab to show them where to go and where to camp.

B. The True Meaning of the Text Does Not Exclude Human Guides.

1. Self-trained men are usually incomplete. Fanciful notions take possession of the solitary thinker, and peculiarities of character that would have been kept in check, and might have become aids in the symmetrical development of the whole man, if they had been reduced and modified in society, get swollen into deformities in solitude.

2. Much of God's guidance is through men. God's guidance does not make man's needless, for a very large part of God's guidance is ministered to us through men. And wherever a man's thoughts and words teach us to understand God's thoughts and words more clearly, to love them more earnestly, or to obey them more gladly, there human guidance is discharging its noblest function.

C. The Danger to Be Avoided.

We are ever apt to feel that we cannot do without the human leader. Our weakness of faith in the unseen is ever tending to pervert the relation between teacher and taught into practical forgetfulness that the promise of the new covenant is, "They shall be all taught of God" (John 6:45).

1. Avoid overemphasizing human guidance.

2. Avoid underestimating Divine guidance.

III. THE TRUE LEADER OF OUR MARCH.

A. Israel's True Leader.

The true leader of the children of Israel in their wilderness journey was not Moses, but the Divine Presence in the cloud with a heart of fire, that hovered over their camp for a defense and sailed before them for a guide (Exodus 13:21).

B. The Christian's True Leader.

In sober reality we have God's presence; and waiting hearts which have ceased from self-will may receive leading as real as ever the pillar gave to Israel.

C. The Christian's Responsibility to His Leader.

1. Obedient step-by-step following. No doubt in all our lives there come times when we seem to have been brought into a blind alley, and cannot see where we are to get out; but it is very rare indeed that we do not see one step in advance, the duty which lies next to us. And be sure of this, that if we are content to see but one step at a time, and take it, we shall find our way made plain.

2. Certainty of God's will. Do not seek to outrun God's guidance, to see what you are to do a year hence or to act before you are sure of what is His will; do not let your wishes get in advance of the pillar and the ark, and you will be kept from many a mistake and led into a region of deep peace.

3. Reverent following. "Go after the ark, yet there shall be a space between it and you; come not near it, that ye may know the way ye ought to go" (Joshua 3:3, 4). If we impatiently press too close on the heels of our guide we lose the guidance. There must be a reverent following which allows indications of the way full time to develop themselves and does not fling itself into new circumstances on the first flush of apparent duty.

IV. THE CRAVING FOR A HUMAN GUIDE HAS BEEN MET IN THE GIFT OF CHRIST.

A. Hobab's Qualification.

Moses sought to secure this Midianite guide because he was a native of the desert and had travelled all over it. His experience was his qualification.

B. Christ's Qualification.

He travelled every foot of the road by which we have to go. He knows "how to encamp in this wilderness," for He Himself has "tabernacled among us" and by experience has learned the weariness of the journey and the perils of the wilderness.

C. The Believer's Pattern.

His life is our pattern. Our marching orders are brief and simple: Follow your leader, and plant your feet in His footprints.

CONCLUSION

If we only ask Him to be with us "instead of eyes" and accept His gentle leading, we shall not walk in darkness, but may plunge into the thickest night and the most unknown land, assured that He will "lead us by the right way to the city of habitation" (Psalm 107:7).

THE EAGLE AND ITS BROOD

As an eagle stirreth up her nest, fluttereth over her young, spreadeth abroad her wings, taketh them, beareth them on her wings.
—DEUTERONOMY 32:11

THIS is an incomplete sentence in the Authorized Version, but really it should be rendered as a complete one, the description of the eagle's action including only the two first clauses, and (the figure being still retained) the person spoken of in the last clauses being God Himself. That is to say, it should read thus, "As an eagle stirreth up his nest, fluttereth over his young, He spreads abroad His wings, takes them, bears them on His pinions." While the text primarily refers to the infant nation in the forty years wanderings, it carries larger truths about us all; and sets forth the true meaning and importance of life.

I. A GRAND THOUGHT ABOUT GOD.

A. The Metaphor Used: The Vulture.

Now it may come as something of a shock if I say that the bird that is selected for the comparison is not really an eagle, but one which, in our estimation, is of a very much lower order such as, the carnivorous vulture. Our modern repugnance to the vulture as feeding on carcasses was probably not felt by the singer of this song. What he brings into view are the characteristics common to the eagle and the vulture; superb strength in beak and claw, keenness of vision almost incredible, magnificent sweep of pinion, and power of rapid, unwearied flight.

B. The Purpose of the Use of the Metaphor:

The purpose is to show the analogy between the characteristics of the bird and the Divine nature. And these characteristics, we may say, have their analogies in the Divine nature, and the emblem not unfitly shadows forth one aspect of the God of Israel, who is "fearful in praises," who is strong to destroy as well as to save, whose all-seeing eye marks every foul thing, and who often pounces on it swiftly to rend it to pieces, though the sky seemed empty a moment before.

C. The Lesson Taught by the Metaphor.

The action described in the text is not destructive, terrible, or fierce. The monarch of the sky busies itself with tender cares for its brood. Then, there is gentleness along with the terribleness. The impression of this blending of power and gentleness is greatly deepened, as it seems to me, if we notice that it is the male bird that is spoken about in the text, which should be rendered: "As the eagle stirreth up *his* nest and fluttereth over *his* young."

II. AN ILLUMINATING THOUGHT OF THE MEANING OF LIFE.

A. The Purpose of Life.

The purpose of life: a training school fitting the child of God for heaven. What is it all for? To teach us to fly, to exercise our half-fledged wings in the short flights, that may prepare us for, and make it possible to take, longer ones. Every event that befalls us has a meaning beyond itself; and every task that we have to do reacts upon us, the doers, and either fits or hinders us for larger work. Life as a whole, and in its minutest detail, is worthy of God to give, and worthy of us to possess, only if we recognize the teaching that is put into the picturesque form in this text—that the meaning of all which God does to us is to train us for something greater beyond.

B. The Importance of the Purpose of Life.

It is the key to the mystery of life. No man gets to the heart of the mystery of life or has in his hand the key which will enable him to unlock all the doors and difficulties of human experience, unless he gets to this—that it is meant as training.

C. The Necessity to Carry Out This Conviction of the Purpose of Life in the Small Things.

If we could only carry that clear conviction with us day by day into the little things of life, what different things these, which we call the monotonous trifles of our daily duties, would become. The things may be small and unimportant, but the way we do them is not unimportant. The same fidelity may be exercised and must be brought to bear in order to do the veriest trifle of our daily lives rightly, that needs to be invoked, in order to get us safely through the crises and great times of life.

III. A CALMING THOUGHT AS TO THE VARIETY OF GOD'S METHODS WITH US.

A. God's Loving Compulsion to Effort: "As the Eagle Stirreth Up His Nest."

1. To "stir up the nest" means to make a man uncomfortable where he is.

2. The methods of stirring up the nest are varied—sometimes by the prickings of man's conscience, sometimes by changes of circumstances, and oftentimes by sorrows.

3. The reason for stirring up the nest. We all shrink from change. What would we do if we had it not? We should stiffen into habits that would dwarf and weaken us. We all recoil from storms. What should we do if we had them not? Sea and air would stagnate, and would become heavy and putrid and pestilential, if it was not for the wild west wind and the hurtling storms. So all our changes and all our sorrows should be recognized as being what they are, loving summonses to effort.

B. God's Hovering Presence: "Fluttereth Over His Young." It is a very beautiful word that is employed here which "flutter" scarcely gives us. It is the same that is used in the first chapter of Genesis, about the Spirit of God "brooding on the face of the waters"; and it suggests how near, how all protecting, with expanded wings the Divine Father comes to the child whose restfulness He has disturbed.

C. God's Sustaining Power.

"He spreadeth abroad His wings; He taketh them; beareth them on His wings." On those broad pinions we are lifted and by them we are guarded. It is a picturesque way of saying, "Thou canst do all things through Christ which strengtheneth thee." The Psalmist sang that angels' hands should bear up God's servant. That is little compared with this promise of being carried heavenwards on Jehovah's own pinions.

CONCLUSION

During life this training will go on; and after life, what then? Then, in the deepest sense, the old word will be true, "Ye know how I bore you on eagle's wings and brought you to myself"; and the great promise shall be fulfilled, when the half-fledged young brood are matured and full grown, "They shall mount up with wings as eagles; they shall not be weary; they shall walk and not faint."

Alexander Maclaren

SERMON FOUR

UNPOSSESSED POSSESSIONS

And the King of Israel said unto his servants,
Know ye that Ramoth in Gilead is ours, and we be still,
and take it not out of the hand of the King of Syria?
—I KINGS 22:3

THIS city of Ramoth in Gilead was an important fortified place on the eastern side of the Jordan and had been captured by the northern neighbors in the kingdom of Syria. The people of Israel backed up by a powerful alliance with Jehoshaphat of Judah determined to make a dash to get back what was theirs.

I. WHAT IS OURS AND NOT OURS.

Every Christian man has large tracts of unannexed territory, unattained possibilities, unenjoyed blessings, things that are his and yet not his.

A. Some Unpossessed Possessions.

1. Undisturbed peace. There may be a peace in our hearts deep as life; a tranquillity which may be superficially disturbed, but is never thoroughly, and down to the depths broken. The peace of God is ours; but ah! in how sad a sense it is true that the peace of God is *not* ours.

2. Absolute surrender. It is well within the reach of every Christian soul that he or she should live day by day in the continual and utter surrender of himself or herself to the will of God. But instead of this absolute submission of ourselves to Him, what do we find?

3. Fulness of power. The Divine gift to the Christian community and to the individuals who compose it is of fulness of power for all their work. And yet look how all through the ages the church has been beaten by the corruption of the world.

C. The Threefold Title and Charter to Our Possessions.

1. God's purpose. God's purpose, which is nothing less for every one of us than that we should be "filled with all the fulness of God" (Ephesians 3:19), and that He should supply all our needs "according to His riches in glory" (Philippians 4:19)—that is the first of the parchments on which our title depends.

2. Christ's purchase. And the second titledeed is Christ's purchase; for the efficacy of His death and the power of His triumphant life have secured for all that trust Him the whole fulness of this Divine Gift.

3. Holy Spirit's influence. And the third of our claims and titles is the influence of the Holy Spirit that Jesus Christ gives to every one of His children to dwell in Him. There is working in you, if you have any faith in that Lord, a power that is capable of making you perfectly pure, perfectly blessed, strong with an immortal strength, and glad with a "joy unspeakable and full of glory."

II. OUR STRANGE CONTENTMENT IN IMPERFECT POSSESSION.

A. The Reasons for This Strange Contentment.

Ahab's remonstrances with his servants seem to suggest that there were two reasons for their acquiesence in the domination of a foreign power on a bit of their soil. They had not realized that Ramoth was theirs and they were too lazy and cowardly to go and take it.

1. Ignorance of unattained possibilities in the Christian life. That unfamiliarity with the thought of unattained possibilities in the Christian life is a curse of thousands of people who call themselves Christians. They do not think, they never realize that it is possible for them to be all unlike what they are now.

2. Love of ease. Another reason for the woeful disproportion between what we have and what we utilize is the love of ease, such as kept these Israelites from going up to Ramoth-Gilead. On the whole it was more comfortable to sit at home or look after their farms and their merchandise than to embark on the unromantic attempt to win back a city that had not been theirs for ever so long and that they had got on very well without.

B. The Seriousness of This Strange Contentment.

And is not that something like despising the birthright? Is it not a criminal thing for Christian people thus to neglect and put aside and never seek to obtain all these great gifts of God? There they lie at our doors and they are ours for the taking.

1. Is it not like despising our birthright?

2. Is it not a criminal thing?

III. THE EFFORT THAT IS NEEDED TO MAKE OUR OWN OURS.

A. The Christian Must Take His Possessions.

"We be still, and take it not out of the hands of the King of Syria." Then these things that are ours, by God's gift, by Christ's purchase, by the Spirit's influence will need our effort to secure them. And that is no contradiction nor any paradox. God does exactly in the same way with regard to His spiritual ones. He gives them to us, but we hold them on this tenure, that we put forth our best efforts to get and to keep them. His giving them does not set aside our taking.

1. They are God's gifts.

2. They are to be taken by the Christian.

B. The Necessity of Familiarizing Ourselves with the Possibilities of Unattained Possessions.

1. This applies to all spheres of life. One large part of the discipline by which men make their own their own is by familiarizing themselves with the thought of the larger possibilities of unattained possessions which God has given them. That is true in everything. To recognize our present imperfection and to see stretching before us glorious and immense possibilities is the salt of life in every region.

2. Failure in this results in failure in growth. Whosoever has once lost, or found becoming dim, the vision before him of a possible better than his present best, in any region, is in that region condemned to grow no more. If we desire to have any kind of advancement it is only possible for us when there gleams before us the untravelled road, and we see at the end of it unattained brightnesses and blessings.

CONCLUSION

Let us put away from ourselves this slothful indifference to our unattained possessions. "Know ye that Ramoth is ours?" "Let us be still no longer." "All things are yours, whether the world, or life, or death, or things present, or things to come: all are yours if ye are Christ's."

PRIDE OVERCOMING WANT

But Naaman was wroth, and went away, and said,
Behold, I thought he will surely come out to me, and stand,
and call on the name of the Lord his God, and strike
his hand over the place, and recover the leper.

— II KINGS 5:11

WITH soldier-like quickness of temper and pride, he flashes all at once into a blaze. Leper as he is, and having come there to beg a cure, he cannot stand this with patience; and in his wrath he lets us see curiously and naturally enough all his expectations, and what he thinks his reasonable ground of anger. The characteristics which offended Naaman are the characteristics of God's cure for the leprosy of our spirits.

I. THE UTTER INDIFFERENCE OF THE GOSPEL TO ALL DISTINCTIONS AMONG MEN.

A. The Fact That the Gospel Deals with All Men on the Same Level.

1. The fact illustrated in Naaman's experience. Naaman wanted to be treated as a great man that happened to be a leper: Elisha treated him as a leper that happened to be a great man. He did so not out of rudeness or caprice, but to bring this thought home to him: Your adventitious distinctions are of very small consequence as long as your skin shines with the ghastly whiteness of death.

2. The fact stated. The Gospel deals with all men as on one level. The community in the sickness of sin destroys all distinctions.

B. The Reasons for the Gospel's Dealing with All Men on the Same Level.

1. All men are sinners. "All the world is guilty before God!" You cannot refute and you will not mend that old saying about man's condition. No other theory is so profoundly and accurately true, as that on which the Bible proceeds—the universal fact of sin, the universal guilt of sin, the universal burden of sin.

2. Christ died for all men. "He hath shut up all in unbelief that He might have mercy upon all" (Romans 11:32). As sin and death, so God's love and Christ's work know nothing of our superficial distinctions.

C. The Glory of the Gospel's Dealing with All Men on the Same Level.

The superb indifference of the Gospel to all the distinctions of man from man, is its true glory and has wrought wonderful things.

1. The glory of the Gospel is seen in that it, without respect of persons, delivers from sin's bondage. The Gospel, the true democracy, came and struck the bonds from the slave.

2. The glory of the Gospel is also seen in that it, without respect of persons, unifies believers. We being many are one bread, "for we are all partakers of that one bread" (I Corinthians 10:17).

II. THE NAKED SIMPLICITY OF GOD'S GOSPEL.

A. Man's Way.

1. The tendency of men portrayed in Naaman. "Behold, I thought he will come and stand and call on the name of the Lord his God, and strike his hand over the place, and so by all that ceremonial he will recover the leper."

2. The tendency of man is to look for some tangible object for his wavering confidences to lay hold upon.

B. God's Method.

1. God's method with Naaman. It was like God to contradict the desire and to give him instead—only a promise to grasp and a command to obey.

2. God's method in the Gospel. The one power that cleanses is His blood for pardon, His Spirit for holiness. The one condition of receiving these is simple faith in Him; all externals are nothing.

C. Dangers to Be Avoided.

1. Sacramentalism. The sense-bound materialism which sways us all lays hold of the pure Gospel which Christ wrought and gives and deforms it by tacking on to it an incongruous and heterogeneous appendage of rites and ceremonies and by investing the simple ordinances which He enjoined with mysterious power.

2. The formalism of the nonconformist. We are tempted to attach a false kind of value to church membership and to outward participation in Christian ordinances. We are constantly tempted to put the form in the place of the Spirit.

III. THE UTTER REJECTION BY THE GOSPEL OF ALL MAN'S COOPERATION IN HIS OWN CLEANSING.

A. A Reason for Naaman's Rejection of the Requirement for Cleansing.

The words of Naaman himself do not explicitly contain his refusal to do what was required, on the ground it was so small a thing. But that was evidently in his mind, as well as the other grounds of offence; and it comes out distinctly in the common-sense remonstrance by which his servants brought their angry master to reason —"If the prophet had bid thee do some great thing, wouldest thou not have done it? How much rather then, when he saith to thee, 'Wash and be clean'" (II Kings 5:13).

B. The Gospel Rejects Man's Cooperation in Salvation.

The characteristic of the Gospel is that it will have none of our work. Salvation, though not secured without our faith, cannot be said to be procured by our cooperation.

C. The Gospel Rejects Man's Cooperation in Salvation because the Gospel Demands Faith.

1. What faith is. An essential part of faith is the consciousness that we can do nothing, the forsaking and going out of ourselves, accompanying the flight to Him. The underside of faith is self-abnegation; the upper side is confidence in Christ. Therefore, the proclamation that we are justified by faith is at the same time the absolute refusal to give men any share in their own healing.

2. What faith does. Faith is not the means of our cure, but only the bringing of our sickness into contact with the means. God's love in Christ, Christ's Spirit poured out—these are the energies that heal; faith is but lifting the eyelids that the light may fill the eyes, but opening the door that the physician may enter.

CONCLUSION

It is the glory of the Gospel that it proclaims a work in which we have no share. Christ will do it all. Nay, Christ has done it all. "Not by works of righteousness, but according to His mercy He saved us" (Titus 3:5).

Alexander Maclaren

PRUDENCE AND FAITH

_And Amaziah said to the man of God, "But what shall
we do for the hundred talents which I have given to the
army of Israel?" And the man of God answered, "The Lord
is able to give thee much more than this."_
—II CHRONICLES 25:9

WHEN Amaziah came to the throne he immediately began to aim at
conquests. In order to strengthen himself he hired "a hundred thousand
mighty men of valor" out of Israel for a hundred talents of silver. In the
prophet's eyes, to seek help from Israel was equivalent to flinging off help
from God. So a man of God comes to him and warns him that the Lord is
not with Israel and that the alliance is not permissible for him. Instead of
yielding to the prophet's advice, Amaziah parries it with this misplaced
question.

I. A MISPLACED QUESTION.

A. The Reason This Was a Misplaced Question.

I call it misplaced because Amaziah's fault, and the fault of a great
many of us, was, not that he took consequences into account, but that he
took them into account at the wrong time. The question should have come
second, not first. Amaziah's first business should have been to see clearly
what was duty; and then, the next business should have been to consider
consequences.

1. It was not a misplaced question because it took account of consequences.

2. It was a misplaced question because it took account of consequences at the wrong time.

B. The Right Place and Way of Asking This Question.

1. The tragedy of the failure to consider consequences. Many of us make shipwreck of our lives because, with our eyes shut, we determine upon some grand design and fall under the condemnation of the man that "began to build and was not able to finish." If a man does not open his eyes to a clear vision of the consequences of his actions his life will go to water in all directions.

2. The wisdom of considering consequences in the Christian life. There is no region in which such clear insight into what is going to follow upon my determinations and the part that I take, is more necessary than in the Christ's life. Let us face the facts of what is involved in the way of sacrifice, surrender, loss, if we determine to be on Christ's side; and then, when the difficulties come we shall neither be perplexed nor swept away.

C. The Right Thing in the Wrong Place.

1. In the life of the individual. Amaziah thought nothing about duty. There sprang up in his mind the cowardly and ignoble thought, "I cannot afford to do what is right because it will cost me a hundred talents." He that allows the clearest perception of disagreeable consequences to frighten him out of the road that he knows he ought to take is a fool, a coward, and recreant to his own conscience.

2. In the life of the church. All the churches are too apt to let their eyes wander from reading the plain precepts of the New Testament to looking for the damaging results to be expected from keeping them.

3. In the life of the nation. The nation takes a leaf out of Amaziah's book and puts aside many plain duties for no better reason than that it would cost too much to do them. "What is the use of talking about suppressing the liquor traffic. Think of the cost." The hundred talents block the way and bribe the national conscience.

II. THE TRIUMPHANT ANSWER.

A. The Meaning of the Prophet.

1. The ability of God to give. I suppose this prophet did not mean more than the undeniable truth that God was able to give Amaziah more than a hundred talents.

2. The probability of God's giving. He simply meant, "You will very likely get more than the one hundred talents that you have lost, if you do what pleases God."

B. The Wrong Application of the Prophet's Answer.

1. In the Old Testament material prosperity did not always follow righteousness. In the Old Testament we have instances enough that prosperity did not always attend righteousness. In the Old Testament we find the book of Job and the book of Ecclesiastes and many a Psalm, all of which were written in order to grapple with the question, "How is it that God does *not* give the good man more than the hundred talents he has lost for the sake of being good?"

2. Today material prosperity does not always follow righteousness. It is not true, and it is a dreadful mistake to suggest that it is true that a man in this world never loses by being a good, honest, consistent Christian. He often does lose a great deal as far as this world is concerned; and he has to make up his mind to lose it.

C. The Right Application of the Prophet's Answer.

1. The gaining of nobility and strength of character. The "much more" that Christianity has educated us to understand is meant in the depths of such a promise as this is, first of all, character. Every man that sacrifices anything to convictions of duty gains more than he loses thereby, because he gains in inward nobleness and strength, to say nothing of the genial warmth of an approving conscience.

2. The gaining of a fuller capacity for a fuller possession of Christ. He wins not only character, but a fuller capacity for a fuller possession of Jesus Christ Himself and that is infinitely more than anything that any man has ever sacrificed for the sake of that dear Lord. Do you remember when it was that there was granted to the Apostle John the vision of the enthroned Christ? It was "when I was in Patmos for the Word of God, and for the testimony of Jesus." He lost Ephesus; he gained an open heaven and a visible Christ.

CONCLUSION

Fling out the ballast if you wish the balloon to rise. Let the hundred talents go if you wish to get the "more than this." And listen to the New Testament variation of this Old Testament promise, "If thou wilt have treasure in heaven, go and sell all that thou hast and follow Me."

Alexander Maclaren

SERMON SEVEN

A PATTERN PRAYER

Bow down Thine ear, O Lord, hear me; for I am poor and needy.
Preserve my soul; for I am holy: O Thou my God, save Thy servant
that trusteth in Thee. Be merciful unto me, O Lord: for I cry unto
Thee daily. Rejoice the soul of Thy servant: for unto Thee, O Lord,
do I lift up my soul. For Thou, Lord, art good, and ready to forgive;
and plenteous in mercy unto all them that call upon Thee.

—PSALM 86:1–5

"WHEN ye pray, use not vain repetitions, as the heathen do." But earnest reiteration is not vain repetition. The one is born of doubt; the other of faith. This faithful and prevailing reiteration remarkably characterizes the striking series of supplications in these verses.

I. THE INVOCATIONS.

A. The General Idea of Invocation.

When we call upon the name of God aright we do three things:

1. Contemplate the character of God. We summon up before our thoughts that aspect of the Divine character which lies in the name that we utter.

2. Profess to trust in that character of God revealed in the name. We say in effect: "This aspect of Thy Divine all sufficiency, this fragment of Thine ineffable perfection, on this I build and to this I make my appeal."

3. Profess to believe that God responds to the obligations that are involved therein. It is as saying: "I bring Thee myself and in Thy mighty name, for the sake of what it declares, I ask that these goods may be bestowed upon me."

B. The Comprehensiveness and Variety of God's Names Used by the Psalmist.

1. Jehovah. This name has a double force in Scripture—one derived from its literal, philological meaning; the other derived from its historical use and development. As concerns the former the word substantially implies eternal, timeless beings, underived self-existence. As to the latter, it was given as a seal of the covenant, as the ground of the great deliverance from Egyptian bondage.

2. My God. The word "God" implies the abundance and fullness of power. This general conception becomes special on the Psalmist's lips by the personal pronoun "my" he prefixes to the name.

3. Lord. The name "Lord" is not the same word as that which is rendered *LORD* in verse 1. That, as we have said, is Jehovah. This means just what our English word "lord" means; it conveys the general idea of authority and dominion.

II. THE PETITIONS.

A. The Basis of Petitions: The Cry That God Will Hear.

1. An act of the will is included in the hearing of prayer. There is an act of loving will which is most clearly conveyed by that strong, and yet plain and intelligible metaphor, "Bow down thine ear," as an eager listener puts his hand to his ear and bends the lobe of it in the direction of the sound.

2. Hearing embodied in an act of deliverance. With God to hear is to answer.

B. A Description of the Process of Deliverance and the Need and Weakness of the Suppliant: the petition for protection, safety, and mercy.

1. The deliverance contemplated. The first petition, "preserve my soul," might be rendered, "guard" or "watch" my soul. Looking at all three we see that the first prays for protection; the second prays for the happy issue of that protection, in safety, and the third prays for that mercy which is the sole foundation of both the protection and the safety it ensures.

2. The suppliant's need and weakness revealed. These three petitions also embody varying thoughts of the need and weakness of the suppliant. In the two former (verse 2) he regards himself as defenseless and in peril. In the last (verse 3) he thinks of himself as lowly and unworthy—for "mercy" is love shown to inferiors or to those who deserve something else.

3. A significant omission. In all this variety of petitions for deliverance there is not a word about the exact manner of it. The way in which God's mercy is to guard and save is left, with meek patience, to God's decision.

C. The Petition for Gladness: Rejoice the Soul of Thy Servant.

1. All of God's obedient children have a claim on God for joy. All His creatures have a claim on Him for blessedness according to their capacity, as long as they stand where He has set them.

2. God's disobedient children may have joy in returning to Him. The persons who have departed from that obedience which is joy, may yet, in penitent abasement, return to Him and ask that He would rejoice the soul of His servant (Psalm 51:8).

III. THE PLEAS.

A. The Psalmist Pleads His Necessities.

He is "poor and needy," or rather, perhaps, "afflicted and poor," borne down the pressure of outward calamity and destitute of inward resources. Circumstances and character both constitute an appeal to God.

1. Circumstances: the evils that oppress from without.

2. Character: the lack of power within to bear up against outward circumstances.

B. The Psalmist Pleads His Relation to God and His Longing for Communion with God.

1. His relationship expressed. (a) "I am holy." The word in the original means "one who is the recipient or object of mercy." "One whom Thou favorest." It sets forth the relation between God and His suppliant from the divine side. (b) "Thy servant that trusteth in Thee." This is the same relation contemplated from the human side. I am knit to Thee, as a servant I belong to Thy household, and the Master's honor is concerned in His dependent's safety.

2. *His longing for fellowship expressed.* "Unto Thee do I lift up my soul." This expresses the conscious effort to raise his whole being above earth, to lift the heavy grossness of his nature bound in the fetters of sense to this low world, up and up to the Most High who is his home.

C. The Psalmist Pleads God's Own Character.

1. *This is the forceful plea with God.* The one prevalent plea with God is the faithful recounting of all that grace and pity which He is and has exercised.

2. *God is the reason and source of all our deliverance.* Because we can pray by none other, we implore Him by Himself, for the sake of His own holy Name, because He is that He is, to have mercy upon us.

CONCLUSION

When we call upon the name of Jesus Christ our Lord and ask that our prayers be heard "for the sake of Christ," we are taking no other plea into our lips than that ancient and all prevalent one of this Psalm.

Alexander Maclaren

FROM THE DEPTHS TO THE HEIGHTS

Out of the depths have I cried unto Thee O Lord. Lord hear my voice; let Thine ears be attentive to the voice of my supplications. If Thou, Lord, shouldest mark iniquities, O Lord! who shall stand? But there is forgiveness with Thee, that Thou mayest be feared. I wait for the Lord, my soul doth wait, and in His Word do I hope. My soul waiteth for the Lord more than they that watch for the morning: I say, more than they that watch for the morning. Let Israel hope in the Lord; for with the Lord there is mercy, and with Him is plenteous redemption. And He shall redeem Israel from all his iniquities.

—PSALM 130

IT is a "song of degrees," as the heading tells us, that is, a "song of goings up." Whatever that very enigmatical phrase may mean, there is a sense in which this Psalm, at any rate, is distinctly a song of ascent, in that it starts from the very lowest point of self-abasement and consciousness of evil and rises steadily up to the tranquil summit, led by the consciousness of the Divine Presence and grace.

I. THE CRY FROM THE DEPTHS (Verses 1–2).

A. The Meaning of "the Depths."

1. It is not merely the depth of the recognition of man's insignificance, sorrow, or despondency.

2. It is primarily the depth of the recognition of man's sinfulness.

B. The Truths Suggested by the Cry from the Depths.

1. The depths are the place for us all. Every man amongst us has to go down there, if we take the place that belongs to us.

2. Unless a man has cried to God from the depths he has never cried to Him at all. Unless you come to Him as a penitent, sinful man, with the consciousness of transgression awakened within you, your prayers are shallow.

3. Nothing more than a cry is needed to draw a man from the depths. God has let down the fulness of His forgiving love in Jesus Christ our Lord, and all that we need is the call, which is likewise faith, which accepts while it desires, and desires in its acceptance; and then we are lifted up "out of a horrible pit and the miry clay," and our feet are set upon a rock, and our goings established (Psalm 40:2).

II. A DARK FEAR AND A BRIGHT ASSURANCE (Verses 3–4).

A. The Fear That God Will Mark Iniquities.

1. To "mark iniquities" means to impute them to us. The word, in the original, means to *watch,* that is to say, to remember in order to punish.

2. The impossibility of any man sustaining the righteous judgment of God. Like a man having to yield ground to an eager enemy, or to bend before the blast, every man has to bow before that flashing brightness and to own that retribution would be destruction.

B. The Assurance of Forgiveness.

1. The significance of the term "forgiveness." Forgiveness! The word so translated here in my text has for its literal meaning, "cutting off," "excision."

2. The area of forgiveness. Men may say, "There cannot be forgiveness; you cannot alter consequences." But forgiveness has not to do only with consequences, but also and chiefly with the personal relation between me and God, and that can be altered.

3. The basis of godliness is forgiveness. No man reverences and loves and draws near to God so rapturously, so humbly, as the man that has learned pardon through Jesus Christ. "There is forgiveness with Thee, that Thou mayest be feared" (verse 4).

III. DEPENDENCE UPON GOD (Verses 5–6).

A. Its Nature.

1. It is a permanent dependence. A continual dependence upon God.

2. It is a peaceful dependence. They that have tasted that the Lord is gracious can sit very quietly at His feet and trust themselves to His kindly dealings, resting their souls upon His strong word, and looking for the fuller communication of light from Himself. This is a beautiful picture of a tranquil, continuous, ever-rewarded, and ever-fresh waiting upon Him and reliance upon His mercy.

B. The Desire of the Man Depending Upon God.

And so the man waits quietly for the dawn, and his whole soul is one absorbing desire that God may dwell with him and brighten and gladden him.

1. That God may dwell with him.

2. That God may brighten and gladden him.

IV. THE MISSIONARY CALL (Verses 7–8).

A. The Extent of the Invitation.

1. In his first cry the Psalmist was only interested in himself and God (verse 1). There was no room for anything in his heart when he began this psalm except his own self in his misery and that Great One high above him. There was nobody in all the universe to him but himself and God, at his first cry from the depths.

2. Now his interest extends to his fellow men. But there is nothing that so knits him to all his fellows and brings him into such wide-reaching bonds of amity and benevolence as the sense of God's forgiving mercy for his own soul. So the call bursts from the lips of the pardoned man, inviting all to taste the experience and exercise the trust which have made him glad: "Let Israel hope in the Lord."

B. The Content of the Invitation.

1. There is plenteous redemption (verse 7). Not only forgiveness, but redemption. It is "plenteous"—multiplied, as the word might be rendered.

2. There is inexhaustible redemption (verse 8). It is inexhaustible redemption, not to be provoked, not to be overcome by any obstinacy of evil—available for every grade and every repetition of transgression.

CONCLUSION

"With Him is plenteous redemption; He shall redeem Israel from all his iniquities." This is the Old Testament prophecy. Let me leave on your hearts the New Testament fulfilment of it. "Thou shalt call His name Jesus, for He shall save His people from their sins" (Matthew 1:21). That is the fulfilment, the vindication, and explanation of the Psalmist's hope.

Alexander Maclaren

THE SLUGGARD IN HARVEST

*The sluggard will not plough by reason of the cold;
therefore shall he beg in harvest and have nothing.*
—PROVERBS 20:4

LIKE all the sayings of this book this is simply a piece of plain, practical common sense. It is intended to inculcate the lesson that men should diligently seize the opportunity while it is theirs. The sluggard is one of the pet aversions of the Book of Proverbs, which, unlike most other manuals of Eastern wisdom, has a profound reverence for honest work.

I. THE PRINCIPLES CRYSTALIZED IN THIS PICTURESQUE PROVERB.

A. Present Conduct Determines Future Conditions.

1. This principle is true about life in general. The position which a man fills, the tasks which he has to perform, and the whole host of things which make up the externals of his life, depend on far other conditions than any that he brings to them. But yet, on the whole, it is true that what a man does, and is, settles how he fares.

2. This principle is especially true about youth. You can, I was going to say, be anything you make up your minds to, and within reasonable limits, this bold saying is true. "Ask what thou wilt and it shall be given to thee" is what nature and Providence, almost as really as grace and Christ, say to every young man and woman.

B. The Easy Road Is Generally the Wrong Road.

1. The certainty of obstacles in the way of a noble life. There are always obstacles in the way of a noble life. If a man is going to be anything worth being or to do anything worth doing he must start with and adhere to the resolve "to scorn delights and live laborious days."

2. The condition to be met in order to live a noble life. Self-denial and rigid self-control, in its two forms, of stopping your ears to the attractions of lower pleasures and of cheerily encountering difficulties is an indispensable condition of any life which shall at last yield a harvest worth the gathering.

C. The Season Let Slip Is Gone Forever.

1. The tragedy of lost opportunity. Opportunity is bald behind and must be grasped by the forelock. Life is full of tragic might-have-beens. No regret, no remorse, no self-accusation, no clear recognition that I was a fool will avail one jot. "Too late" is the saddest of human words.

2. The solemn admonition to faithful discharge of duties. As the stages of our lives roll on, unless each is filled with the discharge of the duties and the appropriation of the benefits which it brings, then, to all eternity that moment will never return and the sluggard may beg in harvest that he may have the chance to plough once more, and have none.

II. THE APPLICATION OF THE PRINCIPLES CRYSTALIZED IN THE PICTURESQUE PROVERB.

A. The Application to Daily Secular Work.

1. The necessity of hard work. Do not trust to any way of getting on by dodges or speculation, or favor, or by anything but downright hard work. Don't shirk difficulties, don't try to put the weight of the work upon some colleague or other, that you may have an easier life of it.

2. The blessing of work. "In all labor there is profit." Whether the profit comes to you in the shape of advancement, position, promotion in your offices, partnerships perhaps, wealth and the like, or no, the profit lies in the work. Honest toil is the key to pleasure.

B. The Application to Intellectual Activity.

1. The intellect is a gift of God. Carry these principles with you in the cultivation of that important part of yourself—your intellects. Some of you, perhaps, are students by profession; I should like all of you to make a conscience of making the best of your brains, as God has given them to you in trust.

2. Man's responsibility in the use of his intellect. Amidst all the flood of feeble, foolish, flaccid literature with which we are afflicted at this day, I wonder how many of you ever set yourselves to some great book or subject that you cannot understand without effort. Unless you do you are not faithful stewards of God's gift of that great faculty which apprehends and lives upon truth.

C. The Application to the Formation of Character.

1. Nobility of life is the result of toil and divine grace. Nothing will come to you noble, great, or elevating in that direction unless it is sought, and sought with toil. Wisdom and truth and all their elevating effects upon human character absolutely require for their acquirement effort and toil.

2. Character is formed during the impressionable years of life. In the making of character we have to work as a painter in fresco does, with a swift brush on the plaster while it is wet. It sets and hardens in an hour. And men drift into habits which become tyrannies and dominant before they know where they are.

D. The Application to the Christian Life.

1. The wisdom and necessity of beginning the Christian life at the earliest moment. If you do not yield yourselves to Jesus Christ in your early days and take Him for your Savior and rest your souls upon Him and then take Him for your Captain and Commander, for your Pattern and Example, for your Companion and your Aim, you will lose what you can never make up by any future course.

2. *The present life in relation to the future.* This life as a whole is to the future life as the ploughing time is to the harvest and there are awful words in Scripture which seem to point in the same direction in reference to the irrevocable and irreversible issue of neglected opportunities on earth as this proverb does in regard to the ploughing and harvests of this life.

CONCLUSION

I dare not conceal what seems to me the New Testament confirmation and deepening of the solemn words of our text, "He shall beg in harvest and have nothing," by the Master's words, "Many shall say to Me in that day, Lord! Lord! And I will say, I never knew you." Now, while it is called day harden not your hearts.

Alexander Maclaren

THE CHARGE OF THE PILGRIM PRIESTS

*Watch ye, and keep them, until ye weigh them . . .
at Jerusalem, in the chambers of the house of the Lord.*
—EZRA 8:29

THE little band of Jews returning from Babylon had just started on a long pilgrimage and made a brief halt in order to get everything in order for their transit across the desert; when their leader, Ezra, taking count of his men, discovers that amongst them there are none of the priests or Levites. He then takes measures to reinforce his little army with a contingent of these and entrusts to their care a very valuable treasure in gold and silver and sacrificial vessels which had been given to them for use in the house of the Lord.

I. THE PRECIOUS TREASURE.

A. The Treasure of Ourselves.

The metaphor is capable of two applications. The first is to the rich treasure and solemn trust of our own nature, of our own souls; the faculties and capacities, precious beyond all count, rich beyond all else that a man has ever received. The precious treasure of your own natures, your own hearts, your own understandings, wills, consciences, desires—keep these until they are weighed in the house of the Lord.

B. *The Treasure of the Gospel.*

And in like manner, taking the other aspect of the metaphor—we have given to us, in order that we may do something with it, that great deposit and treasure of truth, which is all embodied and incarnated in Jesus Christ our Lord. It is bestowed upon us that we may use it for ourselves and in order that we may carry it triumphantly all through the world. Possession involves responsibility always. It is given to us in order that we may keep it safe and carry it high up across the desert as becomes the priests of the most high God.

II. THE GUARDIANSHIP OF THE TREASURE.

"Watch ye, keep them." I cannot do more than touch upon some of the ways in which this charge may be worked out or in its application for ourselves.

A. *Unslumbering Vigilance.*

First of all, no slumber; not a moment's relaxation; or some of those who lie in wait for us on the way will be down upon us and some of the precious things will go. While the rest of the wearied camp slept, the guardians of the treasure had to outwatch the stars. While others might straggle on the march, lingering here and there or resting on some patch of green, they had to close up round their precious charge; others might let their eyes wander from the path, they had ever to look to their care.

B. *Lowly Trust.*

Ezra said in effect, "Not all the cohorts of Babylon can help us; and we do not want them. We have one strong hand that will keep us safe." His confidence was, "God will bring us all safe out to the end there and we shall carry every glittering piece of precious things that we brought out of Babylon right into the Temple of Jerusalem." "I know whom I have believed, and am persuaded that He is able to keep that which I have committed unto Him against that day" (II Timothy 1:12).

C. *Punctilious Purity.*

"I said unto them, Ye are holy unto the Lord; the vessels are holy unto the Lord." It was fitting that the priests should carry the things that belonged to the temple. To none other guardianship but the guardianship of the possessors of a symbolic and ceremonial purity could the vessels of a symbolic and ceremonial worship be entrusted; and to none others but the possessors of real and spiritual holiness can the treasures of the true temple, of an inward and spiritual worship, be entrusted. The only way to keep our treasure undiminished and untarnished is to keep ourselves pure and clean.

D. Constant Use.

Although the vessels which those priests bore through the desert were used for no service during all the weary march, they weighed just the same when they got to the end as at the beginning though, no doubt, even their fine gold had become dim and tarnished through disuse. But if we do not use the vessels that are entrusted to our care they will not weigh the same. Gifts that are used fructify. Capacities that are strained to the uttermost increase. Service strengthens the power of service.

III. THE ACCOUNTING OF THE TREASURE.

And lastly think of that weighing in the house of the Lord. Cannot you see the picture of the little band when they finally reach the goal of their pilgrimmage; and three days after they arrived, as the narrative tells us, went up into the temple and there, by number and weight, rendered their charge and were clear of their responsibility?

A. The Encouragement of Anticipation of the Day of Accounting.

Oh, how that thought of the day when they would empty out the rich treasure upon the marble pavement and clash the golden vessels into the scales, must have filled their hearts with vigilance during all the weary watches, when desert stars looked down upon the slumbering encampment and they paced wakeful all the night.

B. The Joy of Anticipation of the Day of Accounting.

How the thought, too, must have filled their hearts with joy when they tried to picture to themselves the sigh of satisfaction and the sense of relief with which, after their perils, their "feet would stand within thy gates, O Jerusalem," and they would be able to say, "That which Thou has given me I have kept and nothing of it is lost."

CONCLUSION

Though it cannot be that you and I shall meet the trial and the weighing of that great day without many a flaw and much loss, yet we may say, "I know whom I have believed, and that He is able to keep my deposit—whether it be in the sense of that which I have committed unto Him, or in the sense of that which He has committed unto me—against that day." We may hope, that, by His gracious help and His pitying acceptance, even such careless stewards and negligent watchmen as we are, may lay ourselves down in peace at the last saying, "I have kept the faith"; and may be awakened by the word, "Well done, good and faithful servant."

THE JOY OF THE LORD

The joy of the Lord is your strength.
—NEHEMIAH 8:10

HERE, in the incident before us, there has come a time in Nehemiah's great enterprise, when the law, long forgotten, long broken by the captives, is now to be established again as the rule of the newly founded commonwealth. Naturally enough there comes a remembrance of many things in the past history of the people; and tears not unnaturally mingle with the thankfulness that again they are a nation, having a Divine worship and a Divine law in their midst. The leader of them, knowing for one thing that if the spirits of his people once began to flag, they could not face nor conquer the difficulties of their position, said to them, "Neither be ye sorry, for the joy of the Lord is your strength." And that is as true, brethren, with regard to us, as it ever was in these old times.

I. THE JOY OF THE LORD IS THE NATURAL RESULT OF CHRISTIAN FAITH.

A. The Gospel's Provision for Joy.

1. The Gospel provides joy by what it brings. It gives us what we well call a sense of acceptance with God, it gives us God for the rest of our spirits, it gives us the communion with Him which in proportion as it is real, will be still; and in proportion as it is still, will be all bright and joyful.

2. The Gospel provides joy by what it takes away. It takes away from us the fear that lies before us, the strifes that lie within us, the desperate conflict that is waged between a man's conscience and his inclinations, between his will and his passions, which tears the heart asunder, and always makes sorrow and tumult wherever it comes. It takes away the sense of sin.

B. Sorrow Is a Foundation Upon Which Rests the Joy of the Lord.

1. The reason for the believer's sorrow. If we think of what our faith does; of the light that it casts upon our condition, upon our nature, upon our responsibilities, upon our sins, and upon our destinies, we can easily see how, if gladness be one part of its operation, no less really and truly is sadness another.

2. The importance of sorrow as a foundation for joy. There is nothing more contemptible in itself, and there is no more sure mark of a trivial round of occupation than unshaded gladness, that rests on no deep foundations of quiet, patient grief; grief, because I know what I am and what I ought to be; grief, because I have learned the "exceeding sinfulness of sin"; grief, because, looking out upon the world, I see as other men do not see, hellfire burning at the back of the mirth and the laughter, and know what it is that men are hurrying to.

3. Joy and sorrow are not contradictory. These two states of mind, both of them the natural operations of any deep faith, may coexist and blend into one another, so that the gladness is sobered and chastened and made manly and noble; and that the sorrow is like some thundercloud all streaked with bars of sunshine that go into its deepest depths. The joy lives in the midst of the sorrow; the sorrow springs from the same root as the gladness.

II. THE JOY OF THE LORD IS A MATTER OF CHRISTIAN DUTY.

A. The Reasons Why It Is a Christian Duty.

1. It is a commandment of God's Word. It is a commandment here (Nehemiah 8:10) and it is a commandment in the New Testament (Philippians 4:4).

2. The Christian can, to a great extent, regulate his emotions. To rejoice in the Lord is a duty, a thing that the Apostle enjoins; from which, of course, it follows that somehow or other it is to a large extent within one's power and that even the indulgence in this emotion and the degree to which a Christian life shall be a cheerful life is dependent in a large measure on our own volitions and stands on the same footing as our obedience to God's other commandments.

3. The Christian can determine his thoughts which regulate his emotions. To lose thoughts of ourselves in God's truth about Himself is our duty.

B. The Hindrances to This Christian Duty.

1. Temperament. Some of us are naturally fainthearted, timid, skeptical of any success, grave, melancholy, or hard to stir to any emotion. To such there will be an added difficulty in making quiet confident joy any very familiar guest in their home or in their place of prayer. But even such should remember that the "powers of the world to come," the energies of the Gospel, are given to us for the very express purpose of overcoming, as well as of hallowing natural dispositions.

2. Deficiency in the depth and reality of our faith. It is only where there is much faith and consequent love that there is much joy. If there is but small faith, there will not be much gladness.

3. Failure to take the position a Christian has a right to take. You must cast yourselves on God's Gospel with all your weight, without any hanging back, without any doubt, without even the shadow of a suspicion that it will give—that the firm, pure floor will give and let you through into the water.

III. THE JOY OF THE LORD IS A SOURCE OF STRENGTH.

A. It Affects Our Efficiency.

1. Because man's force comes from his mind and not his body. All gladness has something to do with our efficiency; for it is the prerogative of man that his force comes from his mind and from his body.

2. Because joy lightens work. If we have souls at rest in Christ or the wealth and blessedness of a tranquil gladness lying there, work will be easy.

3. Because joy repels temptations. If the soul is full, and full of joy, what side will be exposed to the assault of any temptation?

B. It Is Necessary to Effective Christian Service.

1. The things which cannot strengthen a man. No vehement resolutions, no sense of your own sinfulness, nor even contrite remembrance of past failures ever made a man strong.

2. Joy is essential to strength. For strength there must be joy.

3. The most dangerous opponent to Christian work—despondency and simple sorrow.

CONCLUSION

You are weak unless you are glad; you are not glad and strong unless your faith and hope are fixed in Christ and unless you are working from and not toward the assurance of salvation.

Alexander Maclaren

SERMON TWELVE

THE INHABITANT OF THE ROCK

Thou wilt keep him in perfect peace, whose mind is stayed on Thee; because he trusteth in Thee. Trust ye in the Lord forever; for in the Lord Jehovah is everlasting strength.
— ISAIAH 26:3–4

THERE is an obvious parallel between these verses and the two preceding ones. The safety which is there set forth as the result of dwelling in a strong city is here presented as the consequences of trust. The emblem of the fortified place passes into that of the Rock of Ages. In the two preceding verses we have the triumphant declaration of security followed by a summons to "open the gates," so here we have the declaration of perfect peace followed by a summons to "trust in the Lord forever."

I. THE NATURE OF TRUST.

A. The Meaning of Trust Stated.

Now the literal meaning of the expression here rendered "to trust" is to lean upon anything. As we say, trust is reliance.

B. The Meaning of Trust Illustrated and Applied.

As a weak man might stay his faltering, tottering steps upon some strong staff or might lean upon the outstretched arm of a friend, so we, conscious of our weakness, aware of our faltering feet, and realizing the roughness of the road and the smallness of our strength, may lay the whole weight of ourselves upon the loving strength of Jehovah.

II. THE STEADFAST PEACEFULNESS OF TRUST.

A. Trust Produces Steadfastness.

1. Steadfastness is not a characteristic of the average man's life. Most men's lives are blown about by winds of circumstance, directed by gusts of passion, shaped by accidents, and are fragmentary and jerky, like some ship at sea with nobody at the helm, heading here and there as the force of the wind or the flow of the current may carry them.

2. Steadfastness is the result of trusting in God. No man can steady his life except by clinging to a holdfast outside of himself. Some of us look for that stay in the fluctuations and fleetingnesses of creatures and some of us are wiser and saner and look for it in the steadfastness of the unchanging God. Only they who stay themselves upon God are steadfast and solid.

B. The Steadfast Mind Is Kept of God.

1. The necessity to have an attitude of confidence. In order to receive the full blessed effects of trust into our characters and lives we must persistently and doggedly keep on in the attitude of confidence. There must be a steadfast working if there is to be a continual flow.

2. The certainty that God keeps the steadfast mind in perfect peace. It is the mind that cleaves to God which God keeps. I suppose there was floating before Paul's thought some remembrance of this great passage of the evangelical prophet when he said, "The peace of God which passeth understanding shall keep your hearts and minds through Christ Jesus" (Philippians 4:7). It is the steadfast mind that is kept in perfect peace.

C. The Steadfast Mind Is Filled with Peace.

1. The character of the peace. There is something very beautiful in the prophet's abandoning the attempt to find any adjective which adequately characterizes the peace of which he has been speaking. He falls back upon an expedient which is a confession of the impotence of human speech worthily to portray its subject when he simply says, "Thou shalt keep in peace,

peace . . . because he trusteth in Thee." The reduplication expresses the depth and completeness of the tranquility which flows into the heart.

2. The dependence of peace. The possession of this deep, unbroken peace does not depend on the absence of conflict, distraction, trouble, or sorrow, but on the presence of God.

III. THE WORTHINESS OF THE DIVINE NAME TO EVOKE AND THE POWER OF DIVINE CHARACTER TO REWARD THE TRUST.

A. The Meaning of the Words, "In the Lord Jehovah Is Everlasting Strength."

1. The literal translation of "everlasting strength." The words feebly rendered in the Authorized Version "everlasting strength" are literally "the Rock of Ages."

2. The significance of "Lord Jehovah." Here we have the name of Jehovah reduplicated. In Jah Jehovah is the Rock of Ages. In adoration he contents himself with twice taking the name upon his lips in order to *impress* what he cannot *express,* the majesty and the sufficiency of that name.

B. The Truth Expressed by the Words "In the Lord Jehovah Is Everlasting Strength."

1. Jehovah is the unchangeable, self-existent, covenant keeping God. Jehovah, in its grammatical signification, puts emphasis upon the absolute, underived and therefore unlimited, unconditioned, unchangeable, eternal being of God. "I Am that I Am" (Exodus 3:14). It is the name of the God who entered into covenant with His ancient people and remains bound by His covenant to bless us.

2. The child of God has an unchangeable defence. The metaphor needs no expansion. We understand that it conveys the idea of unchangeable defence. They who fasten themselves to that Rock are safe in its unchangeable strength. "The conies are a feeble folk, yet they make their houses in the rocks" (Proverbs 30:26). So our weakness may house itself there and be at rest.

IV. THE SUMMONS TO TRUST.

A. It Is a Merciful Summons.

Surely, the blessed effects of trust, of which we have been speaking, have a voice of merciful invitation summoning us to exercise it. The promise of peace appeals to the deepest, though often neglected and misunderstood longings of the human heart. Storms live in the lower regions of the atmosphere; get up higher and there is peace.

B. It Is a Summons to Faith.

Surely the name of the Rock of Ages is an invitation to us to put our trust in Him. If a man knew God as He is, he could not choose but trust Him.

C. It Is a Summons Addressed to All.

It is a summons addressed to us all. "Trust ye"—whoever you are—"in the Lord forever."

CONCLUSION

When from the cross there comes to all our hearts the merciful invitation, "Believe on the Lord Jesus Christ, and thou shalt be saved" (Acts 16:31), why should not we each answer,

"Rock of Ages, cleft for me,
Let me hide myself in Thee"?

Alexander Maclaren

A THREEFOLD DISEASE AND A TWOFOLD CURE

I will cleanse them from all their iniquity,
whereby they have sinned against Me; and
I will pardon all their iniquities, whereby
they have sinned, and whereby they have
transgressed against Me.
— JEREMIAH 33:8

JEREMIAH was a prisoner in the palace of the last King of Judah. The long, national tragedy had reached almost the last scene of the last act. The prophet never faltered in predicting its fall, but he as uniformly pointed to a period behind the impelling ruin when all should be peace and joy. That fair vision of the future begins with the offer of healing and cure, and with the exuberant promise of my text.

I. A THREEFOLD VIEW OF THE SAD CONDITION OF HUMANITY.

A. The Three Words Used by the Prophet to Describe the Sad Condition of Humanity.

You see there are three expressions which roughly may be taken as referring to the same ugly fact, but yet not meaning quite the same—"iniquity, or iniquities, sin, transgression." These three all speak about the same sad element in your experience and mine, but they speak about it from somewhat different points of view, and I wish to try to bring out that difference for you.

1. Iniquity.

2. Sin.

3. Transgression.

B. The Significance of the Three Words Used by the Prophet to Describe the Sad Condition of Humanity.

1. A sinful life is a twisted or warped life. The word rendered "iniquity" in the Old Testament in all probability literally means something that is not straight; that is, bent, or, as I said, twisted or warped. All sin is a twisting of the man from his proper course. Here is a straight road and there are the devious footpaths that we have made, many a coming back instead of going forward.

2. A sinful life is a life that misses the mark. The meaning of the word (sin) in the original is simply "that which misses the mark." There are two ways in which that thought may be looked at. Every wrong thing that we do misses the aim, if you consider what a man's aim ought to be. All godlessness, all the low, sinful lives that so many live, miss the shabby aim which they set before themselves.

3. A sinful life is a rebellious life. The expression which is translated in our text "transgressed," literally means "rebelled." And the lesson of it is, that all sin is, however little we think it, a rebellion against God. When we do wrong we lift up ourselves against our Sovereign King, and we say, "Who is the Lord that we should serve Him? Who is Lord over us? Let us break His bands asunder, and cast away His cords from us."

II. THE TWOFOLD BRIGHT HOPE WHICH SHINES THROUGH THE DARKNESS.

If sin combines in itself all these characteristics that I have touched upon, then clearly there is guilt and clearly there are stains; and the gracious promise of this text deals with both the one and the other.

A. Pardon.

1. The meaning of pardon. What do you fathers and mothers do when you forgive your child? You may use the rod or you may not. Forgiveness does not lie in letting him off the punishment; but forgiveness lies in the flowing to the child, uninterrupted, of the love of the parent heart, and that is God's forgiveness. "Thou wast a God that forgavest them, though Thou tookest vengeance of their inventions" (Psalm 99:8).

2. The need of pardon. Do you need pardon? What does the sense of remorse say? What does conscience say? There are tendencies to ignore the fact that all sin must necessarily lead to tremendous consequences of misery. It does so in this world, more or less. A man goes into another world as he left this one and you and I believe —"after death, the judgment" (Hebrews 9:27).

3. The basis of pardon. "Himself bore our sins in His own body on the tree" (I Peter 2:24). Jesus Christ, the Son of God, died that the loving forgiveness of God might find its way to man's heart, whilst yet the righteousness of God remained untarnished. I know not any Gospel that goes deep enough to touch the real sore place in human nature except the Gospel that says, "Behold the Lamb of God that taketh away the sin of the world" (John 1:29).

B. Cleansing.

1. The reason for cleansing. But forgiveness is not enough, for the worst results of past sin are the habits of sin which it leaves within us; so that we all need cleansing.

2. The impossibility of man to cleanse himself. Can we cleanse ourselves? Let experience answer. Did you ever try to cure yourself of some little trick of gesture, or manner, or speech? And did you not find out then how strong the trivial habit was? You never know the force of a current till you try to row against it. "Can the Ethiopian change his skin?" (Jeremiah 13:23).

3. The secret of cleansing. So, again, we say that Jesus Christ who died for the remission of sins that are past, lives that He may give to each of us His own blessed life and power, and so draw us from our evil and invest us with His good.

CONCLUSION

Pardon and cleansing are our two deepest needs. There is one hand from which we can receive them both, and one only. There is one condition on which we shall receive them, which is that we trust in Him "who was crucified for our offences" and lives to hallow us into His own likeness.

Alexander Maclaren

A PAIR OF FRIENDS

Can two walk together, except they be agreed?
—AMOS 3:3

THE "TWO" whom the prophet would see walking together are God and Israel and his question suggests not only the companionship and communion with God which are the highest form of religion and the aim of all forms and ceremonies of worship, but also the inexorable condition on which alone that height of communion can be secured and sustained. Two may walk together, though the one be God and the other be I. But they have to be agreed thus far, at any rate, that both shall wish to be together and both be going the same road.

I. THE POSSIBLE BLESSED COMPANIONSHIP WHICH MAY CHEER A LIFE.

A. *Three Aspects of Divine Companionship.*

1. Walking before God (Genesis 17:1). Sometimes we read about "walking before God," as Abraham was bid to do. That means ordering the daily life under the continued sense that we are "ever in the great Taskmaster's eye."

2. Walking after God (Deuteronomy 13:4). This means conforming the will and active efforts to the rule that He has laid down, setting our steps firm on the paths that He has prepared that we should walk in them and accept His providences.

3. Walking with God (Genesis 5:22). High above both of these conceptions of a devout life is the one which is suggested by the text and was realized in the case of the patriarch Enoch—walking "with God." To "walk with Him" implies a constant, quiet sense of His divine presence which forbids loneliness, guides and defends, floods the soul, and fills the life.

B. The Possibility of Divine Companionship.

1. The certainty of its possibility. Far above us as such experience seems to sound, such a life is a possibility for every one of us. We may be able to say, as truly as our Lord said it, "I am not alone, for the Father is with Me" (John 16:32).

2. The necessary requirement. It is possible that the dreariest solitude of a soul may be turned into blessed fellowship with Him. But that solitude will not be so turned unless it is first painfully felt. We need to feel in our deepest hearts that loneliness on earth before we walk with God.

C. The Blessings of Divine Companionship.

1. It results in mutual communications. If we are so walking it is no piece of fanaticism to say that there will be mutual communications. As two friends on the road will interchange remarks about trifles and if they love each other, the remarks about trifles will be weighed with love, so we can tell our smallest affairs to God.

2. It is the secret of all blessedness. It is the only thing that will make a life absolutely sovereign over sorrow and fixedly unperturbed by all tempests and invulnerable to all "the slings and arrows of outrageous fortune."

II. THE SADLY INCOMPLETE REALITY IN MUCH CHRISTIAN EXPERIENCE WHICH CONTRASTS WITH THIS POSSIBILITY.

A. The Failure of Many Christians.

1. To be habitually conscious of divine companionship. I am afraid that very, very few so-called Christian people habitually feel, as they might do, the depth and blessedness of this communion.

2. To actually have unbroken Divine companionship. And sure I am that only a very small percentage of us have anything like the continuity of companionship which the text suggests as possible. Is it a line in my life or is there but a dot here and a dot there and long breaks between? The long embarrassed pauses in a conversation between two who do not know much of, or care much for, each other are only too like what occurs in many professing Christians' intercourse with God.

B. A Description of the Failure of Many Christians.

It is broken at the best, and imperfect at the completest, and shallow at the deepest.

1. Broken companionship.

2. Imperfect companionship.

3. Shallow companionship.

III. THE EXPLANATION OF THE FAILURE TO REALIZE THE LORD'S CONTINUAL PRESENCE.

A. Failure of Agreement.

The two are not agreed; and that is why they are not walking together.

1. The sensitiveness of the consciousness of God's presence. The consciousness of God's presence with us is a very delicate thing. It is like a sensitive thermometer which will drop when an iceberg is a league off over the sea and scarcely visible.

2. The reason for the failure of agreement. We do not wish His company, or we are not in harmony with His thoughts, or we are not going His road and therefore, of course, we part.

B. Sin.

1. This is the primary factor. At bottom there is only one thing that separates a soul from God, and that is sin—sin of some sort, like tiny grains of dust that get between two polished plates in an engine, that ought to move smoothly and closely against each other. The obstruction may be invisible and yet be powerful enough to cause friction which hinders the working of the engine and throws everything out of gear.

2. It may be that the Christian is unconscious of it. A light cloud that we cannot see may come between us and a star, and we shall only know it is there because that star is not visibly there. Similarly, many a Christian, quite unconsciously, has something or other in his habits or in his conduct or in his affections which would reveal itself to him, if he would look, as being wrong, because it blots out God. There may be scarcely any consciousness of parting company at the beginning. Let the man travel on it far enough and the two will be so far apart that he cannot see God or hear Him speak.

CONCLUSION

If we have parted from our Friend there should be no time lost ere we go back. May it be true of us that we walk with God, so that at last the great promise may be fulfilled about us, "that we shall walk with Him in white" being by His love accounted "worthy," and so "follow" and keep company with "the Lamb whithersoever He goeth."

Alexander Maclaren

BARTIMAEUS

. . . Blind Bartimaeus, the son of Timaeus,
sat by the highway side begging.
—MARK 10:46
(READ MARK 10:46–52)

THE NARRATIVE of this miracle is contained in all the three first Gospels. Mark's account is evidently that of an eyewitness. It is full of little particulars which testify thereto. Whether Bartimaeus had a companion or not, he was obviously the chief actor and spokesman. And the whole story seems to me to lend itself to the enforcement of some very important lessons, which I will try to draw from it.

I. THE BEGGAR'S PETITION AND THE ATTEMPTS TO SILENCE IT (Verses 47–48).

A. The Beggar's Cry.

1. It expresses an insight into Christ's place and dignity. He cried, "Jesus, Thou Son of David," distinctly recognizing our Lord's Messianic character, His power and authority, and on that power and authority he built a confidence. He is sure of both the power and the will.

2. It expresses a sense of need. He individualizes himself, his need, Christ's power and willingness to help him.

3. It expresses an insight into our Lord's unique character and power. Unless we know Him to be all that is involved in that august title, "the son of David," I do not think our cries to Him will ever be very earnest.

B. The Attempts to Stifle the Beggar's Cry.

1. The people, undoubtedly, considered their efforts to stifle the cry a defense of the Master's dignity.

2. The people were ignorant of the fact that the cry of wretchedness was sweeter to the Lord than the shallow hallelujahs.

3. The people failed to stifle the beggar's cry. The more they silenced him, the more a great deal he cried.

II. CHRIST'S CALL AND THE SUPPLIANT'S RESPONSE (Verses 49–50).

A. The Call of the Savior.

1. The setting of the Savior's call. He was on His road to His cross and the tension of spirit which the evangelist's notice as attaching to Him then and which filled the disciples with awe as they followed Him, absorbed Him, no doubt, at this hour so that He heard but little of the people's shouts.

2. The interest of the Savior in the beggar. But He did hear the blind beggar's cry and He arrested His march in order to attend to it.

3. The present interest of the Savior in the cries of the needy. The living Christ is as tender a friend, has as quick an ear, is as ready to help at once, today, as He was when outside the gate of Jericho. Christ still hears and answers the cry of need.

B. The Response of the Suppliant.

Notice the suppliant's response. That is a very characteristic right-about-face of the crowd, who one moment were saying, "Hold your tongue and do not disturb Him," and the next moment were all eager to encumber him with help, and to say, "Rise up! Be of good cheer; He calleth thee." And what did the man do?

1. The beggar arose. "Sprang to his feet"—as the word rightly rendered would be.

2. The beggar flung away his garment. And flung away his disordered and offensive rags that he had wrapped round him for warmth and softness of seat, as he waited at the gate.

3. The beggar came to Jesus. Brethren, "casting aside every weight and the sin that doth so easily beset us; let us run" to the same Refuge (Hebrews 2:1).

III. THE QUESTION OF ALL-GRANTING LOVE AND THE ANSWER OF CONSCIOUS NEED (Verse 51).

A. The Interrogation.

1. The meaning of the question. It was the implicit pledge that whatever he desired he should receive.

2. The reason for the question. Jesus knew that the thing this man wanted was the thing that He delighted to give.

3. The authority of the Questioner. Think of a man doing as Jesus Christ did—standing before another and saying, "I will give you anything that you want." He must be either a madman, or a blasphemer, or "God manifest in the flesh," Almighty power guided by infinite love.

B. The Response.

1. The content of the answer. He had no doubt what he wanted most—the opening of those blind eyes of his.

2. It was the answer of a wise man. If you are a wise man, if you know yourself and Him, your answer will come as swiftly as the beggar's—Lord! Heal me of my blindness and take away my sin and give me Thy salvation.

3. Man's greatest need is expressed in the answer.

IV. SIGHT GIVEN AND THE RECEIVER FOLLOWING (Verse 52).

A. The Gift of Sight.

1. The cure was in answer to the beggar's cry. Bartimaeus had scarcely ended speaking when Christ began. He was blind at the beginning of Christ's little sentence; he saw at the end of it.

2. The cure was immediate. The answer came instantly and the cure was as immediate as the movement of Christ's heart in answer.

3. The immediateness of salvation. As soon as we desire we have and as soon as we have we see.

B. The Condition by Which Christ's Mercy Rushes into a Man's Soul.

1. Faith made it possible for Christ's power to make the beggar whole. Here we have a clear statement of the path by which Christ's mercy rushes into a man's soul. "Thy faith hath saved thee" (Verse 52).

2. Physical miracles do not always require trust in Christ but the possession of Christ's salvation does.

CONCLUSION

Now, this story should be the story of each one of us. One modification we have to make upon it, for we do not need to cry persistently for mercy, but to trust in, and to take, the mercy that is needed. One other difference there is between Bartimaeus and many of my hearers. He knew what he needed, and some of you do not. But Christ is calling us all and my business now is to say to each of you . . ., "Rise! Be of good cheer; He calleth thee."

Alexander Maclaren

HOW THE LITTLE MAY BE USED TO GET THE GREAT

He that is faithful in that which is least is faithful also in much, and he that is unjust in the least is unjust also in much. If, therefore, ye have not been faithful in the unrighteous mammon, who will commit to your trust the true riches? And if ye have not been faithful in that which is another man's, who shall give you that which is your own?

—LUKE 16:10–12

THESE are very revolutionary words in more than one aspect. There are two things remarkable about them. One is the contrast which is seen in all three verses between what our Lord calls "mammon" (that is, simply outward good) and the inward riches of a heart devoted to and filled with God and Christ. But another striking thing about the words is the broad, bold statement that a man's use of the lower goods determines, or is at least an element in determining, his possession of the highest.

I. A NEW STANDARD OF VALUE.

A. The Antithesis between "Small" and "Great" (Verse 10).

1. They imply a comparison with each other.

2. They imply a common standard of value for both. "Small" and "great," of course, are relative terms; they imply a comparison with each other, and imply also a reference of both to a common standard of value.

3. The common standard of value stated. What are these two classes of good measured by, but their respective power of filling the heart.

B. The Antithesis between "Unrighteous Mammon" and the "True Riches" (Verse 11).

1. The meaning of "unrighteous." If we keep strictly to the antithesis, "unrighteous" must be the opposite of "true." The word would then come to mean very nearly the same as deceitful, that which betrays.

2. The deception of material good. No man ever found in any outward good, when he got it, that which he fancied was in it when he was chasing after it.

3. The true riches. But the inward riches of faith, true holiness, lofty aspirations, Christ centered purposes, all these are true. They bring more than they said they would.

C. The Antithesis between "Another's" and "Your Own" (Verse 12).

1. The term "another's" may signify stewardship. Another's? Well, that may mean God's; and therefore you are stewards, as the whole parable that precedes the text has been teaching.

2. The term "another's" implies the limitations and defects of outward possessions of outward good. There is no real possession, even while there is an apparent one . . . the possession is transient as well as incomplete.

3. The term "another's" suggests that accidents of life rob men of outward possessions. What can be taken out of man's hands by death has no right to be called his. Each, for the moment says "Mine!" and Christ says "No! No! Another's!"

4. The term "your own" refers to the things we are. That which is your own is that which you can gather into your heart and keep there, and which death cannot take away from you.

II. THE HIGHEST USE OF THE LOWEST GOOD.

A. The Essence of the Principle (Verses 10–12).

1. The statement of the principle. Our Lord . . . distinctly asserts here, as a principle, that our manner of employing the lesser goods of outward possessions is an element in determining the amount of our possession of the highest blessing.

2. The Christian's fear concerning this principle. Good people are sometimes cautious of asserting that with the plain emphasis with which it is here asserted, for fear they should damage the central truth that God's mercy and the gifts of His grace come to men through faith, not through their conduct.

3. The necessity of faith in receiving the "true riches." A man receives into his heart "the true riches" simply on condition of his desiring them and of his trusting Jesus Christ to give them.

B. Conduct May Help or Hinder a Man in the Possession and Exercise of Faith.

1. This does not militate against the central truth of the Gospel.

2. The love of the world is a hindrance to salvation. There are plenty of people who are kept from being Christians because they love the world too much.

3. The love of the world is a hindrance to Christians. And is it not true about many Christians that their too high estimate of, and too great carefulness about, and too niggardly disposal of the goods of this lesser life, are hindering their Christian career?

C. The Principle of the World and the Principle of Christ Contrasted.

1. The principle of the world stated. The world thinks that the highest use of the highest things is to gain possession of the lowest.

2. The principle of Christ stated. Christ's teaching of the relationship is exactly the opposite, that all the outward is then lifted to its noblest purpose when it is made rigidly subordinate to the highest.

III. THE FAITHFULNESS WHICH UTILIZES THE LOWEST AS A MEANS OF POSSESSING MORE FULLY THE HIGHEST.

You will be "faithful" if, through all your administration of your possessions there run the principles of stewardship, sacrifice, and brotherhood.

A. Stewardship.

1. Consciousness of stewardship a requisite to faithfulness. "Of thine own have we given thee" (I Chronicles 29:14) is to be always our conviction, for all is God's.

2. The obligation of stewardship. One of the plainest duties of stewardship is that we bring conscience and deliberate consideration to bear upon our administration of this world's goods.

3. The extent of stewardship—personal and domestic expenditure, savings, and gifts.

B. Sacrifice.

1. It is a fundamental law of the Christian life.

2. It must be applied in the region of outward possessions. It must be applied especially in his region of outward possession where the opposite law of selfishness works most strongly.

3. It is based on God's mercies.

C. Brotherhood.

1. The Christian's obligation is to share blessings with fellow believers. It and they and we all belong to God.

2. The reason for the obligation is to share blessings. We get everything in order that we may transmit it to others.

3. The sphere of blessings shared, outward goods, faculties of the mind and heart, wisdom, sympathy, the gifts of the Gospel.

CONCLUSION

Here and now we may win a greater possession of the love and likeness of God, and may have our spirits widened to receive more of all that makes us noble and calm, hopeful and strong, by our Christian administration of earthly goods. It will make us more capable of a larger possession of the life and the grace of God hereafter.

Alexander Maclaren

THE TRANSLATION OF ELIJAH AND THE ASCENSION OF CHRIST

*And it came to pass, as they still went on, and talked,
that, behold, there appeared a chariot of fire, and horses
of fire, and parted them both asunder; and Elijah went
up by a whirlwind into heaven.*
—II KINGS 2:11

*And it came to pass, while He blessed them, He was departed
from them, and carried up into heaven.*
—LUKE 24:51

I COULD wish no better foil for the history of the ascension than the history of Elijah's rapture. The comparison rings out contrasts at every step, and there is no readier way of throwing into strong relief the meaning and purpose of the former than holding up beside it the story of the latter.

I. THE CONTRAST BETWEEN THE MANNER OF ELIJAH'S TRANSLATION AND THE MANNER OF OUR LORD'S ASCENSION.

A. The Manner of Elijah's Translation.

1. It was a tempestuous translation. The prophet's end was like the man. It was fitting that he should be swept up into the skies in tempest and fire. The impetuosity of his nature and the stormy energy of his career had already been symbolized (I Kings 19:11–12).

2. It was a translation by external power. It suggests very plainly that Elijah was lifted to the skies by power acting on him from without. He did not ascend; he was carried up; the earthly frame and the human nature had no power to rise.

B. The Ascension of Christ.

1. It was quiet. The silent gentleness, which did not strive nor cry nor cause His voice to be heard in the streets, marks Him even in that hour of lofty and transcendent triumph. No blaze of fiery chariots nor agitation of tempest is needed to bear Him heavenwards.

2. It was by inherent power. Our Lord's ascension by His own inherent power is brought into boldest relief when contrasted with Elijah's rapture and is evidently the fitting expression, as it is the consequence, of His sole and singular Divine nature.

II. THE CONTRAST BETWEEN THE LIFE'S WORK OF EACH WHICH PRECEDED THE TWO EVENTS.

A. Elijah Leaves His Work Unfinished.

1. The symbol of transference. The falling mantle of Elijah has become a symbol known to all the world for the transference of unfinished tasks and the appointment of successors to departed greatness. It was the symbol of office and authority transferred.

2. The powerlessness of Elijah to make the transference. Elisha asked that he might have a double portion of his master's spirit, not twice as much as his master, but the eldest son's share of the father's possessions. His master had no power to bestow the gift and had to reply as one who has nothing that he has not received and cannot dispose of the grace that dwells in him.

B. Christ Completes His Work.

None are hailed as His successors. He has left no unfinished work which another may perfect. He has done no work which another may do again for new generations.

1. He has no successors.

2. His work needs no repetition.

III. THE TWO EVENTS CONTRASTED IN RELATION TO THE TRANSITION TO A CONTINUOUS ENERGY FOR AND IN THE WORLD.

A. The Translation of Elijah Was Not a Transition to a Continuous Energy for and in the World.

Clearly the narrative derives all its pathos from the thought that Elijah's work is done. His task is over and nothing more is to be hoped for from him.

1. His work was over.

2. Nothing more is to be hoped from him.

B. The Ascension of Christ Was a Transition to a Continuous Energy for and in the World.

1. The ascension of Christ did not end His activity for men, but cast it in a new form. When He ascended up on high He relinquished nothing of His activity for us, but only cast it into a new form which in some sense is yet higher than that which it took on earth.

2. The nature of Christ's present activity. He works with His servants. He has gone up to sit at the right hand of God. The session at God's right hand means the repose of a perfected salvation, the communion of divine worship, the exercise of all the omnipotence of God, the administration of the world's history.

IV. THE TWO EVENTS CONTRASTED AS TO THE BEARING ON THE HOPES OF HUMANITY FOR THE FUTURE.

A. Elijah's Translation in Relation to the Prophets.

1. It gave them a deepened conviction of Elijah's mission and perhaps a clearer faith in the future life. The prophet is caught up to the glory and the rest for himself alone, and the sole share which the gazing follower or sons of the prophets had in his triumph was a deepened conviction of this prophet's mission and perhaps some clearer faith in a future life.

2. It did not shed any light on their future. No light streamed from it on their own future. The path they had to tread was still a common road into the great darkness, as solitary and unknown as before.

B. Christ's Ascension in Relation to Man.

1. It assures the child of God of presence with Him. His resurrection assures us that "them which sleep in Jesus will God bring with him" (I Thessalonians 4:14). His passage to the heaven assures us that "they who are alive and remain shall be caught up together with them" (I Thessalonians 4:17), and that all of both companies shall with Him live and reign, sharing His dominion, and molded to His image.

2. It assures us of Christ's personal return. "Ye men of Galilee, why stand ye gazing up into heaven? This same Jesus, which is taken up from you into heaven, shall so come in like manner as ye have seen Him go into heaven" (Acts 1:11). "So"—that is to say, personally, corporeally, on clouds—"and His feet shall stand in that day upon the Mount of Olives" (Zechariah 14:4).

CONCLUSION

That parting on Olivet cannot be the end. Such a leaving is the prophecy of happy greetings and an inseparable reunion. So let us take our share in the great joy with which the disciples returned to Jerusalem, left like sheep in the midst of wolves as they were, and "let us set our affections on things above, where Christ is, sitting at the right hand of God."

Alexander Maclaren

THE CROSS, THE GLORY OF CHRIST, AND GOD

Therefore, when he was gone out, Jesus said, "Now is the Son of Man glorified, and God is glorified in Him. If God be glorified in Him, God shall also glorify Him in Himself, and shall straightway glorify Him.
—JOHN 13:31–32

IN IMMEDIATE connection with the departure of the traitor comes this singular burst of triumph in our text. What Judas went to do was the beginning of Christ's glorifying. We have here, then, a triple glorification—the Son of Man glorified in His cross; God glorified in the Son of Man; and the Son of Man glorified in God.

I. THE SON OF MAN GLORIFIED IN HIS CROSS.

A. Christ's Twofold Attitude toward the Cross.

1. The innocent shrinking of His manhood. On the one hand we mark in Him an unmistakable shrinking from the cross, the innocent shrinking of His manhood expressed in such words as "I have a baptism to be baptized with, and how am I straitened till it be accomplished" (Luke 12:50); and in such incidents as the agony in Gethsemane.

2. The triumphant anticipation. And yet, side by side with that, not overcome by it, but not overcoming it, there is the opposite feeling, the reaching out almost with eagerness to bring the cross nearer to Himself.

211

B. The Twofold Manner in Which the Cross Glorified Christ.

1. It was the revelation of His heart. All His lifelong He had been trying to tell the world how much He loved it. His love had been, as it were, filtered by drops through His words, through His deeds, through His whole demeanor and bearing; but in His death it comes in a flood and pours itself upon the world.

2. It was the throne of His saving power. The paradoxical words of our text rest upon His profound conviction that in His death He was about to put forth a mightier and diviner power than ever He had manifested in His life. They are the same in effect and in tone as the great words: "I, if I am lifted up, will draw all men unto Me" (John 12:32).

II. GOD GLORIFIED IN THE SON OF MAN.

A. The Glorification of God in the Cross of Christ.

1. The indwelling of God in Christ. God was in Christ in some singular and eminent manner. If all His life was a continual manifestation of the Divine character, if Christ's words were the Divine wisdom, if Christ's compassion was the Divine pity, if Christ's loveliness was the Divine gentleness, if His whole human life and nature were the brightest and cleanest manifestation to the world of what God is, we can understand that the cross was the highest point of the revelation of the Divine nature to the world.

2. The death of Christ was substitutionary. The words involve as it seems to me, not only that idea of a close, unique union and indwelling of God in Christ, but they involve also this other: that the sufferings bore no relation to the deserts of the Person who endured them. "God was in Christ reconciling the world to Himself" (II Corinthians 5:19).

B. God Is Glorified in the Cross of Christ because it Is a Revelation of His Love.

1. It is the greatest revelation of God's love. The cross upon which Christ died towers above all other revelations as the most awful, the most sacred, the most tender, the most complete, the most heart-touching, the most soul-subduing manifestation of the Divine nature.

2. It is the revelation which has brought the greatest blessing to men. Has it not scattered doubts that lay like mountains of ice upon man's heart? Has it not swept the heavens clear of clouds that wrapped it in darkness?

III. THE SON OF MAN GLORIFIED IN THE FATHER.

A. *The Nature of the Glorification.*

1. The statement of the glorification of the Son of Man in the Father. "He shall also glorify Him in Himself" (vs. 32).

2. The explanation of statement of the glorification of the Son of Man in the Father. Mark that—"in Himself." That is the obvious antithesis to what has been spoken about in the previous clause, a glorifying which consisted in a manifestation to the external universe, whereas this is a glorifying within the depths of the Divine nature. And the best commentary upon it is our Lord's own words: "Father! Glorify Thou Me with the glory which I had with Thee before the world was" (John 17:5).

B. *The Person of the Glorification.*

1. It is the Son of Man. That is to say, the man Christ Jesus, "bone of our bone and flesh of our flesh," the very Person that walked upon earth and dwelt amongst us . . .

2. It is the Son of Man incorporated into the heart of God. He is taken up into the heart of God and in His manhood enters into that same glory which from the beginning the eternal Word had with God.

C. *The Time of the Glorification.*

1. It began in paradise. We have the glorifying set forth as commencing immediately upon the completion of God's glorifying by Christ upon the cross. "He shall straightway glorify Him" (verse 32). It began in that paradise into which we know that upon that day He entered.

2. It was manifested to the world at the resurrection and the ascension. It was manifested to the world when He raised Him from the dead and gave Him glory. It reached a still higher point when they brought Him near unto the Ancient of Days.

3. It will be more fully manifested at the second coming of Christ. It shall rise to its highest manifestation before an assembled world when He shall come in His glory.

CONCLUSION

This, then, was the vision that lay before the Christ in that upper room, the vision of Himself glorified in His extreme shame because His cross manifested His love and His saving power; of God glorified in Him above all other of His acts of manifestation when He died on the cross, and revealed the very heart of God; and of Himself glorified in the Father when, exalted high above all creatures, He sitteth upon the Father's throne and rules the Father's realms.

Alexander Maclaren

THE TRUE VISION OF THE FATHER

Philip said unto Him, "Lord, show us the Father, and it sufficeth us."
Jesus said unto him, "Have I been so long time with you, and yet hast
thou not known Me, Philip? He that hath seen Me hath seen the Father;
and how sayest thou then, show us the Father? Believest thou not that I
am in the Father, and the Father in Me? The words that I speak unto
you I speak not of Myself: but the Father that dwelleth in Me, He doeth
the works. Believe Me that I am in the Father, and the Father in Me:
or else believe Me for the work's sake."
— JOHN 14:8–11

THE VEHEMENT burst with which Philip interrupts the calm flow of our Lord's discourse is not the product of mere frivolity or curiosity. As an Old Testament believer he knew that Moses had once led the elders of Israel up to the mount where "they saw the God of Israel," and to many others had been granted sensible manifestations of the Divine presence. His petition is childlike in its simplicity, beautiful in its trust, noble and true in its estimate of what men need. He longs to see God. He believes that Christ can show God; he is sure that the sight of God will satisfy the heart.

I. THE REVELATION OF GOD IN CHRIST IS SUFFICIENT TO ANSWER MEN'S LONGINGS (Verses 8–9).

A. All Men Need a Visible Revelation of God.

1. The history of heathendom shows us this need. In every land men have said, "The gods have come down to us in the likeness of men."

2. The cultured have the same need. The highest cultivation of this highly cultivated self-conscious century, has not removed men from the same necessity that the rudest savage has, to have some kind of manifestation of the Divine nature other than the dim and vague ones which are possible apart from the revelation of God in Christ.

3. The whole world has this need.

4. It is a personal need. Your heart and mind require it.

B. Man's Need of a Visible Revelation of God Is Met in Christ.

1. Abstract qualities are made visible through the deeds of the body. Wisdom, love, and purity are only seen through the deeds of the body.

2. The invisible God is made visible through the incarnate Christ. He is the manifestation to the world of the unseen Father.

C. The Revelation of God in Christ Is Sufficient for Man.

If we can see God it suffices us. Then the mind settles down upon the thought of Him as the basis of all being, and of all change; and the heart can twine itself round Him, and the seeking soul folds its wings and is at rest; and the troubled spirit is quiet, and the accusing conscience is silent, and the rebellious will is subdued.

1. It is sufficient for the mind.

2. It is sufficient for the heart.

3. It is sufficient for the will.

II. THE REVELATION OF GOD IN CHRIST IS MADE POSSIBLE BY THE DIVINE AND MUTUAL INDWELLING OF THE FATHER AND THE SON (Verse 10).

A. Christ's Claim to the Oneness of Unbroken Commission.

1. "I am in the Father" indicates the suppression of all independent and therefore rebellious will, consciousness, thought, and action.

2. "The Father in Me" indicates the influx into that perfectly filial manhood of the whole fulness of God in unbroken, continuous, gentle, deep flow.

B. Christ's Claim to Oneness of Complete Cooperation.

1. Correspondence of statements. "The words that I speak unto you, I speak not of Myself" corresponds to "I am in the Father." "The Father that dwelleth in Me, He doeth the works" corresponds to "The Father in Me."

2. The teaching of the corresponding statements. The two put together teach us this, that by reason of that mysterious and ineffable union of communion, Jesus Christ in all His words and works is the perfect instrument of the Divine will.

C. Consideration Drawn from Christ's Two-fold Claim.

1. No deflection or disharmony between Christ and the Father. Everything that Jesus Christ said He knew it to be God's speaking; everything that He did He knew it to be God's acting.

2. A testimony to Christ's deity. If Jesus had this consciousness (such as the oneness of unbroken communion and the oneness of complete cooperation) either He was mistaken and untrustworthy, or He is what the Church in all ages confessed Him to be, "the everlasting Son of the Father."

III. THE REVELATION OF GOD IN CHRIST AND HIS UNION WITH GOD IS THE BASIS OF THE INVITATION TO BELIEVE IN CHRIST (Verse 11).

A. Faith Is the Bond of Union between Men and Jesus Christ.

Faith really is the outgoing of the whole man—heart, will, intellect, and all—to a person whom its grasps.

B. Faith Is Seeing and Knowing.

Philip said, "Show us the Father." Christ answers, "Believe, and thou dost see." The true way to knowledge and to a better vision than the uncertain vision of the eye is faith. In certitude and directness the knowledge of God that we have through faith in the Christ whom our eyes have never seen is far ahead of the certitude and the directness that attach to our mere bodily sight.

C. Faith Based on Lower Grounds than the Highest Is Faith and Is Acceptable to God.

"Or else believe Me for the very works sake."

1. The highest ground of faith is the image of Christ obliging man to trust Him.

2. The lower ground of faith is the works of Christ. The "works" are mainly, though not exclusively, His miracles. If so, we are here taught that if a man has not come to that point of spiritual susceptibility in which the image of Jesus Christ lays hold upon his heart and obliges him to trust Him, and to love Him, there are yet the miracles to look at; and the faith that grasps them, and by help of that ladder climbs to Him, though it be second best, is yet real.

CONCLUSION

To each of us Christ addresses His merciful invitations, "Believe Me that I am in the Father, and the Father in Me." May we all answer, "We believe that Thou art the Christ, the Son of the living God!"

Alexander Maclaren

WITNESSES OF THE RESURRECTION

Wherefore of these men which have companied with us all the time that the Lord Jesus went in and out among us . . . must one be ordained to be a witness of His resurrection.
—ACTS 1:21–22

THE words of the text are the Apostle Peter's own description of what was the office of an apostle—"to be a witness with us of Christ's resurrection." And the statement branches out into three considerations. First, we have here the witnesses; secondly, we have the sufficiency of their testimony; thirdly, we have the importance of the fact to which they bear their witness.

I. THE WITNESSES.

A. Their Qualification.

The qualifications are only personal knowledge of Jesus Christ in His earthly history, because the function is only to attest His resurrection.

B. Their Function.

1. Their work during Christ's earthly ministry. The work of the apostles in Christ's lifetime embraced three elements, none of which were peculiar to them—to be with Christ, to preach, and to work miracles.

2. Their work after Christ's ascension. Their characteristic work after His ascension was witness bearing.

II. THE SUFFICIENCY OF THE TESTIMONY.

A. The Method of Establishing a Historical Fact: The Personal Testimony of an Eyewitness.

The way to establish a fact is only one—that is, to find somebody that can say, "I know it, for I saw it."

B. The Character of the Testimony to the Resurrection.

1. The testimony of the Pauline epistles written not later than a quarter of a century after the resurrection. The dates assigned to the four epistles—Romans, First and Second Corinthians and Galatians—by anybody, believer or unbeliever bring them within twenty-five years of the alleged date of Christ's resurrection. We find in all of them reference to the resurrection.

2. The testimony of Paul's vision of the risen Christ ten years after the resurrection. There is the reference to his own vision of the risen Savior (I Corinthians 15:8) which carries us up within ten years of the alleged fact. So, then, by the evidence of admittedly genuine documents which are dealing with the state of things ten years after the supposed resurrection there was a unanimous concurrence of belief on the part of the whole primitive church, so that even the heretics could be argued with on the ground of their belief in Christ's resurrection.

C. The Implications of the Testimony of the Resurrection.

1. The statement of the implications. If the resurrection be not a fact, then that belief was either a delusion or a deceit.

2. The impossibility of the implications. Not a delusion, for such an illusion is altogether unexampled; and it is absurd to think of it as being shared by a multitude like the early church. This is not a fond imagination giving an apparent substance to its own creation, but sense recognizing first the fact, "He is dead," and then, in opposition to expectation and when hope had sickened to despair, recognizing the astounding fact, "He liveth that was dead."

Not deceit. For the character of the men, and the characters of the associated morality, and the obvious absence of all self-interest, and the persecutions and sorrows which they endured, make it inconceivable that the fairest building that ever has been reared in the world, and which is cemented by men's blood, should be built upon the mud and slime of conscious deceit!

III. THE IMPORTANCE OF THE FACT.

A. With the Resurrection of Jesus Christ Stands or Falls the Deity of Christ.

1. The declaration of the Scriptures. "Declared to be the Son of God, with power by the resurrection from the dead" (Romans 1:4). "God hath made this same Jesus, whom ye have crucified, both Lord and Christ" (Acts 2:36). "He will judge the world in righteousness by that man whom He hath ordained, whereof He hath given assurance unto all men, in that He hath raised Him from the dead" (Acts 17:31).

2. The claims of Christ. Christ lived as we know and in the course of that life claimed to be the Son of God. He made such assertions as these—"I and the Father are one" (John 10:30). "I am the way, and the truth, and the life" (John 14:6). "He that believeth on Me shall never die" (John 11:25, 26). "The Son of Man must suffer many things—and the third day He shall rise again" (Luke 9:22). If He be risen from the dead then His loftiest claims are confirmed from the throne and we can see Him—the Son of God.

B. With the Resurrection of Jesus Christ Stands or Falls Christ's Whole Work for Our Redemption.

1. If Christ is not risen He died only as a martyr. If He died, like other men—if that awful bony hand has got its grip upon Him too, then we have no proof that the cross was anything but a martyr's cross.

2. If Christ is not risen there is no salvation. His resurrection is the proof of His completed work of redemption. It is the proof that His death was the ransom for us. His resurrection is the condition of His present activity. If He has not risen, He has not put away sin; and if He has not put it away by the sacrifice of Himself, none has, and it remains.

CONCLUSION

There is nothing between us and darkness, despair, death, but the ancient message, "I declare unto you the Gospel which I preached, by which ye are saved if ye keep in memory what I preached unto you, how that Christ died for our sins according to the Scriptures, and that He was raised the third day according to the Scriptures" (I Corinthians 15:1–4).

Alexander Maclaren

SONS AND HEIRS

If children, then heirs, heirs of God and joint heirs with Christ.
—ROMANS 8:17

THERE is a sublime and wonderful mutual possession of which Scripture speaks much wherein the Lord is the inheritance of Israel, and Israel is the inheritance of the Lord. This being clearly understood at the outset, we shall be prepared to follow the apostle's course of thought while he points out the conditions upon which the possession of that inheritance depends. It is children of God who are heirs of God.

I. NO INHERITANCE WITHOUT SONSHIP.

A. Natural Blessings Require a Natural Capacity to Receive Them.

1. Only the eye perceives the light. Always and necessarily the capacity or organ of reception precedes and determines the bestowment of blessings. The light falls everywhere, but only the eye drinks it in.

2. Lower orders of creatures do not participate in the gifts belonging to higher forms of life. Man has higher gifts simply because he has higher capacities. All creatures are plunged in the same boundless ocean of Divine beneficence and bestowment, and into each there flows just that, and no more, which each, by the make and constitution that God has given him, is capable of receiving.

B. Spiritual Blessings Require a Spiritual Capacity for Their Reception.

1. Man must be adapted and prepared for the present blessings of salvation. Inasmuch as God's deliverance is not a deliverance from a mere arbitrary and outward punishment: inasmuch as God's salvation, though it be deliverance from the penalty as well as from the guilt of sin, is by no means chiefly a deliverance from outward consequences, but a removal of the nature and disposition that makes these outward consequences certain. Therefore, a man cannot be saved upon any other condition than this, that his soul shall be adapted and prepared for the reception and enjoyment of the blessing of a spiritual salvation.

2. Man must be adapted and prepared for the future blessings of salvation. There is no inheritance of heaven without sonship; because all the blessings of that future life are of a spiritual character. God is the heritage of His people.

II. NO SONSHIP WITHOUT A SPIRITUAL BIRTH.

A. Sonship Is Not Innate, but Men Become Sons of God after Birth by a Divine Act.

1. The distinction between the general manifestation of God to all men and the specific relationship of God to some men by virtue of their faith. John 1:9, 12. Whatever else may be taught in John's words, surely they do teach us this, that the sonship of which he speaks does not belong to man as man, is not a relation into which we are born by natural birth, that we become sons after we are men, that those who become sons are not coextensive with those who are lighted by the Light, but consist of so many of that greater number as receive Him.

2. The contrast between the sons of God and the world. I John 3:10; John 8:42, 44. These are but specimens of a whole cycle of Scripture statements which in every form of necessary implication, and of direct statement, set forth the principle that he who is born again of the Spirit, and he only, is a son of God.

B. The Implications of Sonship.

1. Communication of life. It involves that the Father and the child shall have kindred life—the Father bestowing and the child possessing a life which is derived; and because derived, kindred; and because kindred, unfolding itself in likeness to the Father that gave it.

2. Reciprocity of love. It requires that between the Father's heart and the child's heart there shall pass, in blessed interchange and quick correspondence, answering love, flashing backwards and forwards like the lightning that touches the earth and rises from it again.

III. NO SPIRITUAL BIRTH WITHOUT CHRIST.

A. Man Cannot Save Himself.

1. Because the new life is in full accord with God. It unfolds itself in certain holy character and affections and desires, the throbbing of the whole soul in full accord and harmony with the Divine character and will.

2. Because man is sinful. Man cannot make the new life for himself because of the habit of sin and because of the guilt and punishment of sin.

B. Christ Came to Save Men.

1. The nature of the salvation He procured. Christ came to make you and me live again as we never lived before—possessors of God's love, tenanted and used by the Divine Spirit, with affections we could not kindle, with purposes in our souls which we never could put there.

2. The cost of the salvation He procured. Christ has carried in the golden urn of His humanity a new spirit and a new life which He has set down in the midst of the race; and the urn was broken on the cross of Calvary, and the water flowed out, and whithersoever that water comes there is life and whithersoever it comes not there is death!

IV. NO CHRIST WITHOUT FAITH.

It is not enough, brethren, that we should go through all these steps, if we then go utterly astray at the end, by forgetting that there is only one way by which we become partakers of any of the benefits and blessings that Christ has wrought out. Unless we are wedded to Jesus Christ by the simple act of trust in His mercy and His power, Christ is nothing to us.

A. The Necessity of Faith.

1. The benefits wrought by Christ are received only on the basis of faith.

2. Without faith Christ is nothing to us.

B. The Meaning of Faith.

1. It is trust.

2. It is rest.

CONCLUSION

If you have not your foot upon the lowest rung of the ladder (faith) you will never come within sight of the blessed face of Him who stands at the tip of it, and who looks down to you at this moment, saying to you, "My child, wilt thou not cry unto Me, 'Abba, Father'?"

Alexander Maclaren

SUFFERING WITH CHRIST, A CONDITION OF GLORY WITH CHRIST

Joint heirs with Christ, if so be that we suffer with Him,
that we may be also glorified together.
—ROMANS 8:17

IN THE former part of this verse the apostle tells us that in order to be heirs of God we must become sons through and joint heirs with Christ. The one, being sons or "joint heirs with Christ," is the root of the whole matter; the other, "the suffering with Him," is but the various process by which from the root there come "the blade, and the ear, and the full corn in the ear." Given the sonship—if it is to be worked out into power and beauty, there must be the suffering with Christ. But unless there be sonship, there is no possibility of inheriting God; discipline and suffering will be of no use at all.

I. SONSHIP WITH CHRIST NECESSARILY INVOLVES SUFFERING WITH HIM.

A. The Believer's Fellowship in Christ's Sufferings.

The sufferings of Christ, both because of the nature which bore them, and of the aspect which they wore in regard to us are in their source, in their intensity, in their character, and consequences, unapproachable, incapable of repetition. But then, do not let us forget that the very books and writers in the New Testament that preach Christ's sole, all-sufficient, eternal redemption for the world by His sufferings and death, turn around and say to us, too, "Be planted together in the likeness of His death"; "fill up that which is behind of the sufferings of Christ."

1. Christ's sufferings caused by His contact with the world.

2. Christ's sufferings caused by His temptations. There was no sin within Him, no tendency to sin, no yielding to the evil that assailed. But yet, when that dark power stood by His side and said, "If Thou be the Son of God, cast Thyself down," it was a real temptation and not a sham one.

3. The death of Christ typical of the believer's daily dying. The death of Christ [in addition to its redemptive aspect—Ed.] is a type of the Christian's life, which is to be one long-protracted and daily dying to sin, to self, to the world.

B. The Companionship of Christ with the Suffering Believer.

1. It is a consoling fact that Christ is with us in our afflictions. We need not hold that there is no reference here to that comforting thought, "In all our affliction, He is afflicted."

2. It is a consoling fact that Christ has trod the path of suffering before us. Brethren, you and I have—each of us—one in one way, and one in another, all in some way, all in the right way, none in too severe a way, none in too slight a way—to tread in the path of sorrow; and is it not a blessed thing, as we go along through that dark valley of the shadow of death down into which the sunniest paths go sometimes, to come amidst the twilight and gathering clouds, upon tokens that Jesus has been on the road before us?

3. It is a consoling fact that no affliction is too small for Him to bear with us. Whether it be a poison from an serpent sting, or whether it be poison from a million of buzzing tiny mosquitoes; if there be an affliction, go to Him and He will help you bear it. He will do more, He will bear it with you, for if so be that we suffer with Him, He suffers with us. Our oneness with Christ brings about a community of possessions whereby it becomes true of each trusting soul in its relations to Him, that "all mine (joys and sorrows alike) are thine and all thine are mine."

II. THIS COMMUNITY OF SUFFERING IS A PREPARATION FOR THE COMMUNITY OF GLORY.

A. *The Way a Man Is Made Fit for Glory.*

1. It is not by discipline. One thing at any rate is very certain, it is not the discipline that fits. That which fits goes before the discipline, and the discipline only develops the fitness.

2. It is a past act. "God *hath made* us meet for the inheritance of the saints in light," says the apostle. This is a past act.

3. It is when a man turns to Christ. The preparedness for heaven comes at the moment—if it be a momentary act—when a man turns to Christ. "This day thou shalt be with Me in paradise"—fit for the inheritance.

B. *The Development of Man's Fitness for Glory.*

1. Discipline develops man's fitness for heaven. In His mercy He is leaving you here, training you, disciplining you, cleansing you, making you to be polished shafts in His quiver.

2. Discipline is a seal of sonship.

3. Discipline prepares the believer for greater rewards in heaven. And so learn to look upon all trial as being at once the seal of your sonship and the means by which God puts it within your power to win a higher place, a loftier throne, a nobler crown.

III. INHERITANCE IS THE NECESSARY RESULT OF SUFFERING.

A. *The Ground of Possessing the Inheritance.*

1. It is not merely compensation. It is not only because the joy hereafter seems required in order to vindicate God's love to His children, who here reap sorrow from their sonship, that the discipline of life cannot but end in blessedness.

2. It is union with Christ. The suffering results from our union with Christ. That union must needs culminate in glory.

B. The Certainty of Possessing the Inheritance.

1. Union with Christ. But the inheritance is sure to all who here suffer with Christ, because the one cause—union with the Lord—produces both the present result of fellowship in His sorrows and the future result in His joy, of possession.

2. Christ's present possession of the inheritance.

3. The design of trials to prepare us for heaven. The inheritance is sure because earth's sorrows not merely require to be repaid by its peace, but because they have an evident design to fit us for it and it would be destructive to all faith in God's wisdom, and God's knowledge of His own purposes, not to believe that what He has wrought for us will be given to us.

CONCLUSION

Measure the greatness of the glory by what has preceded it. God takes all these years of life and all the sore trials and afflictions that belong inevitably to an earthly career and works them in, into the blessedness that shall come.

Alexander Maclaren

WHAT LASTS

Whether there be prophecies, they shall fail; whether there
be tongues, they shall cease; whether there be knowledge,
it shall vanish away . . . And now abideth faith,
hope, charity, these three . . .
—I CORINTHIANS 13:8, 13

WE discern the apostle's thought best by omitting the intervening verses and connecting these two. When we thus unite them there is disclosed the apostle's intention of contrasting two sets of things, three in each. There also, comes out distinctly that the point mainly intended by the contrast is the transiency of the one and the permanence of the other.

I. THE THINGS THAT ARE TRANSIENT.

A. Present Modes of Apprehension.

1. They shall cease because the imperfect shall be absorbed into the perfect. "Knowledge, it shall cease," and as the apostle goes on to explain, in the verses which I have passed over for my present purpose, it shall cease because the perfect will absorb into itself the imperfect, as the inrushing tide will obliterate the little pools in the rocks on the seashore.

2. They shall cease because they are indirect and there it shall be immediate. For another reason, the knowledge, the mode of apprehension belonging to the present will pass—because here it is indirect and there it will be immediate. "We shall know face to face," which is what philosophers call intuition.

B. Present Modes of Utterance.

1. There will be new methods of communication in heaven. Modes of utterance will cease. With new experiences will come new methods of communication; as a man can speak and a beast can only growl or bark. So a man in heaven, with new experiences, will have new methods of communication.

2. The comparison between the present mode of communication and that of the future. The comparison between that mode of utterance which we now have and that which we shall then possess will be like the difference between the old-fashioned semaphore that used to wave about clumsy wooden arms in order to convey intelligence, and the telegraph.

II. THE THINGS THAT ARE PERMANENT.

A. Faith.

1. Its relation to hope and love. "So then, abideth these three, faith, hope, love." Paul takes these three nouns and couples them with a verb in the singular. Do not correct the grammar and spoil the sense, but discern what he means, that the two latter come out of the former and that without it they are nought and that it without them is dead.

2. Its essence. The essence of faith is not the absence of the person trusted, but the emotion of trust which goes out to the person, present or absent. In its deepest meaning of absolute dependence and happy confidence, faith abides through all the glories and the lustres of the heavens.

B. Hope.

1. The difference between earthly and Christian hope. Our hopes, apart from the revelation of God in Jesus Christ, are but the balancings of probabilities and the scale is often dragged down by the clutch of eager desires. Only the Christian has a rock foundation on which he can build his hope.

2. The reason hope abides. The future presents itself to us as the continual communication of an inexhaustible God to our progressively capacious and capable spirits. In that continual communication there is continual progress. Wherever there is progress there must be hope.

C. Love.

1. The abiding nature of love. I need not, I suppose, enlarge upon that thought which nobody denies, that love is the eternal form of the human relation to God. It, too, like the mercy which it clasps, "endureth forever."

2. The reason love is greatest. It is greater than its linked sisters, because whilst faith and hope belong only to a creature and are dependent and expectant of some good to come to themselves and correspond to something which is in God in Christ, the love which springs from faith and hope not only corresponds to, but resembles that from which it comes and by which it lives. The love that is in man is like the love that is in God.

III. THE THINGS THAT FOLLOW FROM ALL THIS.

A. The True Understanding of Abiding Love.

1. A false notion of love. I do not use the word charity. Charity has come to mean an indulgent estimate of other people's faults or the giving of money to other people's necessities. These are what the people who do not care much about Paul's theology generally suppose that he means here. But these do not exhaust his meaning.

2. The true idea of love. Paul's notion of love is the response of the human love to the Divine, which Divine is received into the heart by faith in Jesus Christ. And his notion of love which never fails is love to men, which is but one stream of the great river of love to God.

B. The Highest Conception of the Christian's Future Condition.

1. A danger to be avoided. It is very easy to bewilder ourselves with speculations and theories of another life. It is easy to let ourselves be led away by turning rhetoric into revelation and accepting the symbols of the New Testament as if they carried anything more than images of the realities.

2. The essence of life in heaven. The elements of the imperfect, Christlike life of earth are the essence of the perfect, Godlike life in heaven. "Now abide these three: faith, hope, love."

C. The Christian's Life Should Be Shaped in Accordance with These Certainties.

1. The relation of the transient and the permanent in the Christian's life. The dropping away of the transient things is no argument for neglecting or despising them; for our handling of them makes our characters and our characters abide. But it is an excellent argument to use the transient as that it shall help us toward that which does not pass.

2. The importance of preparing for the future. Suppose you knew that you were to go somewhere and you never did a single thing toward getting ready or preparing yourself. Would you be a wise man? But that is what a great many are doing.

CONCLUSION

Cultivate the high things, the permanent things; then death will not wrench you violently from all that you have been and cared for; but it will usher you into the perfect form of all that you have been and done upon earth.

Alexander Maclaren

TRANSFORMATION BY BEHOLDING

We all with open face beholding as in a glass the glory of the Lord, are changed into the same image.
—II CORINTHIANS 3:18

JUDAISM had the one lawgiver who beheld God, while the people tarried below. Christianity leads us all to the mount of vision. Moses veiled the face that shone with the irradiation of Deity. We with unveiled faces are to shine among men. He had a momentary gleam; we have a perpetual light. Moses' face shone, but the luster was but skin deep. But the light that we have is inward and works transformation into its own likeness.

I. THE CHRISTIAN LIFE IS A LIFE OF CONTEMPLATING AND REFLECTING CHRIST.

A. The Meaning of "Beholding in a Glass."

1. The requirement of the context. It is a question whether the single word rendered "beholding as in a glass" means that, or "reflecting as a glass does." The latter seems more in accordance with the requirements of the context and with the truth of the matter in hand. On the whole, it seems better to suppose that Paul meant "mirroring," than "seeing in a mirror."

2. The actual force of the expression. But, whatever the exact force of the word, the thing intended includes both acts. There is no reflection of the light without a previous reception of the light.

3. The truth presented. Thus, then, we may say that we have in our text the Christian life described as one of contemplation and manifestation of the light of God.

B. The Object of the Vision.

1. It is Jesus Christ.

2. It is the glory of Jesus Christ. The glory which we behold and give back is not the incomprehensible, incommunicable luster of the absolute Divine perfectness, but the glory which was manifested in loving, pitying words, and loveliness of perfect deeds; the glory of the will resigned to God, and of God dwelling in and working through the will; the glory of faultless and complete manhood, and therein of the express image of God.

C. The Nature of the Vision.

1. It is a spiritual perception. That seeing which is affirmed to be possible and actually bestowed in Christ, is the beholding of Him with the soul by faith; the immediate direct consciousness of His presence, the perception of Him in His truth by the mind, the sense of Him in His love by the heart, the contact with His gracious energy in our recipient and opening spirits.

2. It is a perception that all believers may have. "We, all." This vision does not belong to any select handful. Christ reveals Himself to all His servants in the measure of their desire after Him.

3. It is a contemplation involving reflection. What we *see* we shall certainly *show*. Nor is it only that our fellowship with Christ will, as a matter of course, show itself in our characters and beauty born of that communion "shall pass into our face," but we are also called on, as Paul puts it here, to make direct conscious efforts for the communication of the light which we behold.

II. THE LIFE OF CONTEMPLATION IS A LIFE OF GRADUAL TRANSFORMATION.

A. The Contrast between the Brightness on Moses' Face and the Glory Which the Christian Beholds.

1. The brightness on Moses' face lacked permanence and transforming power, thereby illustrating the powerlessness of the law to change the moral character.

2. The glory of the Lord which the Christian beholds has permanence and transforming power, proclaiming Christian progress and assimilation to Christ.

B. The Work of Contemplation.

1. The prerequisite to contemplation: Christ in us. The light must first sink in before it can shine out. In deep inward beholding we must have Christ in our hearts, that He may shine forth from our lives.

2. The nature of contemplation: gaze of love and trust. It is not the mere beholding, but the gaze of love and trust that molds us by silent sympathy into the likeness of His wondrous beauty, who is fairer than the children of men.

3. The practical result of contemplation: Christlikeness. Spirits that dwell with Christ become Christlike. Such transformation, it must be remembered, comes gradually. The language of the text regards it as a lifelong process.

III. THE LIFE OF CONTEMPLATION FINALLY BECOMES A LIFE OF COMPLETE ASSIMILATION.

A. Transformation Issues into Complete Assimilation.

1. It is completed in heaven in corporeal likeness. We look for the merciful exercise of His mighty working to "change the body of our lowliness, that it may be fashioned like unto the body of His glory" (Philippians 3:21); and that physical change in the resurrection of the just rightly bulks very large in good men's expectations.

2. It begins on earth in spiritual likeness. The glorious, corporeal life like our Lord's, which is promised for heaven, is great and wonderful, but it is only the issue and last result of the far greater change in the spiritual nature which by faith and love begins here. His true image is that we should feel as He does, should think as He does, should will as He does; have the same sympathies, the same loves, the same attitude toward God and the same attitudes toward men.

B. The Significance of the Term "Same Image."

1. The image we behold.

2. The likeness of all who become like him. As if he had said, "Various as we are in disposition and character, unlike in the history of our lives, and all the influences these have had upon us, differing in everything but the common relation to Jesus Christ, we are all growing like the same image and we shall come to be perfectly like it and yet each retain his own distinct individuality."

3. The aggregate perfectness of the individual church. In the Epistle to the Ephesians Paul says that the Christian ministry is to continue till a certain point of progress has been reached which he describes as our *all* coming to a "perfect man" (Ephesians 4:13). The whole of us together make a perfect man: the whole make one image.

CONCLUSION

The law of the transformation is the same for earth and for heaven. Here we see Him in part and beholding we grow like Him. There we shall see Him as He is and the likeness will be complete.

Alexander Maclaren

MEASURELESS POWER AND ENDLESS GLORY

Now unto Him that is able to do exceeding abundantly above all that we ask or think, according to the power that worketh in us, unto Him be glory in the Church by Christ Jesus throughout all ages, world without end. Amen.
—EPHESIANS 3:20–21

THE FORM of our text marks the confidence of Paul's prayer. The exuberant fervor of his faith, as well as the natural impetuosity and ardor, comes out in the heaped-up words expressive of immensity and duration. He is gazing on God confident that he has not asked in vain.

I. THE MEASURE OF THE POWER.

A. According to the Riches of His Glory (Ephesians 3:16).

1. Its explanation. The "riches of His glory" can be nothing less than the whole uncounted abundance of that majestic and far-shining nature, as it pours itself forth in the dazzling perfectness of its own self-manifestation.

2. Its effect. Absolute perfectness, the full transmutation of our dark, cold being into the reflected image of His own burning brightness, the ceaseless replenishing of our own spirits with all graces and gladness akin to His, the eternal growth of the soul upward and Godward.

B. According to His Mighty Power, Which He Wrought in Christ When He Raised Him from the Dead (Ephesians 1:19–20).

1. Its purport. The Lord, in the glory of His risen life, and in the riches of the gifts which He received when He ascended up on high, is the pattern for us and the power which fulfils its own pattern.

2. Its purpose. The limits of that power will not be reached until every Christian soul is perfectly assimilated to that likeness nor till every Christian soul is raised to participation in Christ's dignity and sits on His throne.

C. According to the Power Which Works in Us (Ephesians 3:20).

1. Its meaning. What power is that but the power of the Spirit of God?

2. Its outcome. The effects already produced and the experiences we have already had carry in them the pledge of completeness.

II. THE RELATION OF THE DIVINE WORKING TO OUR THOUGHTS AND DESIRES.

A. The Extent of the Divine Working.

1. It is "beyond all things." What he means by this is more fully expressed in the words: "exceeding abundantly above what we ask or think."

2. It refers especially to spiritual blessings. The rapturous words of our text are only true in a very modified and partial sense about God's working for us in the world. It is His work in us concerning which they are absolutely true.

B. The Wonder of the Divine Working.

1. It is the power of the Triune God. As regards the working of God on our spiritual lives, this passing beyond the bounds of thought and desire is but the necessary result of the fact that the only measure of the power is God Himself in that threefold being.

2. It is more than we realize and receive. In every act of His quickening grace, in every God-given increase of our knowledge of God, in every bestowment of His fulness, there is always more bestowed than we receive, more than we know even while we possess it.

C. The Reminders Concerning the Divine Working.

1. While the Divine working exceeds our thoughts and prayers, it is meant to draw them after it. While our thoughts and prayers can never react to the full perception or reception of the gift, the exuberant amplitude with which it reaches far beyond both is meant to draw both after it.

2. Our thoughts and desires determine the amount of grace received. The grace which we receive has no limit or measure but the fulness of God, the working limit, which determines what we receive of the grace, is those very thoughts and wishes which it surpasses. We may have as much of God as we can hold, or as much as we wish.

III. THE GLORY WHICH SPRINGS FROM THE DIVINE WORK.

A. The Doxology.

1. It is both a prophecy and a prayer. This doxology is at once a prophecy that the working of God's power on His redeemed children will issue in setting forth the radiance of His name yet more, and a prayer that it may.

2. The highest exhibition of God's character for reverence and love is in His work on Christian souls and the effect produced. He reckons it His highest praise that He has redeemed men, and by His indwelling them, fills them with His own fulness.

B. The Offerers of the Glory.

1. The persons. The chiefest praise and brightest glory accrues to Him "in the Church in Christ Jesus." His glory is to shine in the Church, the theater of His power, the standing demonstration of the might of His redeeming love.

2. The prerequisite. His glory is to be set forth by men on condition that they are "in Christ," living and moving in Him, in that mysterious but most real union.

IV. THE ETERNITY OF THE WORK AND OF THE PRAISE.

A. *The Scriptural Statement.*

1. The Authorized Version: "throughout all ages world without end."

2. The literal rendering: "to all generations of the age of the ages."

B. *The Meaning of the Scriptural Statement.*

1. "To all generations": expressive of duration as long as birth and death shall last.

2. "The age of the ages": pointing to that endless epoch whose moments are ages.

3. The blending of the two expressions: an unconscious acknowledgement that the speech of earth, saturated with the coloring of time, breaks down in the attempt to express the thought of eternity.

C. *The Compass of the Statement.*

The work is to go on forever and ever and with it the praise. As the ages which are the beats of the pendulum of eternity come and go, more and more of God's power will flow out to us and more and more of God's glory will be manifested in us.

1. Work.

2. Praise.

CONCLUSION

Let His grace work in you, and yield yourselves to Him, that His fulness may fill your emptiness.

Alexander Maclaren

THE RACE AND THE GOAL

This one thing I do, forgetting those things which are behind, and reaching forth unto those things which are before, I press toward the mark for the prize.
—PHILIPPIANS 3:13–14

THE APOSTLE here is letting us see the secret of his own life and telling us what made him the sort of Christian that he was. He counsels wise obliviousness, wise anticipation, strenuous concentration; and these are the things that contribute to success in any field of life.

I. MAKE GOD'S AIM YOUR AIM.

A. The Example of Paul.

1. The testimony of the immediate context. He regards the aim toward which he strains as being the aim which Christ had in view in his conversion (Verses 12, 13b).

2. The summary of the teaching of the immediate context. He took God's purpose in calling and Christ's purpose in redeeming him as being his great object in life. God's aim and Paul's were identical.

B. God's Aim.

1. The aim stated. What, then, is the aim of God in all that He has done for us? The production in us of godlike and God-pleasing character.

243

2. The importance of the aim. For this all the discipline of life is set in motion. For this we were created; for this we have been redeemed. For this Jesus Christ lived and suffered and died. For this God's Spirit is poured out upon the world.

C. The Results of the Acceptance of God's Aim.

1. It changes man's estimate of the meaning and true nature of events. It will give nobleness and blessedness to our lives. How different all our estimates of the meaning and true nature of events would be, if we kept before us that their intention was to mold us to the likeness of our Lord and Savior!

2. It changes a man's estimate of nearer objects and aims. Men take these great powers which God has given them and use them to make money, to cultivate their intellects, to secure the gratification of earthly desires, to make a home for themselves; and all the while the great aim which ought to stand out clear and supreme is forgotten.

II. CONCENTRATE ALL EFFORT ON THIS ONE AIM.

A. The Aim Is Consistent with All Occupations, Except Sin.

It needs not that we should seek any remote or cloistered form of life, nor shear off any legitimate and common interests, but in them all we may be seeking for the one thing, the molding of our characters into the shapes that are pleasing to Him.

B. The Requirements in Order to Keep This Aim Clear.

1. To keep close to God.

2. To be surrendered to God. To keep the aim clear is possible if we will do two things, keep ourselves close to God and be prepared to surrender much, laying our own wills, our own fancies, purposes, eager hopes and plans in His hands, and asking Him to help us that we may never lose sight of the only end which is an end in itself.

3. To concentrate on the aim. The conquering word is, "This one thing I do." If you want to be a Christian after God's pattern you have to make it your business to give the same attention, the same concentration, the same unwavering energy to it which you do to your trade.

III. PURSUE THIS END WITH A WISE FORGETFULNESS.

A. The Meaning of "Forgetting the Things That Are Behind."

1. The meaning stated negatively. He does not mean that we are to cultivate obliviousness as to let God's mercies to us "lie, forgotten in unthankfulness, or without praises to die." Nor does he mean to tell us that we are to deny ourselves the solace of remembering the mercies which may, perhaps, have gone from us.

2. The meaning stated positively. He means that we should so forget as, by the oblivion, to strengthen our concentration.

B. The Application of "Forgetting the Things That Are Behind."

1. Remember and forget past failures and faults. Let us remember them in order that the remembrance may cultivate in us a wise chastening of our self-confidence. Let us forget our failures insofar as these might paralyze our hopes or make us fancy that future success is impossible where past failures frown.

2. Remember and forget past successes and achievements. Remember them for thankfulness, for hope, for counsel and instruction, but forget them when they tend to make us fancy that little more remains to be done; and forget them when they tend to make us think that such and such things are our line and of other virtues and graces and achievements of culture and of character, that these are not our line and not to be won by us.

IV. PURSUE THE AIM WITH A WISE, EAGER REACHING FORWARD.

A. The Expressiveness of "Reaching Forth."

1. The English translation only partially expresses the meaning. The apostle employs a graphic word here, which is only partially expressed by that "reaching forth."

2. The picture presented by the word. "Reaching out over" is the full though clumsy rendering of the word; and it gives us the picture of a runner with his whole body thrown forward, his hand extended and his eye reaching even further than his hand, in eager anticipation of the mark and the prize.

B. The Incentive of the Unattained.

The idealists see the unattained burning so clearly before them that all the unattained seems as nothing in their eyes. So life is saved from commonplace, is happily strung into fresh effort, is redeemed from flagging, monotony, and weariness.

1. It gives an element of nobility to the lives of idealists.

2. It saves life from the commonplace.

C. The Measure of Attainment May Be Estimated by the Extent to Which the Unattained Is Clear to Us.

1. The blessing of having a boundless future. They who have a boundless future before them have an endless source of inspiration, of energy, of buoyancy granted to them.

2. The Christian has the greatest vision of a boundless future. No man has such an absolutely boundless vision of the future as we have if we are Christian people. Only we can look thus forward.

CONCLUSION

Make God's aim your aim; concentrate your life's efforts upon it; pursue it with a wise forgetfulness; pursue it with an eager confidence of anticipation that shall not be put to shame.

Alexander Maclaren

EVERLASTING CONSOLATION AND GOOD HOPE

Now our Lord Jesus Christ Himself, and God, even our Father,
which hath loved us, and hath given us everlasting consolation
and good hope through grace, comfort your hearts, and establish
you in every good word and work.
—II THESSALONIANS 2:16–17

THIS is the second of the four brief prayers in this letter. We do not know the special circumstances under which these were written, but there are many allusions, both in the first and second epistles, which seem to indicate that they specially needed the gift of consolation.

I. THE DIVINE HEARERS OF THE PRAYER.

A. The Recognition of the Deity of Jesus Christ Was a Familiar Truth to the Thessalonian Christians.

1. The accumulation of His august titles. The first striking thing about this prayer is its emphatic recognition of the deity of Jesus Christ as a truth familiar to these Thessalonian converts. Note the solemn accumulation of His august titles, "Our Lord Jesus Christ Himself."

2. The association of His name with the Father's.

3. The order of the names. Note, the most remarkable order in which these two names occur—Jesus first, God second. The reason for the order may be found partly in the context which has been naming Christ, but still more in the fact that while he writes, the apostle is realizing the mediation of Christ and that the order of mention is the order of our approach. The Father comes to us in the Son; we come to the Father by the Son.

B. The Distinct Address to Christ as the Hearer of Prayer.

1. The grammatical peculiarity. The words which follow, that is, "comfort" and "establish," are in the singular, while these two mighty and august names are their nominatives and would therefore, by all regularity, require a plural to follow them.

2. The truth expressed by this grammatical peculiarity. The phraseology is the expression of the great truth, "Whatsoever things the Father doeth, these also doth the Son likewise." And from it there gleam out unmistakably the great principles of the unity of action and the distinction of person between Father and Son in the depths of that infinite and mysterious Godhead.

3. The testimony of this grammatical peculiarity. Now all this is made the more remarkable and the stronger as a witness of the truth from the fact that it occurs in this incidental fashion and without a word of explanation or apology, as taking for granted that there was a background of teaching in the Thessalonian Church which had prepared the way for it and rendered it intelligible, as well as a background of conviction which had previously accepted it.

II. THE GREAT FACT ON WHICH THIS PRAYER BUILDS ITSELF.

A. The Implication of a Definite Historical Act.

1. The statement of the implication. The form of words in the original, "loved" and "given," all but necessarily requires us to suppose that their reference is to some one definite historical act in which the love was manifested, and, as love always does, found voice in giving.

2. The act implied. The gift of Jesus Christ is that in which everlasting consolation and good hope are bestowed upon men. When our desires are widened out to the widest they must be based upon the great sacrifice of Jesus Christ.

B. The Gifts Bestowed.

1. Everlasting comfort. There is one source of comfort which, because it comes from an unchangeable Christ and communicates unfailing gifts of patience and insight and because it leads to everlasting blessedness and recompenses may well be called "external consolation."

2. Good hope. In the cross and in the Christ lie the foundation and the object of a hope which stands unique in excellence and sufficient in its firmness. "A good hope"; good because well founded; good because grasping worthy objects.

C. The Presupposition of Heaven's Logic.

1. The statement of heaven's logic. God has given; therefore God will give.

2. Three suppositions. It presupposes inexhaustible resources, unchangeable purposes of kindness, patience that is not disgusted and cannot be turned away by sin.

III. THE SPECIFICATION OF THE DESIRES INCLUDED IN THE PRAYER.

A. A Comforted Heart.

1. The connection between the past gift of everlasting consolation and the present and future comfort of hearts. God has bestowed the materials for comfort; God will give the comfort for which He has supplied the materials.

2. Man's need met. It is not enough for us that there should be calmness and consolation twining round the cross if we choose to pluck the fruit. We need and we have an indwelling God who, by that Spirit who is the Comforter, will make for each of us the everlasting consolation our individual possession.

B. A Stable Heart.

1. Man's natural instability. We all know how vacillating, how driven to and fro by gusts of passion and winds of doctrine and forces of earth our resolutions and spirits are.

2. The secret of stability. If we have Christ in our hearts He will be our consolation first and our stability next. Our hearts may be like some land-locked lake that knows no tide. "His heart is fixed, trusting in the Lord."

C. A Fruitful Heart.

1. A man's life can be characterized by practical righteousness. There is no reason why each of us should not appropriate and make our own the forms of goodness to which we are least naturally inclined and cultivate and possess a symmetrical, fully-developed, all-round goodness in some humble measure after the pattern of Jesus Christ our Lord.

2. The source of practical righteousness. Practical righteousness, "in every good word and work," is the outcome of all the sacred and secret consolations and blessings that Jesus Christ imparts. We get our goodness where we get our consolation, from Jesus Christ and His Cross.

CONCLUSION

All your hopes will be like a child's castles on the sand unless your hope is fixed on Him. You may have everlasting consolation, you may have a hope which will enable you to look severely on the ills of life. You may have a calm and steadied heart. You may have an all-round, stable, comprehensive goodness. But there is only one way to get these blessings and that is to grasp and make our own by simple faith that great gift, Jesus Christ.

Alexander Maclaren

SERMON TWENTY-EIGHT

THE GOSPEL OF THE GLORY OF THE HAPPY GOD

The glorious Gospel of the blessed God.
—I TIMOTHY 1:11

TWO REMARKS will prepare the way for our consideration of this text. The first is that the proper rendering is given in the Revised Version—"The Gospel of the glory," not "The glorious Gospel." The apostle is not telling us what kind of thing the Gospel is, but what it is about. Then the other remark is with reference to the meaning of the word "blessed." The word which is used here describes Him altogether apart from what man says of Him, as what He is in Himself, the "blessed," or, as we might almost say, the "happy God."

I. THE REVELATION OF GOD IN JESUS CHRIST IS THE GLORY OF GOD.

A. The Significance of the Words "Glory of God."

1. The Old Testament meaning of "the glory." Now what do we mean by "the glory"? I think, perhaps, that the question may be most simply answered by remembering the definite meaning of the word in the Old Testament. There it designates usually, that the supernatural and lustrous light which dwelt between the cherubim, the symbol of the presence and of the self-manifestation of God.

2. The explanation of the phrase "the glory of God." The glory of God is the sum-total of the light that streams from His self-revelation, considered as being the object of adoration and praise by a world that gazes upon Him. The apostle, just because to him the Gospel was the story of the Christ who lived and died, declares that in this story of a human life, patient, meek, limited, despised, rejected, and at last crucified, lies, brighter than all other flashings of the Divine light, the very heart of the luster and palpitating center and frontal source of all the radiance with which God has flooded the world. The history of Jesus Christ is the glory of God.

B. Three Considerations Concerning the Substance of the Gospel.

1. Christ is the self-revelation of God. What force of logic is there in the apostle's words: "God commendeth His love toward us in that while we were yet sinners Christ died for us," unless there is some altogether different connection between the God who commends His love and the Christ who dies to commend it, than exists between a mere man and God. In that man Christ Jesus "we behold His glory, the glory of the only begotten of the Father." We see in Him the manifest deity. Listen to that voice, "He that hath seen Me hath seen the Father," and bow before the story of the human life of Jesus Christ as being the revelation of the indwelling God.

2. The Divine self-communication in Christ. In that wondrous story of the life and death of our Lord Jesus Christ the high-water mark of Divine self-communication has been touched and reached. All the energies of the Divine nature are embodied there. The "riches both of the wisdom of the knowledge of God" are in the cross and passion of our Savior. The whole Godhead, so to speak, flows from the cross of Christ into the hearts of men.

3. The center of the glory of God is the love of God. The text implies still further that the true living, flashing center of the glory of God is the love of God. If we rightly understand the text, then we learn this, that the true heart of the glory is tenderness and love. The Gospel is the Gospel of the glory of God because it is all summed up in the one word—"God so loved the world that He gave His only begotten Son."

II. THE REVELATION OF GOD IN JESUS CHRIST IS THE BLESSEDNESS OF GOD.

A. The Fact of the Blessedness of God.

The Bible's God "delighteth in mercy," rejoiceth in His gifts and is glad when men accept them. If we went no further, to me there is infinite beauty and mighty consolation and strength in that one thought—the happy God. The Psalmist saw deeply into the Divine nature when he exclaimed, "Thou makest us to drink of the rivers of Thy pleasures."

B. The Source of the Blessedness of God.

The context seems to suggest that howsoever the Divine nature must be supposed to be blessed in its own absolute and boundless perfectness, an element in the blessedness of God Himself arises from His self-communication through the Gospel to the world. The blessed God is blessed because He is God. But He is blessed too because He is loving and therefore the giving God.

1. God's own perfectness.

2. God's self-communication through the Gospel to men.

III. THE REVELATION OF GOD IN JESUS CHRIST IS GOOD NEWS TO ALL.

A. The Loss of the Significance of the Gospel.

How the word "Gospel" has become tarnished and enfeebled by constant use and unreflective use, so that it slips glibly off my tongue and falls without producing any effect upon your hearts. It needs to be freshened up by considering what it really means.

1. By constant usage.

2. By thoughtless usage.

B. The True Meaning of the Gospel.

Here are we like men shut up in a beleaguered city, hopeless, helpless, with no power to break out or to raise the seige; provisions failing, death

253

certain. And the message is this: God is love; and that you may know that He is, He has sent you His Son who died on the cross, the sacrifice for a world's sin.

1. The deliverance of captives.

2. The deliverance of captives on the ground of Christ's death.

CONCLUSION

Let me beseech you, welcome the message; do not turn away from the Word from heaven which will bring life and blessedness to all your hearts! Some of you have turned away long enough, some of you, perhaps, are fighting with the temptation to do so again even now. Let me press that ancient Gospel upon your acceptance, that Christ the Son of God has died for you, and lives to bless and help you. So shall you find that "as cold water to a thirsty soul, so is this best of all news from the far country."

Alexander Maclaren

A PRISONER'S DYING THOUGHTS

I am now ready to be offered, and the time of my departure is at hand. I have fought a good fight, I have finished my course, I have kept the faith: henceforth there is laid up for me a crown of righteousness.
—II TIMOTHY 4:6–8

THESE familiar words of our text bring us a very sweet and wonderful picture of the prisoner, so near his end. How beautifully they show his calm waiting for the last hour and the bright forms which lightened for him the darkness of the cell. These words refer to the past, the present, the future. "I have fought—the time of my departure is come—henceforth there is laid up."

I. THE QUIET COURAGE WHICH LOOKS DEATH IN THE FACE WITHOUT A TREMOR.

A. The Tone of the Language of the Text.

As the revised version more accurately gives it, "I am already being offered"—the process is begun, the initial steps of his sacrifice—"and the time of my departure is come." There is no sign of excitement, no tremor of emotion, no affectation of stoicism in the simple sentences.

B. The Occasion of the Text.

He is led to speak about himself only in order to enforce his exhortation to Timothy to put his shoulder to the wheel and do his work for Christ with all his might.

C. The Subject of the Text.

1. Its effect on Paul. The anticipation of death did not dull his interest in God's work in the world as witness the warnings and exhortations of the context. It did not withdraw his sympathies from his companions. It did not hinder him from pursuing his studies and pursuits, nor for providing for small matters of daily convenience. (II Timothy 4:9–22).

2. Its manner of expression. (a) Offering or more particularly a drink offering or libation, "I am already being poured out." No doubt the special reason for the selection of this figure is Paul's anticipation of a violent death. (b) Departure. Death is a going away, or, as Peter calls it, an exodus.

II. THE PEACEFUL LOOK BACKWARDS.

A. The Pauline Estimate of Life.

1. A contest which requires struggle. The world, both of men and things, has had to be grappled with and mastered. His own sinful nature has had to be kept under by sheer force and every moment has been resistance to subtle omnipresent forces that have sought to thwart his aspirations and hamper his performances.

2. A race which requires effort. This speaks of continuous advance in one direction, and more emphatically still, of effort that sets the lungs panting and strains every muscle to the utmost.

3. A stewardship which requires fidelity. He has kept the faith as a sacred deposit committed to him, of which he has been a good steward and which he is now ready to return to the Lord.

B. The Results of the Pauline Estimate of Life.

Such a view of life makes it radiant and fair while it lasts and makes the heart calm when the hour comes to leave it all behind. So thinking of the past there may be a sense of not unwelcome lightening from a load of responsibility when we have all the stress and strain of the conflict behind us.

1. While life lasts it is radiant and fair.

2. When death approaches it makes the heart calm.

C. The Requirement of the Pauline Estimate of Life.

Such an estimate has nothing in common with self-complacency. It coexists with a profound consciousness of many a sin, many a defeat, and much unfaithfulness. It belongs only to a man who, conscious of these, is "looking for the mercy of the Lord Jesus Christ unto eternal life" (Jude 21), and is the direct result of lowly self-abasement, and contrite faith in Him.

1. Absence of self-complacency.

2. Dependence upon God's mercy.

3. Self-abasement.

4. Contrite faith in God.

III. THE TRIUMPHANT LOOK FORWARD.

A. The Reward.

In harmony with the images of the conflict and the race, the crown here is not the emblem of sovereignty, but of victory. The reward then which is meant by the emblem comes through effort and conflict. "A man is not crowned, except he strive" (II Timothy 2:5).

1. It is not a sovereign's diadem.

2. It is the victor's wreath.

B. The Persons Rewarded.

1. The meaning of "crown of righteousness." Righteousness alone can receive the reward. It is not the struggle or the conflict which wins it, not the works of strenuous service, but the moral nature expressed in these. It is, then, the crown of righteousness, as belonging by its very nature to such characters alone.

2. The gift of righteousness. The righteousness which clothes us in fair raiment and has a natural right to the wreath of victory is a gift as truly as the crown itself and is given to us all on the condition of our simple trust in Jesus Christ.

C. The Time of Rewarding.

The crown is given at a time called by Paul "at that day," which is not the near day of his martyrdom, but that of his Lord's appearing. He does not speak of the fulness of the reward as being ready for him at death, but as being "henceforth laid up in heaven." So he looks forward beyond the grave.

1. It is in "that day."

2. It is at the appearing of Jesus Christ.

CONCLUSION

If we can humbly say, "To me to live is Christ," then it is well. Living by Him we may fight and conquer, may win and obtain. Living by Him, we may be ready quietly to lie down when the time comes and may have all the future filled with the blaze of a great hope, that grows brighter as the darkness thickens.

Alexander Maclaren

SERMON THIRTY

A FATHER'S DISCIPLINE

For they verily for a few days chastened us after their own pleasure;
but He for our profit, that we might be partakers of His holiness.
—HEBREWS 12:10

FEW words of Scripture have been oftener than these laid as a healing balm on wounded hearts. They may be long unnoticed on the page, like a lighthouse in calm sunshine, but sooner or later the stormy night falls and then the bright beam flashes out and is welcome. They go very deep into the meaning of life as a discipline; they tell us how much better God's discipline is than that of the most loving and wise of parents and they give that superiority as a reason for our yielding more entire and cheerful obedience to Him than we do to such.

I. LIFE IS ONLY INTELLIGIBLE WHEN IT IS REGARDED AS EDUCATION OR DISCIPLINE.

A. All Which Befalls Us Has a Will Behind It and Operates Together to an End.

Life is not a heap of unconnected incidents, like a number of links flung down on the ground, but the links are a chain and the chain has a staple.

B. Throughout Our Earthly Life We Are in a State of Pupilage.

Life is given to us to teach us how to live, to exercise our powers, to give us habits and facilities of working. There is no meaning worthy of us—to say nothing of God—in anything that we do, unless it is looked upon as schooling.

C. The Whole of This Life is an Education Toward Another.

If this life is education, as is obvious upon its very face, then there is a place where we shall exercise the facilities that we have acquired here and manifest in loftier forms the characters which we here have made our own.

II. THE GUIDING PRINCIPLE OF THAT DISCIPLINE.

A. The Contrast between the Principles of Human and Divine Discipline.

1. Guiding principle of human discipline is the parents' conception of what is good for the child. "They . . . as seemed good to them." Even in the most wise and unselfish training by an earthly parent there will mingle subjective elements, peculiarities of view and thought, and sometimes of passion and whim and other ingredients, which detract from the value of all such training.

2. The guiding principle of Divine discipline is that which is profitable for us. "He for our profit"—with no sidelong look to anything else and with an entirely wise knowledge of what is best for us, so that the result will be always and only for our good.

B. Truths Suggested by the Guiding Principle of Divine Discipline.

There is no such thing as evil except the evil of sin. All that comes is good—of various sorts and various complexions, but all generically the same: The inundation comes up over the fields and men are in despair. It goes down and there is better soil for the fertilizing of our fields. All that men call evil in the material world has in it a soul of good.

1. There is no such thing as evil except evil of sin.

2. All that comes is for our good.

C. The Reality of Pain and Sorrow.

1. It is right that we yield to the impressions made upon us by calamities.
The mission of our troubles would not be effected unless they did trouble

us. The good that we get from a sorrow would not be realized unless we did sorrow. "Weep for yourselves," said the Master, "and for your children" (Luke 23:28).

2. It is wrong, to lose sight of the fact that the calamities are for our good. God sends us many love tokens, and amongst them are the great and the little annoyances and pains that beset our lives and on each of them, if we would look, we should see written, in His own hand, this inscription: "For your good."

III. THE GREAT AIM OF ALL THE DISCIPLINE.

A. The Greatness of the Aim.

God trains us for an eternal end: "that we should be partakers of His holiness." The one object which is congruous with a man's nature and is stamped on his whole being as its only adequate end is that he should be like God. I may have made myself rich, cultured, learned, famous, refined, prosperous; but if I have not at least begun to be like God in purity, in will, in heart, then my whole career has missed the purpose for which I was made and for which all the discipline of life has been lavished upon me.

B. The Means of Reaching the Aim.

That great and only worthy end may be reached by the ministration of circumstances and the discipline through which God passes us. These are not the only ways by which He makes us partakers of His holiness. There is the work of that Divine Spirit who is granted to every believer to breathe into him the holy breath of an immortal and incorruptible life. To work along with these is the influence that is brought to bear upon us by the circumstances in which we are placed and duties which we have to perform.

1. The ministration of circumstances.

2. The ministration of discipline.

3. The ministration of the Holy Spirit.

C. The Intention of Discipline.

1. The statement—They will wean us; they will refine us; they will blow us to His breast, as a strong wind might sweep a man into some refuge from itself.

2. The determining factor is our attitude toward the disciplines of life. But the sorrow that is meant to bring us nearer to Him may be in vain. The same circumstances may produce opposite effects. Take care that you do not waste your sorrows; that you do not let the precious gifts of disappointment, pain, loss, loneliness, ill health, or similar afflictions that come in your daily life, mar you instead of mending you.

CONCLUSION

Let us try to school ourselves into the habitual and operative conviction that life is discipline. Let us yield ourselves to the loving will of the unerring Father. Let us beware of getting no good from what is charged to the brim with good. Let us see to it that out of the many fleeting circumstances of life we gather and keep the eternal fruit of being partakers of His holiness.

Alexander Maclaren

SERMON THIRTY-ONE

MARCUS, MY SON

So doth Marcus, my son.
— I PETER 5:13

MARK was the son of Mary, a woman of some wealth and position. He was a relative, probably a cousin, of Barnabas and possibly like him, a native of Cyprus. The designation of him by Peter as "my son" naturally implies that the apostle had been the instrument of his conversion.

I. THE WORKING OF CHRISTIAN SYMPATHY.

A. The Change of Name of a Disciple of Christ.

1. The fact of a change in name. "John, whose surname was Mark" bore a double name—one Jewish, "John," and one Gentile, "Marcus." As time goes on we do not hear anything more about "John" nor about "John Mark," which are the two forms of his name when he is first introduced to us in the Acts of the Apostles, but he finally appears to have cast aside his Hebrew and to have been only known by his Roman name.

2. The appropriateness of the change in name in relation to his ministry. The change of appellation coincides with the fact that so many of the allusions which we have to him represent him as sending messages of Christian greetings to his Gentile brethren. And it further coincides with the fact that his Gospel is obviously intended for the use of Gentile Christians.

B. *The Significance of the Change in Name.*

1. It intimates a great truth. This change of name may be taken as reminding us of a very important truth, that if we wish to help people, the first condition is that we go down and stand on their level and make ourselves one with them, as far as we can.

2. The importance of the truth intimated. Not only the duty of widening our sympathies, but one of the supreme conditions of being of use to anybody is set forth in the comparatively trifling incident, that this man, a Jew to his fingertips, for the sake of efficiency in his work and of getting close by the side of the people whom he wanted to influence, flung away deliberately that which parted him from them.

II. THE POSSIBILITY OF OVERCOMING EARLY FAULTS.

A. *The Probable Reason of Mark's Failure.*

1. It might have been the lack of courage to do difficult things. He was willing to go where he knew the ground and where there were people that would make things easy for him; but when Paul went further afield Mark's courage ebbed out at his finger ends and he slunk back to the comfort of his mother's house in Jerusalem.

2. The apostle Paul's view of Mark's failure. The writer of the Acts puts Paul's view of the case strongly by the arrangement of clauses in the sentence in which he tells us that the apostle "thought not good to take him with them who withdrew from them from Pamphylia and went not with them to the work" (Acts of the Apostles 15:38).

B. *The Cure of Mark's Failure.*

1. The evidence of the cure. The man that was afraid of dangers and difficulties and hypothetical risks became brave enough to stand by the apostle when he was a prisoner. He won his way into the apostle's confidence and made himself needful for him by his services and his sweetness that the prisoner bids Timothy bring him with himself.

2. The encouragement of the cure to present day believers. Translate that from the particular into the general and it comes to this. Let no man set limits to the possibilities of his own restoration and of his curing faults which are not deeply rooted within himself. Hope and effort should be boundless.

III. THE GREATNESS OF LITTLE SERVICE.

A. *The Nature of Mark's Work.*

1. It was to attend to Paul's comfort. He had to be Paul's man of all work; looking after material things, the commissariat, the thousand and one trifles that someone had to see to if the apostle's great work was to get done.

2. It was his life's work. And he did it all his lifelong. It was enough for him to do thoroughly the entirely "secular" work, as some people would think of it, which it was in his power to do.

B. *The Necessary Requirement to Render Such Service.*

1. Self-suppression. It would have been so natural for Mark to have said, "Paul sends Timothy to be bishop in Crete; and Titus to look after other churches; Epaphroditus is an official here; and Apollos is a great preacher there. I think I'll 'strike' and try and get more conspicuous work." But this "minister," a private attendant and valet of the apostle was glad to do that work all his days.

2. Recognition of the fact that all kinds of work contributing to one end are one sort of work. It was a recognition that all sorts of work which contribute to one end are one sort of work; and that at bottom the man who carried Paul's books and parchments and saw that he was not left without clothes was just as much helping on the cause of Christ as the apostle when he preached.

IV. THE ENLARGED SPHERE THAT FOLLOWS FAITHFULNESS IN SMALL MATTERS.

A. *Mark's Enlarged Ministry.*

The man who began with being a servant of Paul and of Barnabas ends by being the evangelist and it is to him under Peter's direction, that we owe what is possibly the oldest and, at all events, in some aspects, an entirely unique narrative of our Lord's life, "He that is faithful in that which is least is faithful also in much" (Luke 16:10).

B. The Law That Faithfulness in Little Things Brings Greater Responsibilities.

In God's providence the tools do come to the hand that can wield them and the best reward that we can get for doing well our little work is to have larger work to do. And the law will be exemplified most blessedly when Christ shall say, "Well done! good and faithful servant. Thou has been faithful over a few things, I will make thee ruler over many things" (Matthew 25:21).

CONCLUSION

So this faraway figure of the minister evangelist salutes us too and bids us be of good cheer, notwithstanding all faults and failures, because it is possible for us, as he has proved, to recover ourselves after them all.

Alexander Maclaren

THE MASTER AND HIS SLAVES

Denying the Lord that bought them.
—II PETER 2:1

THE APOSTLES glory in calling themselves "slaves of Jesus Christ." That title of honor heads many epistles. In this text we have the same figure expressed with Peter's own energy and carried out in detail. The word in our text for "Lord" is an unusual one, selected to put the idea in the roughest, most absolute form. It is the root of our word "despot" and conveys the notion of unlimited authority.

I. CHRIST'S ABSOLUTE OWNERSHIP.

A. The Sphere of Christ's Lordship.

1. The realm of nature. His lips spoke and it was done when He was here on earth—rebuking disease, and it fled; the wild storm, and there was a great calm; demons, and they came out; death itself, and its dull, cold ear heard and Lazarus came forth.

2. The realm of mankind. His rule in the region of man's spirit is as absolute and authoritative and there too "His Word is with power."

B. The Prerogative of Christ's Lordship.

1. The Master dispenses to His slaves their tasks. The owner of the slave could set him to any work he thought fit. So our Owner gives all His slaves their several tasks. As in some despotic eastern monarchies the sultan's mere pleasure makes one slave his vizier and another his slipper bearer, our King chooses one man to a post of honor and another to a lowly place; none has a right to question the allocation of work.

2. The Master has first claim on His slave's possessions. Whose are our possessions? If we have no property in ourselves, still less can we have property in our property. These things were His before and are His still. The first claim on them is our Master's, not ours.

C. The Slave's Response to Christ's Lordship.

1. Recognition of trusteeship. If we rightly understand our position we shall feel that we are trustees, not possessors. When, like prodigal sons, we "waste our substance" we are unfaithful stewards, also, "wasting our Lord's goods."

2. Submission to the Master. Such absolute submission of will and recognition of Christ's absolute authority over us, our destiny, work, and possessions is ennobling and blessed. So to bow before a man would be degrading were it possible, but so to bow before Him is our highest honor and liberates us from all other submission.

II. THE PURCHASE ON WHICH OUR OWNERSHIP IS FOUNDED.

A. The Expression of the Purchase.

This Master has acquired men by right of purchase. That abomination of the auction block may suggest the better "merchandise of the souls of men" which Christ has made when He bought us with His own blood as our ransom. That purchase is represented in two forms of expression. Sometimes we read that He has bought us with His "blood"; sometimes that He has given "Himself" for us.

1. He bought us with His blood.

2. He gave Himself for us.

B. The Reference of the Statements.

Both expressions point to the same great fact—His death as the price at which He has acquired us as His own.

C. The Implications of the Text.

1. Christ's lordship over men is based on His sacrifice for men. That is a very beautiful and profound thought that Christ's lordship over men is built upon His mighty and supreme sacrifice for men. Nothing short of His utter giving up of Himself for them gives Him the right of absolute authority over them; or, as Paul puts it, "He gave Himself for us" that He might "purchase for Himself a people."

2. Slaves are purchased from previous slavery. The figure suggests that we are bought from a previous slavery to some other master. Free men are not sold into slavery, but slaves pass from one master to another and sometimes are bought into freedom as well as into bondage. Our Kinsman (Christ) bought us back from our bondage to sin and guilt and condemnation, from the slavery of our tyrant lusts, from the slavery to men's censures and opinions, from the dominion of evil and darkness, and making us His, makes us free.

III. THE FUGITIVES OR RUNAWAYS WHO DENY CHRIST'S AUTHORITY.

We do not care to enquire here what special type of heretics the apostle had in view nor to apply them to modern parallels which we may fancy we can find. It is more profitable to notice how all godlessness and sin may be described as denying the Lord.

A. All Sin Is the Denial of Christ's Authority.

It is in effect saying, "We will not have this man to reign over us." It is at bottom the uprising of our own self-will against His rule and the proud assertion of our own independence. It is as foolish as it is ungrateful, as ungrateful as it is foolish.

1. It is the uprising of self-will against Christ's rule.

2. It is the proud assertion of our own independence.

B. The Manifestations of the Denial.

The denial is made by deeds which are done in defiance or neglect of His authority and it is done too by words and opinions.

1. It is shown by deeds.

2. It is shown by words.

CONCLUSION

Let us beware lest the fate of many a runaway slave be ours and we be lost in trackless bogs and perish miserably. Casting off His yoke is sure to end in ruin. Rather, drawn by the cords of love and owning the blessed bonds in which willing souls are held by the love of Christ, let us take Him for our Lord, who has given Himself for our ransom and answer the pleading of His cross with our glad surrender.

Alexander Maclaren

SERMON THIRTY-THREE

FOR THE SAKE
OF THE NAME

For His name's sake.
—III JOHN 7

THE REVISED Version gives the true force of these words by omitting the "His" and reading merely "for the sake of the name." The word rendered "for the sake of" does not merely mean—though it does mean that—"on account of" or "by reason of," but "on behalf of," as if, in some wonderful sense that mighty and exalted name was furthered, advantaged, or benefited by even man's poor services.

I. THE PREEMINENCE IMPLIED IN "THE NAME."

A. The Meaning of "the name."

1. "The name" stands for the person and work of Christ. "The name" means the whole Christ as we know Him or as we may know Him from the Book, in His messiahship, deity, life, words, sacrifice, resurrection, ascension, and present life and reigning work for us at the right hand of God.

2. "The name" indicates the supremacy of Christ in His person and work. It is but a picturesque and condensed way of saying that Jesus Christ, in the depth of His nature and the width of His work, stands alone and is the single, because the all-sufficient object of love and trust and obedience.

B. The Demands of "the name."

The uniqueness and solitariness of "the name" demands an equal and corresponding exclusiveness of devotion and trust.

1. The demand of implicit trust. There is one Christ and there is none other but He. Therefore all the current of my being is to set to Him and on Him alone am I to repose my undivided weight, casting all my cares and putting all my trust only on Him.

2. The demand of implicit devotion. Love none other except Him; for His heart is wide enough and deep enough for all mankind. Obey none other, for only His voice has the right to command. And lifting up our eyes, let us see "No man any more save Jesus only." That name stands alone.

C. The Intimation of "the name."

1. It implies the deity of Christ. The preeminent and exclusive mention of the name carries with it, in fair inference, the declaration of His Divine nature. It seems impossible that a man saturated as this apostle was with Old Testament teaching and familiar as he was as to the sanctity of "the name of the Lord," should have used such language as this of my text unless he had felt, as he has told us himself, that "the Word was God."

2. It implies the common acknowledgement of the deity of Christ by the Apostolic Church. The very incidental character of the allusion gives it the more force as a witness to the common placeness which the thought of the deity of Jesus Christ had assumed to the consciousness of the Christian Church.

II. THE POWER OF THE NAME TO SWAY THE LIFE.

A. There Is Guidance.

1. Wherein it lies. In Him, in the whole fulness of His being, in the wonders of the story of His character and historical manifestation, there lies all guidance for men.

2. What Christ is to us. He is the pattern of our conduct. He is the Companion for us in our sorrow. He is the Quickener but shall have the light of life. "Of the Name" the motto of his life will not walk in darkness, for us in all of our tasks.

B. There Is Power.

1. It is the secret of the transformation of lives. There is nothing else that will go so deep down into the heart and unseal the fountains of power and obedience as that name. There is nothing else that will so strike the shackles off the prisoned will and fan back to their caves the wild beasts that tyrannize within and put the chain round their necks as the name of Jesus Christ.

2. It flows from the cross of Christ. Where in the life and work of Jesus Christ is the dominant summit from which the streams run down? The cross! The love that died for us is the thing that draws out answering love. And answering love is the power that transmutes my whole nature into the humble aspiration to be like Him and to render back myself unto Him for His gift.

III. THE SERVICE THAT WE CAN RENDER TO THE NAME.

A. The Evidence That Believers Can Give Beneficial Service to the Lord.

1. The testimony of the context. There were some Christian people who had gone on a missionary tour and penniless and homeless they had come to a city and had been taken in and kindly entertained by a Christian brother. And says John, these humble men went out "on behalf of the name." Jesus Christ the bearer of the name, was in some sense helped and benefited by the work of these lowly and unknown brethren.

2. The testimony of additional Scriptures. Acts 5:41; 9:16;15:26; 21:13; Romans 1:5. If we put all these together they just come to this, that He has appointed that His name should be furthered by the sufferings, the service, the life, and the death of His followers.

B. The Manner in Which Service Can Be Rendered to the Lord.

1. By word of mouth. "He was extolled with my tongue," says the Psalmist in a rapture of wonder that any words of his could extol God's name. So to you Christians is committed the charge of magnifying the name of Jesus Christ.

2. By life. We can "adorn the doctrine" and make men think more highly of our Lord by our example of faithfulness and obedience. If from us sounded out the name and over all that we did it was written blazing, conspicuous, the world would look and listen and men would believe that there was something in the Gospel.

CONCLUSION

If you are a professing Christian either Christ is glorified or put to shame in you, His saint; and either it is true of you that you do all things in the name of the Lord Jesus and so glorify His name or that through you the name of Christ is "blasphemed among the nations." Choose which of the two it shall be.

Alexander Maclaren

SERMON THIRTY-FOUR

HOW TO KEEP IN THE LOVE OF GOD

But ye, beloved, building up yourselves on your most holy faith,
praying in the Holy Ghost, keep yourselves in the love of God,
looking for the mercy of our Lord Jesus Christ unto eternal life.
—JUDE 20–21

THE MAIN subject of this letter is the warning against certain teachers whose errors of belief and vice of conduct seem to have been equally great. After the denunciation of these the writer turns, as with a sudden movement of revulsion, from the false teachers to exhort his readers to conduct contrary to theirs, and sets forth in these words the true way by which individuals and churches can guard themselves against abounding errors.

I. THE CENTRAL INJUNCTION: "KEEP YOURSELVES IN THE LOVE OF GOD."

A. What Is Meant by the Love of God?

Now "the love of God" here obviously means not ours to Him, but His to us, and the commandment is parallel to and may be a reminiscence of our Lord's great word: "As the Father hath loved Me, so have I loved you. Continue ye in My love" (John 15:9).

1. Negatively stated: it is not our love to God.

2. Positively stated: it is God's love to us.

B. Can a Man Get Out of the Love of God?

1. God's love always extends to all men. No doubt "His tender mercies are over all His works" (Psalm 145:9). No doubt His love holds in a grasp which never can be loosened every creature that He has made.

2. The blessings and consciousness of God's love may be lost. All the best and noblest manifestations of that love and the sweetest, most select aspects of that love cannot come to men irrespective of their moral character and their relation to Him. It is possible for Christian people to lose the consciousness of being surrounded and kept within that warm and sunny circle where God's love falls.

C. Can a Man Always Keep in the Love of God?

1. The ideal set forth in the text. The ideal set forth here is that of unbroken continuity in the flow of that Divine love which falls in its gentlest and mightiest beams only upon the heart that aspires toward Him, and also a continual consciousness on my part that I am within the reach of its rays and that it is well with me because I am.

2. The experience of many Christians. Instead of one unbroken line of light, what do we find? A dot of light and then a stretch of blackness; and then another little sparkle, scarcely visible, and short lived, followed by another dreary tract of murky midnight.

3. The secret of all blessedness. The secret of all blessedness is to live in the love of God. Our sorrows and difficulties and trials will change their aspect if we walk in the peaceful enjoyment and conscious possession of His Divine heart. That is the true anesthetic.

II. THE SUBSIDIARY EXHORTATIONS WHICH POINT OUT THE MEANS OF OBEYING THE CENTRAL COMMAND.

A. A Continual Building Up of a Noble Character on the Foundation of Faith.

1. Faith is only the basis of spiritual progress. The foundation of all that is good and noble in a character is the going out of self to trust in God manifest in Christ. That is the real basis of everything that is great and lofty. But the faith which is thus the foundation of all excellence is only the foundation.

2. Continuous effort is the condition of spiritual progress. Then remember, too, that this building of a noble and godlike and God-pleasing character can be erected on the foundation of faith only by constant effort. Continuous effort is the condition of progress.

3. The importance of continual spiritual progress. They, and only they, have a right to say, "I believe in God the Father and in Jesus Christ His Son," in whom their faith is daily producing growth in the grace as well as in the knowledge which have Him for their object.

B. Holy Spirit Directed Prayer.

1. The necessity of prayer. Who that has ever honestly tried to cure himself of a fault or to make his own some unfamiliar virtue opposed to his natural temperament, but has found that the cry "O God! Help me" has come instinctively to his lips.

2. The nature of prayer. The prayer which helps us to keep in the love of God is not the petulant and passionate utterance of our own wishes, but is the yielding of our desires to the impulses divinely breathed upon us.

3. The effectiveness of prayer. My prayer breaks the bond of many a temptation that holds me. My prayer is the test for many a masked evil that seeks to seduce me. My prayer will be like a drop of poison on a scorpion—it will kill the sin on the instant.

III. THE EXPECTATION ATTENDANT ON THE OBEDIENCE TO THE CENTRAL COMMANDMENT: LOOKING FOR THE MERCY OF THE LORD JESUS CHRIST UNTO ETERNAL LIFE.

A. The Call for Mercy.

The best of us, looking back over our past, will most deeply feel that it is all so poor and stained that all we have to trust to is the forgiving mercy of our Lord Jesus Christ.

B. The Anticipation for Mercy.

That mercy will be anticipated for all the future in proportion as we keep ourselves for the present in the love of God. The more we feel in our hearts the experience that God loves us, the more sure shall we be that He will love us forever.

C. The Ground for Hope in Christ's Future Mercy.

The consciousness of His present love is the surest ground for the hope in Christ's future mercy.

D. The Blessings of Mercy.

That mercy will scatter its pardoning gifts all along the path of life and will not reach its highest issue nor be satisfied in its relation to us until it has brought us into the full and perfect enjoyment of that supereminent degree of eternal life which lies beyond the grave.

CONCLUSION

If you and I keep ourselves in the love of God by effort founded upon faith and prospered by prayer, we may then look quietly forward to that solemn future, knowing our sins indeed, but sure of the love of God and therefore sure of eternal life.

Alexander Maclaren

A NEW NAME

To him that overcometh will I give . . . a new name . . .
which no man knoweth saving he that receiveth it.
—REVELATION 2:17

THE SERIES of sevenfold promises attached to these letters to the
Asiatic churches presents us with a sevenfold aspect of future blessedness.
In the present case the little community at Pergamos was praised because
it held fast Christ's name and so there is promised to it a new name as its
very own.

I. THE LARGE HOPES WHICH GATHER ROUND THIS PROMISE OF
A NEW NAME.

A. The "New Name" Means a New Vision.

We know not how much the flesh, which is the organ of perception
for things sensible, is an obscurity, blind, and impenetrable barrier between us and the loftier order of things unseen. But this we know, that
when the stained glass of life is shattered, the white light of eternity will
pour in. "Now we see through a glass darkly: then, face to face" (I Corinthians 13:12).

B. The "New Name" Means New Activities.

We know not how far these fleshly organs, which are the condition
of our working upon the outward universe with which they bring us into

connection, limit and hem the operations of the spirit. But this we know, that when that which is sown in weakness is raised in power (I Corinthians 15:43), we shall then possess an instrument adequate to all that we can ask it to perform; a perfect tool for a perfected spirit.

C. The "New Name" Means New Purity.

There are two words very characteristic of this book of the Apocalypse. One of them is that word of my text, "new." The other is "white," not the cold, pallid white that may mean death, but the flashing white, as of sunshine upon snow, the radiant white of purity smitten by deity and so blazing up into lustre that dazzles. The one element in the newness of the "new name" is spotless purity and supernal radiance.

D. The "New Name" Means New Joys.

Here and now we know joy and sorrow as a double star, one bright and the other dark, which revolve around one center and with terrible swiftness take each others places. But there, "Thou makest them drink of the river of thy pleasures" (Psalm 36:8). A joy after the pattern of His joy, that was full and abode—an undisturbed and changing blessedness.

II. THE CONNECTION BETWEEN CHRIST'S NEW NAME AND OURS.

A. The Promise That Christ's New Name Will Be Written Upon the Overcomer.

In Revelation 4:12 we read, "Him that overcometh will I make a pillar in the temple of My God, and I will write upon him . . . My new name." The new name of Jesus in a revelation of His character; a new manifestation of Himself to the eyes of those that loved Him when they saw Him amidst the darkness and mists of earth. It implies no antiquating of the old name. Nothing will make the cross of Christ less the center of the revelation of God than it is today.

B. The Significance of Christ's New Name Inscribed Upon the Overcomer.

It is not merely the manifestation of the revealed character of Jesus in new beauty, but it is the manifestation of His ownership of His servants by transformation into His likeness, which transformation is the consequence of their new vision of Him. It is but saying in other words, "The new revelation of My character, which he shall receive, will be stamped upon his character and he shall become like Myself."

III. THE BLESSED SECRET OF THIS NEW NAME.

A. It Is Known Only to the Receiver.

"No man knoweth it saving he that receiveth it." Of course not. There is only one way to know the highest things in human experience and that is by possessing them. That is eminently true about religion and it is most of all true about that perfect future state.

B. It Is a Mystery to All But the Receiver.

That same blessed mystery lies round about the name of each individual possessor, to all but himself. Each eye shall see its own rainbow and each will possess in happy certitude of individual possession a honeyed depth of sweet experience, which will remain unrevealed, the basis of the being, the deep function of the blessedness. But it will be a mystery of no painful darkness, nor making any barrier between ourselves and the saints whom we love.

C. It Guarantees Variety in the Possession of the One Name.

All the surrounding diamonds that are set about the central blaze shall catch the light on their facets, and from one it will come golden, and from another red, and another flashing and pure white. Each glorified spirit shall reveal Christ and yet the one Christ shall be manifested in infinite variety of forms and the total summing up of the many reflections will be the image of the whole Lord.

IV. THE GIVING OF THE NEW NAME TO THE VICTORS.

A. The Condition Laid Down: "To Him That Overcometh."

This renovation of the being, and efflorescence into new knowledges, activities, perfections, and joy is only possible on condition of the earthly life of obedience and service and conquest. It is no arbitrary bestowment of a title. The conqueror gets the name that embodies his victories, and without conquering a man cannot receive it.

B. The Cause Laid Down: "Will I Give."

But while the conquering life here is the condition of the gift, it is nonetheless a gift. It is not a case of evolution but of bestowal by God's free love in Christ. The power by which we conquer is His gift and when He crowns it, it is His own grace in it which He crowns.

CONCLUSION

So my friends, here is the all important truth for us all. "This is the victory that overcometh the world, even our faith (I John 5:4); and that faith is victorious in idea and germ as soon as it begins to abide in a man's heart. We shall either conquer by Christ's strength and so receive His Divine name or else be beaten by the world and the flesh and the devil and so bear the image of our conquerors.

George Whitefield

SERMON OUTLINES

Selected and Edited by
SHELDON B. QUINCER, D. D.

George Whitefield

FOREWORD

One of the greatest revivals of American history was the Great Awakening of the eighteenth century. The beginning of the century saw most of our churches cold and lifeless. A few godly men saw the desperate conditions and were used of God in starting revival fires, but it was not until the arrival of English born George Whitefield in 1740 that the fires were flamed into a blaze that swept the eastern seaboard and Georgia. Under God, Whitefield became the leader of the revival.

He belonged to all denominations—he was ordained as an Anglican, became a Calvanistic Methodist, and was buried under the pulpit of the Federal Street Presbyterian Church of Newburyport, Massachusetts. He preached wherever he had the opportunity, in church buildings regardless of denominational affiliation, and in the open fields.

In thirty-five years of Gospel ministry in the British Isles, West Indies, and America, Whitefield preached eighteen thousand sermons to audiences which sometimes numbered thirty thousand people.

His sermons are both doctrinal and practical. In reading them one is impressed with his emphasis on the total depravity of man, the righteousness of Christ, and the grace of God. To him man is a sinner in need of Christ's imputed righteousness, which he can receive only through God's grace. He firmly held that "salvation is of the Lord."

Born in his father's tavern in Gloucester in December 1714, Whitefield entered Oxford University at the age of eighteen and three years later was converted and soon thereafter began his public ministry of preaching. He died in Newburyport on September 30, 1770.

The editor wishes to acknowledge his indebtedness to the Evangelical Library of London for the loan of several volumes of Whitefield's sermons which have been long out of print.

Sheldon B. Quincer
Grand Rapids, Michigan
January, 1956

THE FIRST PROMISE

And I will put enmity between thee and the woman,
and between thy seed and her seed; it shall bruise thy head,
and thou shalt bruise his heel.
—GENESIS 3:15

UPON CALLING your attention to the words of the text, I may address you in the language of the holy angels to the shepherds that were watching their flocks by night: "Behold, I bring you glad tidings of great joy." This is the first promise that was made of a Savior to the apostate race of Adam. It is wonderful to observe how gradually God revealed His Son to mankind. He began with the promise in the text and this the godly lived upon until the time of Abraham. To him, God made further discoveries of His eternal council concerning man's redemption. Afterwards at various times and in different ways God spoke to the fathers by the prophets until at length the Lord Jesus was manifested in flesh and came and tabernacled among us.

I. THE NEED FOR THE PROMISE.

A. The Reality of the Fall.

1. Temptation. In what odious colors God is here represented: "God doth know that in the day ye eat thereof, ye shall be as gods (equal with God)." Thus the grand temptation was that Adam and Eve should be hereafter under no control; equal, if not superior, to God.

2. Sin. Eve "took of the fruit and did eat and gave also unto her husband." What a complication of crimes in this one act of sin! Here is disbelief of God's threatening, ingratitude to their Maker, and neglect of their posterity who would stand or fall with them. Never again was a crime of such a complicated nature committed by anyone upon earth. Only the devil's apostasy and rebellion could equal it.

B. Realization of the Fall.

The fall of man is written in too legible characters not to be understood. Those who deny it, by their denial prove it. The heathen confess and bewail it. They can see the streams of corruption running through the whole race of mankind, but cannot trace them to the fountainhead. Before God gave a revelation of His Son, man was a riddle to himself. Moses unfolds more in this one chapter, out of which the text is taken, than all mankind could have been capable of finding out of themselves, though they had studied to all eternity.

II. THE MEANING OF THE PROMISE.

A. The Seed of the Serpent.

By the serpent's seed we are to understand the devil and all of his children who are permitted by God to tempt and to sift His children. The Lord Jesus, the seed of the woman, bruised Satan's accursed head through His suffering and death upon the cross. By dying, Christ overcame him who had the power of death, that is the devil. He thereby spoiled principalities and powers, and made a show of them openly, triumphing over them upon the cross.

B. The Seed of the Woman.

By the seed of the woman we are to understand the Lord Jesus Christ, who though God of very God, was for us men and our salvation to have a body prepared for Him by the Holy Spirit and to be born of a woman, and by His obedience and death make an atonement for man's transgression and bring in an everlasting righteousness, work in them a new nature and thereby bruise the serpent's head, that is, destroy his power and dominion over them. Satan bruised His heel when he tempted Him for forty days in the wilderness; when he raised up strong persecution against Him during

His public ministry; especially when our Lord sweat great drops of blood in the garden; when he put it in Judas's heart to destroy Him; most of all when Satan's emissaries nailed Him to the accursed tree.

III. THE FULFILLMENT OF THE PROMISE.

A. By Way of Interpretation.

This promise was literally fulfilled in the person of our Lord Jesus Christ. As we have already seen the promise refers to the seed of the woman, Christ, and His victory on the cross over Satan; and to the seed of the Serpent, Satan and His emissaries, and their defeat at Calvary.

B. By Way of Application.

1. This promise has been fulfilled in the children of God considered collectively. In this promise there is an eternal enmity put between the seed of the woman and the seed of the serpent. Therefore, those that are born after the flesh cannot but persecute those who are born after the Spirit. This enmity showed itself in Cain's persecution of Abel. It continued throughout all the ages before Christ's incarnation as seen in Bible history. It raged after Christ's ascension, as witnessed by the Book of Acts and the history of the early Christians. It now rages and will continue to rage in a greater or less degree to the end of time.

2. This promise has been fulfilled in the children of God considered individually. In every believer there are two seeds, the seed of the woman and the seed of the serpent the—flesh lusting against the Spirit and the Spirit against the flesh. It is with the believer, when quickened with grace in his heart, as it was with Rebekah when she conceived Esau and Jacob in her womb; she felt a struggling. Thus grace and nature struggle, if I may so speak, in the womb of a believer's heart; but grace in the end shall get the better of nature. The promise in the text ensures the perseverance and victory of believers.

CONCLUSION

I know in whom I have believed; I am persuaded He will keep that safe which I have committed unto Him. He is faithful who has promised that the seed of the woman shall bruise the serpent's head. May we all experience a daily completion of His promise, both in the church and in our hearts, until we come to the church of the first born, the spirits of just men made perfect, in the presence and actual fruition of the great God our heavenly Father. To whom, with the Son and the Holy Spirit, be ascribed all honor, power, might, majesty, and dominion now and forever more. Amen.

SERMON TWO

WALKING WITH GOD

And Enoch walked with God; and he was not, for God took him.
—GENESIS 5:24

ENOCH is spoken of in the words of the text in a very extraordinary manner. We have here a short but full and glorious account of his behavior in this world and the triumphant manner of his entry into the next. The former is contained in the words, "And Enoch walked with God." The latter in the words, "and he was not, for God took him."

I. THE IMPLICATIONS OF WALKING WITH GOD.

A. Enmity Has Been Taken Away.

Walking with God implies that the prevailing power of the enmity of a person's heart is taken away by the Spirit of God. The carnal mind is enmity, not only an enemy, but enmity itself, against God. All who know this will acknowledge walking with God requires the destruction of the power of this heart enmity.

B. Reconciliation Has Been Effected.

Walking with God also implies that a person is actually reconciled to God the Father in and through the all-sufficient righteousness and atonement of His Son. When we are justified by faith in Christ, then, but not until then, we have peace with God; and consequently it cannot be said until then that we walk with Him.

C. Fellowship Is Experienced.

"And Enoch walked with God," that is, he maintained a holy, settled, habitual, although undoubtedly not altogether uninterrupted fellowship with God, in and through Jesus Christ. This walking with God consists in a habitual bent of the will for God, in a habitual dependence upon His power and promise, in a habitual voluntary dedication of our all to His glory.

D. Progress in the Christian Life.

The first idea of the word walking seems to suppose progressive motion. A person that walks, though it be more slowly, yet he goes forward and does not continue in one place. So it is with those that walk with God. They go on, as the Psalmist says, "from strength to strength" (Psalm 84:7). Read also II Corinthians 3:18 and II Peter 3:18.

II. THE MEANS OF THE MAINTENANCE OF WALKING WITH GOD.

A. Bible Reading.

Believers maintain their walk with God by reading His Holy Word. "Search the Scriptures," says our Lord, "for these are they that testify of Me" (John 5:39). The Word of God is profitable for reproof, for correction, and for instruction in righteousness, and in every way sufficient to make every true child of God thoroughly furnished unto every good work (II Timothy 3:16–17).

B. Secret Prayer.

A neglect of secret prayer has been frequently an inlet to many spiritual diseases and has been attended with fatal consequences. "Watch and pray that ye enter not into temptation" (Matthew 26:41). If you would keep up your walk with God, pray. When you are about the common business of life, be much in ejaculatory prayer. It will reach the heart of God.

C. Meditation.

Holy and frequent meditation is another blessed means of keeping up a believer's walk with God. "Prayer, reading, temptation, and meditation," says Luther, "make a minister." They also make a perfect Christian. Meditation to the soul is the same as digestion to the body. David found it so and therefore he was frequently employed in meditation, even in the night season.

D. Consideration of God's Providential Dealings.

If we believe the Scriptures we must believe our Lord's words that the hairs of our heads are numbered and the sparrow does not fall without our heavenly Father's knowledge (Matthew 10:29–30). Therefore, if believers would keep up their walk with God they must hear what the Lord has to say concerning them in the voice of His providence.

E. Consideration of the Holy Spirit's Work in the Life.

In order to walk closely with God, His children must watch the workings of His Spirit in their hearts. They must give up themselves to be guided by the Holy Spirit as a little child gives his hand to be led by the parent. It is every Christian's duty to be guided by the Spirit in conjunction with God's written Word.

F. Faithfulness to God.

It is recorded of Zacharias and Elizabeth that they walked in all God's ordinances, as well as commandments, blameless (Luke 1:6). All rightly informed Christians will look upon ordinances as their highest privileges. They will delight to visit the place where God's honor dwelleth and to embrace all opportunities to show forth the Lord's death till He come.

G. Association with the Godly.

If you would walk with God you will associate and keep company with those that walk with Him. The early Christians, no doubt, kept up their vigor and first love by continuing in fellowship one with another. If we look into church history or observe our own times we shall find that as God's power prevails, Christian societies and fellowship meetings prevail.

III. THE MOTIVES FOR WALKING WITH GOD.

A. It Is a Walk That Is Honorable.

Do you consider it a small thing to have the secret of the Lord of lords with you and to be called the friends of God? Such honor have all God's saints. "The secret of the Lord is with them that fear Him" (Psalm 25:14). "Henceforth, I call you not servants, but friends; for the servant knoweth not the will of His master" (John 15:15).

B. It Is a Walk That Is Pleasant.

The wisest of men has told us that "wisdom's ways are ways of pleasantness, and all her paths are peace" (Proverbs 3:17). And I remember Matthew Henry, when he was just about to expire, said to a friend, "You have heard many men's dying words, and these are mine: A life spent in communion with God is the most pleasant life in the world."

C. It Is a Walk Which Ends in Heaven.

There is a heaven at the end of this walk. For, to use the words of Bishop Beveridge, "Though the way be narrow, yet it is not long; and though the gate be straight, yet it opens into everlasting life." Enoch found it so. He walked with God on earth and God took him to sit down with Him forever in the kingdom of heaven.

CONCLUSION

What more can I say to you that are yet strangers to Christ to come and walk with God. Put on the Lord Jesus and make no longer provision for the flesh, to fulfil the lust thereof. The blood, even the precious blood of Jesus Christ, if you come to the Father in and through Him, will cleanse you from all sin.

THE TESTING OF
ABRAHAM

*And He said, "Lay not thine hand upon the lad, neither do thou
anything to him; for now I know that thou fearest God, seeing
thou hast not withheld thy son, thine only son, from Me."*
—GENESIS 22:12

THE APOSTLE Paul informs us that "whatsoever things were written
aforetime were written for our learning, that we through patience and
comfort of the Scriptures might have hope" (Romans 15:4). And as without faith it is impossible to please God or be accepted in the Son of His love;
we may be assured that whatever instances of a more than common faith
are recorded in the Bible, they were designed by God's Spirit for our learning and imitation. (Read Genesis 22:1–14.)

I. ABRAHAM'S TEMPTATION (Verses 1–2).

A. The Time of the Temptation.

The sacred penman begins the narrative thus: "And it came to pass,
after these things, God did tempt Abraham." After these things, that is, after he had undergone many severe trials, after he was old and full of days,
and might flatter himself that the troubles and toils of life were now finished. Christians, you know not what trials you may meet before you die.
Our last trials, in all probability, will be the greatest. We can never say our
trials are finished until we leave this earthly scene.

B. The Meaning of Temptation.

Does not James tell us that God tempts no man (1:13). God tempts no man to evil. However, God may be said to tempt, I mean, to try His servants. In this sense we are to understand the passage where we are told that Jesus was "led up of the Spirit into the wilderness to be tempted of the devil" (Matthew 4:1). In this sense we are to understand the expression before us: "God did tempt (or try) Abraham."

C. The Nature of the Temptation.

It must not only be a son, but "thine only son Isaac, whom thou lovest" (verse 2). It must be his only son, the heir of all, the son of his old age in whom his soul delighted, in whose life his own was wrapped up. This son, this only son, this Isaac, the son of his love, must be taken now and be offered up by his own father for a burnt offering upon one of the mountains of which God would tell him.

II. ABRAHAM'S RESPONSE TO THE TEMPTATION (Verses 3–10).

A. It Was a Response without Consultation with Man.

The humility, as well as the piety of the Patriarch is observable: he saddled his own beast of burden. To show his sincerity, although he took two of his young men and his son Isaac with him, yet he kept his design a secret from them all. He does not so much as tell Sarah his wife. She might hinder him in his obedience to God. The young men, had they known of it, might have forced him away from obeying God's command.

B. It Was a Response of Obedience.

"They came to the place which God had told him of; and Abraham built an altar there, and laid the wood in order, and bound Isaac his son, and laid him upon the altar upon the wood" (verse 9). Here let us pause for awhile and by faith take a view of the place where the father has laid his son. And now the fatal blow is to be given, "And Abraham stretched forth his hand, and took the knife to slay his son" (verse 10).

C. It Was a Response of Faith.

"And Abraham said, 'My son, God will provide Himself a lamb for a burnt offering'" (verse 8). Some think that Abraham by faith saw the Lord

Jesus afar off and here spoke prophetically of the Lamb of God already slain in decree and hereafter to be actually offered up for sinners. This was a Lamb of God's providing, indeed, to satisfy His own justice and to render lim just in justifying the ungodly.

III. ABRAHAM'S OBEDIENCE REWARDED (Verses 11–14).

A. The Call of the Angel of the Lord.

Sing, O heavens and rejoice, O earth! Just as the knife in all probability was near Isaac's throat, "the angel of the Lord (or rather the Lord of angels, Jesus Christ, the Angel of the everlasting covenant) called unto him (probably in an audible manner) from heaven, and said, Abraham, Abraham." The name is spoken twice to engage his attention; and perhaps the suddenness of the call made him draw back his hand just as he was going to strike his son. "And Abraham answered, 'Here am I'" (verse 11).

B. The Message of the Angel of the Lord.

"And He said, 'Lay not thine hand upon the lad, neither do thou anything unto him: for now I know that thou fearest God, seeing thou hast not withheld thy son, thine only son from Me'" (verse 12). Here it was that Abraham received his son Isaac from the dead in a figure. He was in effect offered upon the altar and God looked upon him as offered and given unto Him. Now it was that Abraham's faith, being tried, was found more precious than gold purified seven times in the fire.

C. The Confirmation of God's Promise.

Now as a reward of grace, though not of debt, for this signal act of obedience, by an oath, God gives and confirms the promise that in his seed all the nations of the earth should be blessed (verses 17–19). With what comfort may we suppose Abraham and Isaac went down from the mount and returned to the young men! With what joy may we imagine he went home and related to Sarah all the things which had taken place.

CONCLUSION

We are all fallen creatures and do not love God or Christ as we ought to do. If you admire Abraham's offering up his son, how much more ought you to extol, magnify, and adore the love of God, who so loved the world as to give His only begotten Son, Christ Jesus our Lord, "that whosoever believeth in Him should not perish, but have everlasting life" (John 3:16)? May we not well cry out, "Now we know, O Lord, that Thou hast loved us, since Thou hast not withheld Thine only Son from us."

THE BELOVED OF GOD

And of Benjamin, he said, "The beloved of the Lord shall dwell in safety by Him; and the Lord shall cover him all day long, and he shall dwell between His shoulders."
—DEUTERONOMY 33:12

IF YOU read this chapter you will find how various, yet special, are the blessings which, in a prophetic strain, Moses foretells should attend particular persons or tribes. I have been reading them over, and although I admire them all, I was at a loss from which to speak, until the blessing of Benjamin fixed my attention, not only as sweet, but also instructing.

I. THE IDENTIFICATION OF THE BELOVED OF GOD.

A. An Erroneous Notion.

Some say that the beloved of the Lord signifies all the men that were ever born into the world. That is a broad bridge to take them in, but broad bridges are not always the strongest bridges in the world. Some assert that Judas was as much beloved as Peter or any other of the apostles.

B. The Biblical View.

The beloved of the Lord are the men that the Scriptures always speak of whose constant uniform character is they love God. It is spoken of all the people of God. God help us to apply it to ourselves. The love which God has for the world is quite different from His love for His own children.

II. THE EVIDENCES OF BEING BELOVED OF GOD.

A. Abhorrence and Renunciation of Self-Righteousness.

We are the beloved of the Lord if we are brought to abhor and renounce that which stands between us and the Lord; I mean our cursed self-righteousness. Can I prove that I have renounced my own plans, that I am sick of them, as well as my sins? None but the beloved of the Lord see this; an enemy may have this in his head, but only a friend of the Lord has it in his heart.

B. Love for the Children of God.

If I am beloved of the Lord, having His love in my heart, I will show it by loving those He has loved. As soon as we hear of a sinner turning to God it will rejoice us, and we shall be like the angels in heaven who rejoice over one sinner's repentance more than over ninety-nine just persons who need no repentance (Luke 15:7).

C. Hated by the World.

"If ye were of the world, the world would love his own: but because ye are not of the world, but I have chosen you out of the world, therefore the world hateth you" (John 15:19). You love the Lord and not be hated as was your Lord! I do not say that all are hated alike. In proportion to our successes will we be hated.

D. Living Victoriously over the World.

If I am beloved of the Lord, I really shall live above the world. I remember a dear friend once sent me word how busy he was morning and night, up early and late. "Perhaps," he said, "you will think by this account I am worldly"; but he continued, "No sir, I thank God that my heart is above the world." God grant we may thus prove we love God!

E. Fear of Offending God.

They that love the Lord will endeavor to keep from offending God, not for fear of being condemned, but because sin caused the death of God's Son. There are a great many people who abstain from sin for fear of punishment; but hear what Joseph said, "How can I do this great wickedness and sin against God" (Genesis 39:9), the God who loves me.

F. Willing Service for the Lord.

If we are the beloved of the Lord we shall be willing to work for the Lord. I knew a lady who wanted to be further employed in the service of God. Said she, If Christ would but help me to do such and such a thing I have in view, I would dedicate myself more and more to His honor. A true Christian loves thus to be employed.

G. Desire to See Jesus.

If we have the love of God in our hearts the bent of our minds will be, When shall I see "Him whom my soul loves"? "I am in a strait betwixt two," says Paul; the word signifies a strong intense desire "to be with Christ, which is far better" (Philippians 1:23).

III. A TEMPTATION OF THE BELOVED OF GOD.

A. The Nature of the Temptation.

Can I think God loves me when I am poor or afflicted? If I am beloved of the Lord, how is it that my friends are against me; that my children instead of being a blessing are breaking my heart? If I am beloved of the Lord why have I so many domestic trials; why am I harassed with blasphemous thoughts?

B. The Reminder Concerning the Temptation.

"Whom the Lord loveth He chasteneth, and scourgeth every son whom He receiveth" (Hebrews 12:6). Jesus was never more beloved of His Father than when He cried, "My God! My God! Why hast Thou forsaken Me?" (Matthew 27:46) or in the garden sweating great drops of blood as He cried, "Father, if it be possible, let this cup pass from Me" (Matthew 26:39; Luke 22:44).

IV. THE BLESSINGS OF THE BELOVED OF GOD.

A. They Shall Dwell Safely upon the Earth.

What is to be done to those that are beloved of the Lord? Here it is, "they shall dwell in safety." Why? "They shall dwell between His shoulders." Will God indeed dwell upon the earth? Yes, He dwells in my earthly heart made heavenly by the grace of God. Says the Lord, "I am thy shield" (Genesis 15:1).

B. They Shall Dwell Eternally in Heaven.

Those who are lovers of the Lord Jesus shall dwell safely with God on earth and eternally with Him in heaven. God loves and smiles upon His children and therefore they shall dwell in safety.

CONCLUSION

If any of you who have not the marks of being beloved of the Lord are awakened and convinced, the Lord grant you may not rest until you are God's beloved. Come, throw yourself upon Christ and say, "Lord, pardon my iniquities, for they are great."

FAMILY RELIGION

As for me and my home, we will serve the Lord.
—JOSHUA 24:15

THESE WORDS contain the holy resolution of Joshua, who in a most moving, affectionate discourse recounted to the Israelites the great things God had done for them, and now comes to draw a proper inference from what he had been delivering and acquaint them, in the most pressing terms, that because God had been so gracious to them, they could do no less than dedicate themselves and families to God.

I. THE RESPONSIBILITY OF THE HEAD OF THE FAMILY IN RELATION TO FAMILY RELIGION.

A. The Character of His Responsibility.

Every head of a family ought to look upon himself as obliged to act in three capacities: as a prophet to instruct; as a priest to pray for and with; as a king to govern, direct, and provide for them.

B. The Importance of His Responsibility.

However indifferent some heads of families may be about it, they may be assured that God will require a due discharge of these offices at their hands. For if, as the apostle argues, he that does not provide for his own in temporal things, "hath denied the faith, and is worse than an infidel" (I Timothy 5:8); to what greater degree of apostasy must he have arrived who takes no thought to provide for the spiritual welfare of his family.

C. Examples of Meeting the Responsibility.

What precedents men who neglect their duty in this particular can plead for such omission I cannot tell. Doubtless not the example of holy Job (Job 1:5). Nor can they plead the practice of good old Joshua who in the text we find as much concerned for his household's welfare as his own. Nor that of Cornelius who feared God not only himself but with all his house (Acts 10:2). If Christians had the spirit of Job, Joshua, and the Gentile centurion, they would act like them.

II. THE NATURE OF FAMILY RELIGION.

A. Reading God's Word to the Family.

"Search the Scriptures, for in them ye think ye have eternal life" (John 5:39) is a precept given by our blessed Lord to all; but much more so ought every head of a family to think it in a peculiar manner spoken to himself, because he ought to look upon himself as a prophet and therefore bound to instruct those under his charge in the knowledge of the Word of God. This was the order God gave to Israel (Deuteronomy 6:6–7).

B. Family Prayers.

This is a duty, although as much neglected, yet as absolutely necessary as reading the Scriptures. Reading the Bible is a good preparative for prayer, as prayer is an excellent means to render reading effectual. The reason why every head of a family should join both of these exercises together is plain, because a head of a family cannot perform his priestly office without performing the duty of family prayer.

C. Family Instruction.

Every head of a family should catechize and instruct the entire household and bring them up in the nurture and admonition of the Lord. This is seen in God's commendation of Abraham: "I know that he will command his children and household after him, to keep the way of the Lord, to do justice and judgment" (Genesis 18:19). Parents are commanded in the New Testament to "bring up their children in the nurture and admonition of the Lord" (Ephesians 6:4).

III. THE MOTIVES FOR FAMILY RELIGION.

A. Gratitude to God.

The first motive I shall mention is the duty of gratitude which you who are heads of families owe to God. Providence has given to you a goodly heritage, above many of your fellow men. Therefore, out of a principle of gratitude you ought to endeavor, as much as in you lies, to make every person of your respective households to call upon Him as long as they live. Thus did Abraham and Joshua. Let us go and do likewise.

B. Love for the Family.

If gratitude to God will not, I think love and pity for your children should move you with your families to serve the Lord. Most people express a great fondness for their children and provide, therefore, for their bodily needs; but they forget the salvation of their immortal souls. Is this their way of expressing their fondness for their children? Then was Delilah fond of Samson when she delivered him into the hands of the Philistines?

C. Self-Interest.

This weighs greatly with you in other matters; then be persuaded to let it have a due and full influence on you in this. If it has, and you have faith as a grain of mustard seed, how can you avoid believing that promoting family religion will be the best means to promote your own temporal as well as eternal welfare? "Godliness has the promise of the life that now is, as well as that which is to come" (I Timothy 4:8).

D. Terrors of the Lord.

Let a consideration of the terrors of the Lord persuade you to put into practice the pious resolution of the text. Remember, the time will come, and that perhaps very shortly, when we must all appear before the judgment seat of Christ where we must give a solemn and strict account how we have conducted ourselves in our respective families in this world. How will you endure to see your children, who ought to be your joy and crown of rejoicing in the day of our Lord Jesus Christ, coming out as so many witnesses against you?

CONCLUSION

I hope you have been in some measure convinced by what has been said of the importance of family religion and therefore are ready to cry out: "God forbid that we should forsake the Lord; we will (with our households) serve the Lord" (Joshua 24:16, 21). That there may always be such a heart in you, let me exhort all heads of families often to reflect on the worth of their own souls and the infinite ransom, Christ's blood, which has been paid for them.

SOUL DEJECTION

*Why art thou cast down, O my soul, and why art thou
disquieted within me? Hope thou in God, for I shall yet
praise Him, for the help of His countenance.*

—PSALM 42:5

I HONOR David when I see him yonder tending a few sheep. I admire the young stripling when I see him come out with his sling and stones and aiming at the head of Goliath, the enemy of God; or when exalted and filling the seat of justice. However, to me he never appears greater than when he is bowed down in low circumstances, beset on every side, struggling between sense and faith; and like the sun after an eclipse, breaking forth with greater luster to all the spectators.

I. ASPECTS OF SOUL DEJECTION.

A. The Psalmist Asks the Cause of His Soul Dejection.

Suppose you understand the words as a question. "Why art thou cast down, O my soul" though thou art in such circumstances? What is the cause of being so dejected? The word implies that he was sinking under the weight of his present burden, like a person stooping under a load that lies on his shoulders; and the consequence of this pressure without was turmoil, uneasiness, and anxiety within. There is a connection between soul and body that when one is disordered the other sympathizes with it.

B. The Psalmist Chides Himself for His Soul Dejection.

You may understand it as chiding himself: How foolish is it to be thus drooping and dejected; how improper for one favored of God with so many providences and special privileges to stoop and be made subject to every temptation? Why do you give your enemies cause to find fault with Christianity on account of your gloomy looks and the disquietude of your heart? You see he speaks not to others, but to himself. I would to God we did thus learn to begin with ourselves.

II. THE CAUSES FOR SOUL DEJECTION.

A. Conviction of Sin.

Some poor soul will say, I am cast down with a sense of sin, the guilt of it, the enmity of it; the very aggravated circumstances that attend it appear and set themselves in battle array before me. Once I thought I had no sin, or that sin was not so exceeding sinful; but I now find it such a burden, I could almost say with Cain, "It is greater than I can bear." Perhaps you could say as one man said when under conviction of sin, "I believe God cannot be just unless He damn my wicked soul."

B. Unfaithfulness to God.

I hear someone say, I am cast down because after I knew God to be my God, after I knew Jesus to be my king, the devil and my unbelieving heart threw me down again. Would not God have me cast down? Would He not have me disquieted? You are gone far from your Father's house. If nothing else will do, may your Father whip you back home! Tender hearts, when they reflect how it was once, are cast down.

C. Temptation.

You may say, I am cast down because I am wearied with temptation. I am haunted with this and that evil suggestion until I am a terror to myself. Is it unbelief that dogs you wherever you go? Although it be night, there is some moon, blessed be God, or some stars. If there is a fog that you cannot see, God can quiet His people in the dark; He will make the enemy flee. God will comfort you and punish the devil for tempting you.

D. Trials.

You may say, I have one affliction after another; no sooner is one trial gone, but another follows. I think I shall have a little rest, the tormentor will not come near today, but no sooner has this been said, but another storm comes and the clouds return after the rain. With such experiences we think we must be cast down and ought to be disquieted. This was David's case, "All Thy waves and Thy billows are gone over me" (verse 7). I believe after that there were more waves to come than he had yet felt.

E. Fear.

Perhaps some of you may be cast down with fear, not of death only, but of judgment. I believe many people die a thousand times for fear of dying once. Pour soul, leave this to God, He will take care of your dying hour. "Having loved His own, He loves them to the end." He is a faithful, unchangeable friend that sticketh closer than a brother.

III. TRIUMPH OVER SOUL DEJECTION.

A. The Dejected Psalmist Goes to God.

He goes to God with his case, "O my God, my soul is cast down within me" (verse 6). Oh, that we would learn when in these moods to go more to God and less to man; then we should find more relief and Christianity would be less dishonored.

B. The Dejected Psalmist Trusts in God.

See how faith triumphs in the midst of all. No sooner does unbelief raise its head but faith immediately knocks it down. A never-failing maxim is here proposed, "Hope thou in God," trust in God, believe in Him. I am sure, and all of you who know Jesus Christ are persuaded of it too, that all our troubles arise from our unbelief. Unbelief is an injurious bar to comfort and a source of tormenting fear. On the contrary, faith bears everything.

C. The Dejected Psalmist Assures Himself in God.

The devil tells me my trouble is so great I shall never lift up my head again; but unbelief and Satan are liars. "I shall yet praise Him." My God will carry me through all. I shall praise Him for casting me down; I shall praise Him for that which is the cause of all my unrest. I shall see Him again and be favored with those transforming views with which He favored me in times past.

CONCLUSION

Oh that I could persuade one poor soul to fly to Jesus Christ! Make Him your refuge and then, however you may be cast down, you "shall yet praise Him." God help those who have believed to hope more and more in His salvation until faith be turned into vision and hope into fruition. Even so, Lord Jesus.

George Whitefield

SERMON SEVEN

CHRIST THE BELIEVER'S HUSBAND

For thy Maker is thy husband.
—ISAIAH 54:5

THE WORDS of our text point out to us a relationship which not only comprehends, but, in respect to nearness and dearness, exceeds all other relationships. I mean that of a husband. Although the words were originally spoken to the Jews, yet they are undoubtedly applicable to all believers in all ages. When enlarged upon in a proper manner they will afford us suitable matter of discourse for sinners and saints and for those who once walked in the light of His countenance but are now backslidden from Him.

I. THE REQUIREMENTS FOR THIS RELATIONSHIP.

A. Freedom from All Preengagements.

We are all by nature born under and wedded to the Law as a covenant of works. Hence it is that we are so fond of, and artfully go about to establish a righteousness of our own. But before we can say, "our Maker is our husband," we must be made free from our old husband the Law; we must renounce our own righteousness, our own doings and performances, in point of dependence, whether in whole or part, as dross for the excellency of the knowledge of Christ.

B. Mutual Consent.

Before we can say that "our Maker is our husband" we must be made willing people in the day of God's power. We must be sweetly and effectually persuaded by the Holy Spirit of God that the glorious Emmanuel is willing to accept us just as we are and also that we are willing to accept Him upon His own terms, yea, upon any terms.

C. Union.

We are called Christians after Christ's name, because made partakers of Christ's nature. Out of His fulness believers receive grace for grace. Therefore the marriage state, especially by Paul, is frequently used as a figure of the real and vital union between Christ and believers. This is termed in Ephesians 5:32, "a great mystery." Great as it is, we must all experience it before we can say, "Our Maker is our husband."

II. THE DUTIES IN CONNECTION WITH THIS RELATIONSHIP.

A. Reverence.

"Let the wife see that she reverence her husband" (Ephesians 5:33). May I not apply this caution to you who are married to Jesus Christ? See to it that you reverence and respect your husband. I say, see to it. For the devil will be often suggesting to you hard and mean thoughts about your husband (Christ). Besides, in the eyes of the world, Jesus Christ has no form or comeliness. Therefore, unless you watch and pray you will not keep up such high thoughts of Him as He deserves.

B. Worthy Walk.

"The woman is the glory of the man" (I Corinthians 11:7) even as the church is the glory of Christ. Agreeable to this are the apostle's words, "Whether you eat or drink, or whatsoever you do, do all the glory of God" (I Corinthians 10:31) and "walk worthy of God" (I Thessalonians 2:12). You are His glory and you should so walk that He will be glorified in you.

C. Subjection.

Because wives are to be subject to their own husbands, how much more ought believers, whether men or women, to be subject to Jesus

Christ. He is the head of the church and has purchased her by His blood. Believers therefore are not their own, but are under the highest obligations to glorify and obey Christ in their bodies and souls which are His.

D. Faithfulness.

How carefully ought Christians to keep their souls chaste, pure, and undefiled. There is such a thing as spiritual adultery (James 4:4). Hence it is that the apostle John, in the most endearing manner, exhorts believers to "keep themselves from idols" (I John 5:31). Every time we place our affections upon anything more than Christ we commit spiritual adultery. For then we allow a creature to rival the Creator.

E. Fruitfulness.

If we are married to Jesus Christ we must be fruitful in every good work. We are dead to the law and married to Christ in order "that we should bring forth fruit unto God" (Romans 7:4). Titus is commanded to exhort believers to "be careful to maintain good works" (3:8). "Herein," says Christ, "is My Father glorified, that ye bear much fruit" (John 15:8).

III. THE CONDITION OF THE PERSONS WHO HAVE NEVER EXPERIENCED THIS RELATIONSHIP.

A. They Are Married to the Law.

If you are not married to Jesus Christ you are married to the Law. Do you not hear, you that seek to be justified in the sight of God by your works, what God says to those who are under the Law? "Cursed is everyone that continueth not in all things that are written in the book of the Law, to do them" (Galatians 3:10).

B. They Are Married to the World.

Why are you so wedded to the world? Did it ever prove faithful or satisfactory to any of its votaries? The sum total of worldly happiness is stated by Solomon: "All is vanity and vexation of spirit" (Ecclesiastes 1:14). A greater than Solomon has informed us that a man's life does not consist in the things he possesses (Luke 12:15).

C. They Are Married to the Flesh.

What reasons can you give for being wedded to your lusts? Might not the ancient galley slaves as reasonably be wedded to their chains? Do not your lusts fetter your souls? Do they not have dominion over you? Do they not say, Come, and ye come; Go, and ye go; Do this, and ye do it? Is not he or she who lives in pleasure dead while he lives?

D. They Are Married to the Devil.

How can you bear the thoughts of being wedded to the devil, as is every natural man? How can you bear to be ruled by one who is such a professed, open enemy to the most high and holy God? He will make a drudge of you while you live and be your companion in endless and extreme torment after death.

CONCLUSION

The Lord Jesus is the fountain of wisdom and makes all who come to Him wise unto salvation. As He is wise, so is He holy. Therefore He is called the Holy One of Israel. Nor is His beauty inferior to His wisdom and holiness. "He is altogether lovely." He is altogether loving. His name and His nature is love. He manifested His love by dying for us.

THE POTTER
AND THE CLAY

The word which came to Jeremiah from the Lord, saying, "Arise,
and go down to the potter's house, and there I will cause thee to
hear my words." Then I went down to the potter's house, and, be-
hold, he wrought a work on the wheels. And the vessel that he
made of clay was marred in the hand of the potter: so he made it
again another vessel, as seemed good to the potter to make it. Then
the word of the Lord came to me, saying, "O house of Israel, cannot
I do with you as this potter?" saith the Lord. Behold, as the clay is
in the potter's hand, so are ye in mine hand, O house of Israel.
—JEREMIAH 18:1–6

SOMETIMES God was pleased to send a prophet on some special errand and while he was thus employed a particular message was given to him
which he was ordered to deliver to all the inhabitants of the land. An instruc-
tive instance of this kind is recorded in the passage we are now to consider.
But what Jehovah here says of Israel in general is applicable to every man individually.

I. UNREGENERATE MAN IS A PIECE OF MARRED CLAY.

A. Man's Original State.

1. The Scriptural statement. "And God said, Let us make man in our
image, after our likeness. So God created man in His own image, in the image of God created He him" (Genesis 1:26, 27).

2. The Scriptural statement explained. Man was originally made upright. He was created "after God" in knowledge, as well as righteousness and true holiness.

B. Man's Present State.

Man soon fell from his primeval dignity and by that fall the divine image became defaced.

1. His knowledge is affected. In respect to natural things man's understanding is evidently darkened. He can know only a little and that knowledge which he can acquire is with much weariness of the flesh. In respect to spiritual things his understanding is not only darkened, but has become darkness itself.

2. His will is perverted. Man is the image of God; undoubtedly before the fall man had no other will but his Maker's. There was not the least disunion between them. Now man has a will as directly contrary to the will of God as light is contrary to darkness, or heaven to hell.

3. His affections are defiled. Man's affections when first placed in Eden were always kept within proper bounds and fixed upon proper objects. Now the scene is changed. We are now naturally full of vile affections. We love what we should hate and hate what we should love; we fear what we should hope for and hope for what we should fear.

4. His conscience is corrupted. In the soul of the first man Adam conscience was, undoubtedly, the candle of the Lord and enabled him rightly and instantaneously to discern between right and wrong. Some remains of this are yet left, but it burns dimly and is easily covered or extinguished.

5. His reason is depraved. There will come a time when those who despise and oppose divine revelation will find that what they now call reason is only reason depraved and incapable of itself to guide us into the way of peace or show the way of salvation, as the men of Sodom were unable to find Lot's door when they were struck with blindness.

6. His body is in a state of humiliation. Without attempting to be wise above what is written; we may venture to affirm that originally man had a body which knew no sin, sickness, nor pain; but now its primitive strength and glory has departed.

II. THE NECESSITY FOR THE UNREGENERATE MAN'S RENEWAL.

A. The Fact of Man's Present Condition.

I have been purposely explicit on the unregenerate man's present condition so we may venture to say, "Grant the foregoing doctrine to be true, then you cannot deny the necessity of man's renewal."

B. The Hope of Heaven.

1. Two concepts of heaven. (a) Because the Scriptures, in condescension to the weakness of our capacities, describe heaven by images taken from earthly delights and human grandeur, therefore men are apt to carry their thoughts no higher. (b) Heaven is a state as well as a place. Consequently, unless you are previously disposed by a suitable state of mind you cannot be happy in heaven.

2. The necessity of a moral change. To make us ready to be blissful partakers of the heavenly company this "marred clay," our depraved natures, must undergo a universal moral change. Old things must pass away, all things must become new.

III. THE METHOD OF THE UNREGENERATE MAN'S RENEWAL.

A. Negatively Stated.

1. It is more than moral persuasion. If it is asked how this great change is to be effected, I answer, not by the mere dint and force of moral persuasion. This is good in its place, but it will not produce the necessary change.

2. It is more than the power of free will. "No man," says Christ, "can come to Me unless the Father draw him" (John 6:44). Our own free will, if exercised, may restrain us from committing evil and place us in the way of conversion; but after exerting our efforts, and we are bound in duty to do so, we will find it true that "man since the fall has no power to turn to God."

B. Positively Stated.

1. It is the work of the Holy Spirit. The heavenly Potter is the Spirit of God, the third person of the adorable Trinity. This is the Spirit who moved on the face of the waters, who overshadowed the Holy Virgin. He must move upon the chaos of our souls in order to be sons of God.

2. It is a miraculous work of the Holy Spirit. This miracle of miracles, turning the soul to God, will continue until time shall be no more. True believers are said to be born from above, to be born not of blood, nor of the will of man, but of God (John 3:3, 7; 1:13).

CONCLUSION

To produce this new creation, Jesus left His Father's bosom, led a persecuted life, died an ignominious and accursed death, rose again, and is seated on His Father's right hand. All His precepts and providences, all divine revelation center in these two points: our fallen condition; and to begin, carry on, and complete a change in our souls.

THE LORD OUR RIGHTEOUSNESS

The Lord our righteousness.
—JEREMIAH 23:6

THE RIGHTEOUSNESS of Jesus Christ seems to be one of the first lessons that God taught man after the fall. The coats that God made to put on our first parents were types of the application of the merits of the righteousness of our Lord to the believers' hearts. We may infer that those coats came from animals slain in sacrifice in commemoration of the great sacrifice upon Calvary.

I. THE IDENTIFICATION OF THE LORD.

A. He Is Jesus Christ.

The person mentioned in the text under the character of Lord is Jesus Christ. The Lord our righteousness is the righteous branch of verse 5 and all agree that the righteous branch is Jesus Christ.

B. He Is God.

Because the word "Lord" properly belongs to Christ, He must be God. For as you have it in the margins of your Bibles, the word "Lord" is in the original Jehovah which is the essential title of God Himself. Therefore, He must be very God of very God, or as the apostle devoutly expresses it, "God blessed forever" (Romans 9:5).

II. THE EXPLANATIONS OF THE LORD OUR RIGHTEOUSNESS.

A. *Man's Need.*

The third chapter of Genesis gives us a full but mournful account how our first parents sinned and thereby stood in need of a better righteousness than their own in order to procure their future acceptance with God.

B. *God's Provision.*

Christ not only died, but lived; not only suffered, but obeyed for or in the stead of sinners. Both of these jointly make up that complete righteousness which is to be imputed to us, as the disobedience of our first parents was made ours by imputation. In this sense, and no other, are we to understand that parallel which Saint Paul draws in the fifth chapter of Romans between the first and second Adam.

III. THE CONSIDERATION OF THE OBJECTIONS AGAINST THE DOCTRINE OF THE LORD OUR RIGHTEOUSNESS.

A. *"The Doctrine of Imputed Righteousness Is Destructive of Good Works."*

Never was there a reformation brought about in the church, but by preaching of the doctrine of Christ's imputed righteousness. It excludes works from being any cause of our justification in the sight of God. It requires good works as a proof of our having this righteousness imputed to us and as a declarative evidence of our justification in the sight of men. Then how can the doctrine of imputed righteousness be a doctrine leading to licentiousness?

B. *"The Doctrine of Imputed Righteousness Is Not the Teaching of the Sermon on the Mount."*

In this sermon our Lord speaks of inward piety, such as purity of heart, and hungering and thirsting after righteousness, and then recommends good works as an evidence of our having His righteousness imputed to us, and these graces and divine tempers wrought in our hearts. Then He adds, "Think not that I am come to destroy the moral law—I come not to destroy, to take away the force of it as a rule of life, but to fulfill, to obey it."

C. *"The Doctrine of Imputed Righteousness Is Not the Teaching of Mark 10:17–22."*

Our Lord by referring the young man to the commandments did not in the least hint that his morality would recommend him to God's mercy and favor. He intended thereby to make the Law his schoolmaster to bring him to Himself; that the young man, seeing how he had broken every commandment, might thereby be convinced of his own insufficiency and the absolute necessity of looking for a better righteousness whereon he might depend for eternal life.

D. *"The Doctrine of Imputed Righteousness Is Not the Teaching of Matthew 25:34–36."*

This refers to rewards and not salvation. That the people did not depend on these good actions for their justification in the sight of God is evident from verses 37–39. They were so far from depending on their works for justification in the sight of God that they were filled as it were with a holy blushing to think that our Lord should mention and reward them for their poor works of faith and labors of love.

IV. THE EVIL CONSEQUENCES OF THE REJECTION OF THE DOCTRINE OF THE LORD OUR RIGHTEOUSNESS.

A. *The Rejectors Turn the Word of God into a Lie.*

It would be endless to enumerate the number of Scripture texts that must be false if this doctrine is not true. Let it suffice to affirm in general that if we deny an imputed righteousness we may as well deny a divine revelation all at once. For it is the alpha and omega, the beginning and the end of the book of God. We must either disbelieve the Bible or believe what the prophet has spoken in the text, "the Lord our righteousness."

B. *The Rejector Becomes a Setter Forth of Unscriptural Teaching.*

Suppose I told you that you must intercede with saints in order that they may intercede with God for you; or, that the death of Christ was not sufficient without our death added to it? Might you not then justly call me a setter forth of strange doctrines? Is it not equally absurd and blasphemous to join our obedience, either wholly or in part, with the obedience of Christ—both active and passive?

C. The Rejector Is Doomed to Eternal Torment.

If there be no such thing as the doctrine of an imputed righteousness then those who hold it and bring forth fruit unto holiness are safe. If there be such a thing (as there certainly is), what will become of you who deny it? It is no difficult matter to determine. Your portion must be in the lake of fire and brimstone forever and ever; because you will rely upon your works, by your works you shall be judged.

CONCLUSION

Can anything appear more reasonable, even according to your own way of arguing, than the doctrine of "the Lord our righteousness"? Have you not felt a convincing power go along with the Word? Why then will you not believe on the Lord Jesus Christ in order that He may become the Lord your righteousness? For think you, O sinners, that you will be able to stand in the day of judgment if Christ is not your righteousness? No, that alone is the wedding garment in which you must appear.

George Whitefield

SERMON TEN

CHRIST'S EVERLASTING RIGHTEOUSNESS

And to bring in everlasting righteousness.
—DANIEL 9:24

THE WORDS chosen for the text of the present meditation contain part of a revelation made to the prophet Daniel. If you look back to the beginning of this chapter (verses 2–4), you will find how this good man was employed when God was pleased to give him this revelation. He made the Bible his constant study; for it is the Bible we are to understand by what is here termed books. He prayed and confessed his sins and those of the people.

I. THE EXPLANATION OF RIGHTEOUSNESS.

A. There Is a Righteousness Which Signifies Moral Honesty.

In various passages of Scripture the word righteousness has no other meaning or, at least, bears the meaning of moral honesty, that is, doing justice between man and man. When Paul reasoned with Felix about righteousness (Acts 24:25), he preached to him of the necessity of doing justice because he had been an unjust man; and he put before him the judgment to come in order to make him come to Christ for deliverance from the bad consequences of that judgment.

B. There Is a Righteousness Which Signifies Holiness.

It likewise signifies inward holiness which is wrought in us by the blessed Spirit of God.

C. There Is Righteousness Which Is Imputed.

I believe the word righteousness in the text signifies an imputed righteousness, or the righteousness of the Lord Jesus Christ which is imputed to poor sinners when they believe in Christ as Lord and Savior. By righteousness I understand all that Christ has done and all that Christ has suffered: put these two together and they make up the righteousness of the Lord Jesus Christ. Blessed be God for this righteousness! Blessed be God for the adjective which in the text is used with this righteousness—everlasting righteousness.

II. THE REASON CHRIST'S RIGHTEOUSNESS IS CALLED EVERLASTING.

A. Because It Extends to Mankind from Eternity.

This should deepen our love to God, to think that from all the ages of eternity God had thoughts of us; God intended the Lord Jesus Christ to save our souls; hence it is that God, to endear Jeremiah to Him, tells him, "I have loved thee with an everlasting love." All that we receive in time flows from that inexhaustible fountain, God's everlasting love. Therefore, the righteousness of Jesus Christ may properly be called an everlasting righteousness, because God intended it from everlasting.

B. Because All Saints Are Saved by Christ's Rihteousness.

It is called an everlasting righteousness because the efficacy of Christ's death took place immediately upon Adam's fall. The righteousness of Jesus Christ may be called an everlasting righteousness because all of the saints that have been saved or ever will be saved are all saved by the righteousness of Christ. It was through the faith in Christ that Abel was saved; it was through the sacrifice of Christ that Abraham and the prophets were accepted. Because persons under the law and under the Gospel are saved through Christ, therefore, Christ's righteousness may be called an everlasting righteousness.

C. Because Its Efficacy Will Continue to the End of Time.

The righteousness of Jesus Christ is called an everlasting righteousness because the efficacy thereof will continue until time shall be no more. The efficacy of the Lord Jesus' blood, death, and atonement is as great and effectual now to the salvation of poor sinners as when He bowed His head and gave up His spirit. Whosoever believes on Him now shall see His power, shall taste of His grace, and shall be actually saved by Him the same as if he had been in company with those who saw Him expiring.

D. Because Its Benefit Endures to Everlasting Life.

Christ's righteousness may be called an everlasting righteousness because the benefit of it is to endure to everlasting life. No wicked demon nor your own depraved heart shall be able to separate you from the love of God. God has loved you, He has fixed His heart upon you, and having loved His own, He loves them unto the end. Those who once take hold of Christ's righteousness shall be saved everlastingly by Him. Our salvation depends not upon our own free will, but upon God's free grace.

III. THE SIGNIFICANCE OF THE WORDS "TO BRING IN."

A. It Is Our Lord's Promulgation and Proclamation of His Righteousness to the World.

His righteousness was brought in under the law; but then it was brought in under types and shadows. But Jesus Christ brought life and immortality to light by the Gospel. The light of Moses was only twilight; the light of the Gospel is like the sun at noonday. Therefore, Christ may be said to bring in this everlasting righteousness, because He proclaimed it to the world and commanded it to be preached that God sent His Son into the world that the world through Him might be saved.

B. It Is Our Lord's Working Out His Righteousness on the Cross.

Again, the Lord Jesus Christ brought in this righteousness as He wrought it out for sinners upon the cross. Although man is justified, in God's mind, from all eternity, yet it was not actually brought in until the Lord Jesus Christ pronounced the words, "It is finished"; the grand consummation! Then Jesus brought it in. A new and living way was opened into the holy of holies for poor sinners, by the blood of Christ.

C. It Is the Holy Spirit's Bringing Christ's Righteousness into a Man's Soul.

All that Christ has done, all that Christ has suffered will do us no good unless by the Spirit of God it is brought into our souls. As one expresses it, "an unapplied Christ is no Christ at all." To hear of a Christ dying for sinners will only increase one's damnation, will only sink him deeper into hell, unless he has ground to say by a work of grace wrought in his heart that the Lord Jesus has brought this home to him.

CONCLUSION

Are any of you depending on a righteousness of your own? Do any of you think to save yourselves by your own doings? I say to you, your righteousness shall perish with you. The righteousness of Jesus Christ is an everlasting righteousness wrought out for the very chief of sinners. Christ's righteousness will cover, His blood will cleanse you from the guilt of all sin. Oh, come, come! How will you stand before an angry God without the righteousness of the Lord Jesus Christ?

George Whitefield

THE TEMPTATION
OF CHRIST

Then was Jesus led up of the Spirit into the wilderness,
to be tempted of the devil.
—MATTHEW 4:1

LET US with serious attention consider when, where, and how our Savior fought and overcame the devil. Matthew (4:1–11) is very particular in relating the preparations for, the beginning, the process, and issue of this important combat.

I. THE CIRCUMSTANCES OF THE TEMPTATION.

A. The Time.

1. It was immediately following Christ's baptism. In the close of chapter 3 we are told that Jesus was baptized and inaugurated to His mediatorial office by the opened heavens, descent of the Spirit and the voice from heaven.

2. It was about the time of the beginning of Christ's public ministry. He was about to show Himself openly unto Israel.

3. It was when Christ was full of the Holy Spirit. When He was full of the Holy Spirit (Luke 4:1), even then He was led with a holy unconstrained violence as a champion into the field to engage an enemy whom He was sure to conquer.

B. The Place.

1. It was a lonesome wilderness. But whither is this conqueror led? He is led into a lonesome, wide, howling wilderness. He was probably led, according to Matthew Henry, into the great wilderness of Sinai.

2. It was a wild beast-infested wilderness. It was not only a lonesome wilderness, but inhabited, also, by wild beasts (Mark 1:13). Hither was our Lord led to pray and fast and meet His adversary.

C. The Conditions.

1. He fasted. Neither does He content Himself with praying, but He fasts also, and that forty days and forty nights (Matthew 4:2), even as Moses and Elijah had done many years before; it may be in the very same place.

2. He hungered. We may suppose that during these forty days our Lord felt no hunger. Converse with heaven to Him was instead of meat and drink; but "afterwards He was a hungered"; exceedingly so, no doubt. Now the important fight begins.

II. THE CONFLICT OF THE TEMPTATION.

A. The Nature of the Temptation.

1. To gender doubt. Probably transformed into the appearance of an angel of light, Satan tempts our Lord to nothing less than to doubt that He is the Son of God. "If Thou be the Son of God" (verse 3).

2. To encourage presumption. Because Satan cannot draw Him to distrust or despair, he will now try to prevail on Him to presume. He takes Jesus to the pinnacle of the Temple in Jerusalem and bids Him to cast Himself down to prove His deity (verses 5–6).

3. To appeal to pride. In the third temptation Satan takes Christ into a high mountain and shows Him the kingdoms of the world and their glory; promising them to Him upon the condition of worshipping the Adversary (verses 8–9).

B. The Manner of Meeting the Temptation.

1. The use of God's Word. Although the Lord Jesus had the Spirit of God without measure and might have made use of a thousand other ways, yet He answered the tempter with texts of Scripture. Each time He quoted from Deuteronomy.

2. The use of the word of rebuke. After the third temptation our Lord, filled with a holy resentment, said "Get thee hence, Satan" (verse 10). Get thee hence, I will bear thy insolence no longer.

C. The Outcome of the Temptation.

1. Christ victorious. Now the battle is over. The important combat is ended. Jesus has won the field.

2. Satan defeated. Satan is routed and totally put to flight. "Then," when the devil found that Jesus could withstand even the golden bait, the lust of the eye and the pride of life, in the last two, as well as the lust of the flesh in the first temptation, despairing of the least success, "he leaveth Him."

III. THE CONSIDERATION OF THE LESSONS OF THE TEMPTATION.

A. Solitude May Be Harmful.

1. Proper solitude is profitable. Was our Lord violently beset in the wilderness? Then we may learn that however profitable solitude may be when used in due season, yet when carried too far is hurtful.

2. Extreme solitude encourages temptation. Woe be to him that is always alone! He has not another to lift him when he falls or to advise him when he is tempted. Lord, keep us from leading ourselves into this temptation and support and deliver us when led by Thy providence into it.

B. The Path of Preparation for Christian Service.

1. Exemplified by our Lord. Did our Lord by prayer, fasting, and temptation prepare himself for His public ministry? Surely then all those who profess to be inwardly moved by the Holy Spirit to take upon them the office and administration of the church should be prepared in the same manner.

2. The reason for this need. Without a knowledge of Satan's devices, a minister will be like a physician who prescribes to the sick without having studied medicine. If you would be useful in comforting broken hearts and wounded souls, prepare yourselves for manifold temptation.

C. The Time of Poverty Is the Time of Temptation.

1. The nature of the temptation. Let those of you who are reduced to a low estate learn that an hour of poverty is an hour of temptation, not only to murmuring and doubting our sonship and Divine favor, but also to help ourselves by unlawful means.

2. The responsibility of the tempted. Remember that poverty and temptation are not marks of being cast off by God. Learn of Him not to distrust, but rather to trust in your heavenly Father.

D. The Successful Weapon Against Temptation.

1. The Word of God. Let us learn of our Lord to fight the devil with the Sword of the Spirit, which is the Word of God. We may say of it, as David did of Goliath's sword, "None like this."

2. The power of the Word of God. Had God's children observed to use the Scriptures correctly, how much strange fire would have been extinguished; how many imaginary revelations would have been detected; how many triumphs of Satan would have been prevented!

CONCLUSION

He who conquered for us in the wilderness will make us also more than conquerors over all trials and temptations and over death and hell itself, through His almighty, everlasting, and never-failing love.

George Whitefield

SERMON TWELVE

CHRIST THE SUPPORT
OF THE TEMPTED

Lead us not into temptation.
—MATTHEW 6:13

THE GREAT and important duty of every Christian is to guard against all appearance of evil; to watch against the first risings in the heart of evil and to guard our actions that they may not be sinful or even seem to be so. It is true that the devil is continually tempting us, and our own evil hearts are ready to join with the tempter, to make us fall into sins, that thereby he might obtain a victory over us and we become his slaves. The Lord Jesus seeing how His disciples and others are liable to be overcome by temptation advises them to pray that they might not be led into it.

I. THE TEMPTER.

A. His Identification.

The tempter is Satan, the prince of the power of the air, he that now rules in the children of disobedience (Ephesians 2:2). He is an enemy of God and goodness, he is a hater of all truth. For no other reason did he slander God in paradise. For no other reason did he say to Eve, "You shall not surely die" (Genesis 3:4).

B. His Character.

The tempter is full of malice, envy, and revenge; for what else could enduce him to molest the innocent man in Eden? The person that tempts you is remarkable for his subtlety: for not having power given him from above, he is obliged to wait for opportunities to betray us and to catch us by guile. Therefore he made use of the serpent to tempt our first parent. To lie in wait to deceive is another part of his character. Although this character is given of the devil, if we were to examine our own hearts we would find many of the tempter's characteristics legible in us.

II. THE TEMPTER'S REASONS FOR TEMPTING.

A. Because He Is Envious.

Why he tempts you is the second thing I am to show you. It is out of envy to you and to the Lord Jesus Christ.

B. Because He Wishes to Keep Men from Christ.

If he can keep you from laying hold by faith on Christ, he knows he has you safe enough. The more temptations you are under, and according to their nature and greatness, the more you are disturbed in your minds; and the more unsettled your thoughts and affections are, the more apt you are to conclude that He would not receive you. This is the policy of the tempter, to make you have low and dishonorable thoughts of Christ. Therefore, by degrees he works upon your minds insomuch that you become careless and indifferent about Christ. Nothing will please him more than to see you ruined and lost forever.

III. THE TEMPTER'S METHODS.

A. Flattery.

He endeavors to make you think sin is not so great as it is; that there is no occasion of being overstrict and that you are overly righteous; that you are ostentatious, and will do yourselves harm by it and that you will destroy yourselves. He shows you the bait, but he hides the hook. He shows you the pleasures, profits, and advantages that attend the abundance of his world's goods; but he does not show you the crosses, losses, and vexations that you may have while you are in the enjoyment of the blessings of this world.

B. Doubts and Discouragements.

He throws doubts and discouragements in your mind, whether the way you are in is the true way or not. He may suggest, What! Do you expect to be saved by Christ? Also, he may suggest, Christ did not die for you; you have been too great a sinner; you have lived in sin so long and committed such sins against Christ which He will not forgive.

C. Persecution.

When he finds he cannot allure in some way, he will try you by frowns and the terrors of this world. He will stir up people to point at you. He will stir them up to jeer, scoff, backbite, and hate you. Sometimes when the people of God are met to worship Him, Satan sends his agents, the scoffers, to disturb them.

IV. THE SECRET OF VICTORY OVER TEMPTATION.

A. Confession.

I shall now show you how earnest you ought to be with Jesus Christ, either not to suffer you to be led into temptation or to preserve you under it. Let me beseech you to go to Christ and tell Him how you are assaulted by the Evil One, who lies in wait for your souls. Tell Him you are not able to master the tempter in your own strength.

B. Prayer.

Beg the Lord Jesus' assistance and you will find Him ready to help you. He will give you strength to resist the fiery darts of the devil and therefore, you can nowhere find one so able to relieve you. He knows what it is to be tempted and He will give you the assistance of His Spirit to resist Satan, who will then flee from you. In Christ Jesus you have the strength you need. Fear not, for in the name of the Lord we shall overcome all our spiritual Amalekites. Let them rage, Jesus Christ has them in His power and they shall go no farther than He permits them.

C. Committal.

If Satan and his followers could do us all the mischief they desired, very few of us should be permitted to see our habitations anymore; but blessed be God, we can commit ourselves to His protection. He has been our protector hitherto and He will be so still. Let us keep looking up unto Jesus.

CONCLUSION

You have found Jesus Christ assisting you and supporting you under all the temptations of this life, is not He the chiefest of ten thousand and the altogether lovely One? Now you see a form and beauty in Christ which you never saw before. Oh! How do you and I wish we had known Jesus sooner and that we had more of His love—it is condescending love; it is amazing love, it is forgiving love, it is dying love, it is exalted and interceding love, it is glorified love.

SERMON THIRTEEN

WHAT DO YOU THINK
OF JESUS CHRIST?

What think ye of Christ?
—MATTHEW 22:42

WHEN it pleased the eternal Son of God to tabernacle among men and preach the glad tidings of salvation to a fallen world, different opinions were entertained by different persons concerning Him as to His person and work. Thus today, professing Christians are sadly divided in their thoughts about Him. Therefore, to inform your consciences I will ask you a few questions concerning Christ.

I. WHAT DO YOU THINK OF THE DEITY OF JESUS CHRIST?

A. The Importance of His Deity.

1. It is a foundation stone of the church. The confession of our Lord's deity is the rock upon which God builds His church. If it were possible to take this away, the gates of hell would quickly prevail against the church.

2. It is necessary to salvation. If Jesus Christ is not God, I would never preach the Gospel of Christ again. It would not be Gospel. It would be only a system of moral ethics. It is the deity of our Lord that gives a sanction to His death and makes Him such a high priest as became us, who by the infinite merits of His suffering could fully satisfy an infinitely offended justice.

334

B. The Proof of His Deity.

1. The testimony of inspired apostles. We hear the apostle John pronouncing so positively that the Word (Jesus Christ) was not only with God, but was God (John 1:1). Saint Paul also says that the Lord Jesus was in the form of God: that in Him dwelt "all the fulness of the godhead bodily" (Colossians 2:9).

2. The testimony of Christ Himself. Christ assumed the title which God the Father gave to Himself when He sent Moses to deliver His people Israel: "Before Abraham was, I am" (Exodus 3:14; John 8:58). And again, "I and My Father are one." It is evident that the Jews understood our Lord when He spoke thus as making Himself equal with the Father; otherwise, why did they stone Him as a blasphemer (John 10:30–33)?

II. WHAT DO YOU THINK OF THE MANHOOD OF JESUS CHRIST?

A. The Reason for the Incarnation.

1. Man's present condition is not his original state. It was God who made us. I would willingly think that no person is so blasphemous as to suppose that since God made us, He made such creatures as we now find ourselves to be. This would be giving God's Word the lie, which tells us that "in the image of God (not the image which we now bear on our souls) made He man" (Genesis 1:27).

2. Man's present condition is the result of sin. God placed man in the Garden of Eden and condescended to enter into a covenant with him, promising eternal life upon the condition of obedience and threatening eternal death for disobedience. Man disobeyed, and acting as our representative involved both himself and us in the curse resulting from the fall. The reason why the Son of God took upon Him our nature was the fall.

B. The Purpose of the Incarnation.

1. The eternal provision. The eternal God, foreseeing how Satan would bruise the heel of man, had in His eternal counsel provided a means whereby He might bruise that accursed serpent's head. The Lord Jesus, the only begotten Son of God, offered to die to make an atonement for man's transgression and to fulfill all righteousness in his stead.

2. The fulfillment of the eternal provision. Because it was impossible for Christ to die for our sins in that He was God and also because man had offended, it was necessary that atonement should be made in the person of man. Therefore, rather than that we should perish, Christ, the everlasting God, became man to fulfill the law and die for us in order to procure a union between God and our souls.

III. WHAT DO YOU THINK OF JUSTIFICATION THROUGH JESUS CHRIST?

A. False Views of Justification.

1. Justification apart from Christ. What do you think about being justified by Christ? I believe I can answer for some of you. Many, I fear, think to be justified, that is, looked upon as righteous in God's sight, without Jesus Christ. However, such will find themselves dreadfully mistaken: for out of Christ, "God is a consuming fire."

2. Universal justification. Others satisfy themselves with believing that Christ came into the world to save sinners in general; whereas their chief concern should be how they may be assured that Christ came to save them in particular. He "gave Himself for me" (Galatians 2:20). It is this immediate application of Christ to our own hearts that renders His merits effectual to our eternal salvation.

3. Cooperative justification. Others there are who go still further. They believe that Jesus Christ is the God-man. They hold that He is to be applied to their hearts and that they can be justified in God's sight only in and through Him. But they make Him only in part a Saviour because they are for doing what they can themselves and then Jesus Christ is to take up the deficiencies of their righteousness.

B. Scriptural Teaching on Justification.

1. It is through faith. We are justified through faith in Jesus Christ, without any regard to any work or fitness foreseen in us. All we have to do is to lay hold on His righteousness by faith. The very moment we apprehend it by a living faith, that moment we may be assured that the blood of Jesus Christ has cleansed us from all sin.

2. It is gratuitous. Salvation is the free gift of God. In the great work of man's redemption boasting is entirely excluded; which could not be if any one of our works were to be joined with the merits of Christ. Our salvation is all of God, from the beginning to the end. It is not of works, lest any man should boast; man has no hand in it (Ephesians 2:8–9).

CONCLUSION

This is glad tidings of great joy to all that feel themselves poor, lost, undone, condemned sinners. "Ho, every one that thirsteth, come unto the waters of life, and drink freely; come and buy, without money and without price" (Isaiah 55:1). Behold a fountain opened in your Savior's side for sin and for all uncleanness. "Look unto Him whom ye have pierced:" look unto Him by faith and you shall be saved.

George Whitefield

SERMON FOURTEEN

BLIND BARTIMEUS

And Jesus said unto him, "Go thy way, thy faith hath made thee whole." And immediately he received his sight, and followed Jesus in the way.
—MARK 10:52

WHEN the apostle Peter was recommending Jesus of Nazareth in one of his sermons to the Jews, he gave Him a short, but withal a glorious and exalted character, "that He went about doing good." It was His meat and drink to do the works of Him who sent Him while the day of His public ministry lasted. He ministered to both the physical and spiritual needs. Sometimes the same person was the subject of both mercies. Such an example is Bartimeus (read Mark 10:46–52).

I. THE MAN'S NEED.

A. He Was Blind.

He had lost his sight. His case is still the more pitiful if he was, as some think his name indicates, the blind son of a blind father. Happy was it for Bartimeus that he could hear, though he could not see: for in all probability, upon hearing the noise and clamor of the people who followed our Lord, his curiosity led him to enquire about the cause of it.

B. He Was a Beggar.

Bartimeus, not being able to dig, begs for his living; and in order to make it a better trade, sat by the side of the highway—in all probability without or near the gate of the city where people must necessarily pass in and out.

338

II. THE MAN'S CRY.

A. It Was a Cry of Faith.

Although the eyes of his body were shut, yet the eyes of his mind were in some degree opened so that he saw, perhaps, more than most of the multitude that followed Jesus. As soon as he heard of it he began to cry out; which he would not have done had he not heard of Him before and believed that Christ was able and willing to restore sight to the blind.

B. It Was a Cry of Recognition of Jesus' Messiahship.

Bartimeus styles Him, "Jesus Thou Son of David." Thereby he gives evidence that he believed Him to be the Messiah who was to come into the world, unto whom the Lord God was to give the throne of His father David and of whose kingdom there was to be no end, of whom it had been long foretold (Isaiah 35) that when He should come "the eyes of the blind should be opened."

C. It Was a Cry of Confession of Need.

"He began to cry out." This implies that he had a deep sense of his own misery and the need of a cure. He began to cry out in order that Jesus might hear Him above the noise of the throng. He began to cry out as soon as he heard that Jesus was passing by, not knowing whether he might ever enjoy such an opportunity again.

D. It Was a Cry for Mercy.

"Have mercy upon me," the natural language of a soul brought to lie down at the feet of a sovereign God. Here is no laying claim to a cure by way of merit; no proud self-righteousness; no bringing in a reckoning of performances, nor any doubting of Jesus' power or willingness to heal him. He speaks out of the abundance of his heart and in the language of the poor, broken-hearted publican, he cries out, "Jesus, Thou Son of David, have mercy on me."

III. THE EFFECT OF THE MAN'S CRY.

A. The Effect in Relation to the Crowd.

We would think that such a moving petition as Bartimeus's would have melted the whole multitude, but instead of that, we are told that "many charged him." The word in the original seems to imply a charge attended with threatening, and spoken in an angry manner. They charged him "to hold his peace." It may be that they threatened to beat him if he did not. They looked upon him as beneath the notice of Jesus.

B. The Effect in Relation to Jesus Christ.

1. Jesus heard. How does the Son of David treat the blind beggar? Does He join with the multitude and charge him to hold his peace? Does He go on, thinking him to be beneath His notice? No; for Mark relates: "And Jesus stood still." Although on a journey and in haste, it is not losing time to stop now and then to do a good deed by the way.

2. Jesus called. Jesus "commanded him to be called." Why so? To teach us to be condescending and kind even to poor beggars and tacitly to reprove the misguided zeal of the people who had charged Bartimeus to hold his peace. By this also our Lord prepares the multitude the better to take more notice of the blind man's faith and of His own mercy and power extended in the healing of him.

3. Jesus healed. In reply to Jesus' question, "What wilt thou that I should do unto thee?" blind Bartimeus requested sight for his blinded eyes. "Jesus said unto him, Go thy way, thy faith hath made thee whole. And immediately he received his sight." With the word there went a power; and He that spoke light out of darkness, saying, "Let there be light, and there was light," commanded light into this poor blind beggar's eyes and behold there was light. The miracle was instantaneous: immediately he received his sight.

CONCLUSION

How do you find your hearts affected at the relating of this notable miracle which Jesus wrought? Are you not ready to break out into the language of the song of Moses and to say, "Who is like unto Thee, O Lord, glorious in holiness, fearful in praises, continually doing wonders!" Come unto Him, all ye that are weary and heavy laden, and He will refresh you, He will give you rest. Be not afraid, you seek Jesus; behold He comes to meet you.

George Whitefield

SERMON FIFTEEN

A REPENTANT HEART

Except ye repent, ye shall all likewise perish.
—LUKE 3:3

WHEN we consider how heinous and aggravating our offences are in the sight of a just and holy God, that they bring down His wrath upon our heads and occasion us to live under His indignation; how ought we thereby to be deterred from evil, or at least, to repent thereof and not commit the same again. Repentance denotes an abhorrence of evil and forsaking of it.

I. THE NATURE OF REPENTANCE.

A. It Is Sorrow for Sin.

Our sorrow and grief for sin must not spring merely from a fear of wrath; for if we have no other ground than that, it proceeds from self-love and not from any love to God. If love to God is not the chief motive of your repentance, your repentance is in vain and not to be considered true.

B. It Is Hatred of Sin.

It is not just your confessing yourselves to be sinners, it is not merely knowing your condition to be sad and deplorable. This is in vain so long as you continue in your sins. Your care and endeavors should be to get the heart thoroughly affected therewith, that you may feel yourselves to be lost and undone creatures. If you are enabled to groan under the weight and burden of your sins, then Christ will ease you and give you rest.

C. It Is the Forsaking of Sin.

Resolve to leave all of your sinful lusts and pleasures. Abhor, renounce, forsake your old sinful course of life and serve God in holiness and righteousness the rest of your life. If you lament and bewail past sins and do not forsake them, your repentance is in vain; you are mocking God and deceiving your own soul. You must put off the old man with his deeds before you can put on the new man, Christ Jesus.

II. THE CAUSES OF REPENTANCE.

A. It Is God.

Now, as to the causes of repentance. The first cause is God. He is the Author, for "we are born of God" (John 1:13). God has begotten us, even God, the Father of our Lord Jesus Christ. It is He that stirs up to will and to do of His own good pleasure.

B. It Is God's Grace.

Another cause of repentance is God's free grace; it is owing to "the riches of His grace" (Ephesians 1:7), my brethren, that we have been prevented from going down to hell long ago; it is because the compassions of the Lord fail not, they are new every morning and fresh every evening.

C. It May Be through the Instrumentality of a Saint of God.

Sometimes the instruments are very unlikely. A poor despised minister or other member of the body of Christ may, by the power of God, be made the means in His hands of bringing men to true evangelical repentance. This may be done to show that the power is not in men, but that it is entirely owing to the good pleasure of God.

III. THE NECESSITY FOR REPENTANCE.

A. Because Man Is a Sinner.

Since we have sinned it is necessary to repent. A holy God could not, nor ever can, or will, admit anything that is unholy into His presence. There must be a change in heart and life before there can be a dwelling with God. No unclean person can stand in the presence of God; it is contrary to the holiness of His nature. There is a contrariety between the holy nature of God and the unholy nature of carnal and unregenerate men.

B. Because There Can Be No Communication between God and the Sinner.

What communication can there be between a sinless God and creatures full of sin; between a God of purity and impure creatures? If you were to be admitted into heaven in your inpenitent condition, heaven would be a hell to you; the songs of angels would be intolerable to you. Therefore you must be changed, you must be holy as God is holy (I Peter 1:15–16). He must be your God on earth and you must be His people or you will never dwell together throughout eternity.

C. Because a Sinner Cannot Be Admitted into Heaven.

Singing praises to Him who sits upon the throne and to the Lamb is the employment of all who are admitted into heaven where neither sin nor sinner is allowed to enter, where no scoffer can come without repentance from his evil ways. This must be done before anyone can enter the glorious mansions of God which are prepared for all who love the Lord Jesus Christ in sincerity and truth.

IV. THE EXHORTATION CONCERNING REPENTANCE.

A. The Exhortation Addressed to Sinners.

There is no hope of any who live and die in their sins. They will dwell with demons and lost souls throughout all eternity. Consider, therefore, while you are going on in a course of sin and unrighteousness, the consequence that will attend your thus misspending your precious time. It is worth your while to be concerned about your souls. Will it not be deplorable when your good things on earth are past and your unconcern about eternity will gnaw at your soul?

B. The Exhortation Addressed to Believers.

Be thankful to God for His mercies toward you. Be thankful for this unspeakable mercy. As your life was formerly devoted to sin and the pleasures of this world, let it now be spent wholly in the ways of God. Let Christ's love to you keep you humble. Do not be high-minded, keep close to the Lord. Let the love of Jesus be in your thoughts continually. His love for you is unfathomable.

CONCLUSION

Come and behold Christ crucified for you; see His hands and feet nailed to the cross. Come and see His pierced side. There is a fountain open for sin and for uncleanness. Come and see His head crowned with thorns. Can you think of a bleeding, dying Savior and not be filled with pity? He underwent all this for you. Come to Him by faith; there is mercy for every soul that will come to Him.

George Whitefield

SERMON SIXTEEN

A SCRIPTURAL VIEW
OF SELF-DENIAL

And He said unto them all, "If any man will come after Me,
let him deny himself."
—LUKE 9:23

WHOEVER reads the Gospel sincerely will find that our Lord took all opportunities of reminding His disciples that His kingdom was not of this world. He reminded them that His doctrine was a doctrine of the cross and that their profession of being His followers would call them to a constant state of voluntary suffering and self-denial.

I. THE NATURE OF SELF-DENIAL.

A. It Must Extend to Our Understanding.

We must not lean to our own understanding, but we must submit our short-sighted reason to the light of divine revelation. There are mysteries in Christianity which are above, but not contrary to our natural reason. We must in all humility and reverence embrace the truths revealed in the Scriptures; thus only can we become truly wise, even "wise unto salvation."

B. It Must Extend to Our Wills.

We must deny our wills, that is, we must not make our wills a principle of action. Do not imagine that we have no pleasure in anything we do—

"wisdom's ways are ways of pleasantness"; but pleasing ourselves must be only the subordinate end of our actions. As we must renounce our wills in doing, so likewise we must renounce them in suffering, the will of God. Whatever befalls us we must say, "Father not my will, but Thine be done."

C. It Must Extend to Our Affections.

We must deny ourselves the pleasurable indulgence and self-enjoyment of riches. We must look upon ourselves as stewards and not proprietors of the manifold gifts of God. We must renounce our affection for relatives when they stand in opposition to our love of and duty to God. We must deny ourselves the things that are indifferent in themselves, that is, the things lawful, but not expedient; for the immoderate use of them is harmful.

D. It Must Extend to Our Own Righteousness.

We must renounce our own righteousness. If we should give all our goods to feed the poor and our bodies to be burned, yet, if we in the least depend on that and do not wholly rely on the perfect all-sufficient righteousness of Jesus Christ, it will profit us nothing. "Christ is the end of the law for righteousness to every one that believeth." We are complete in Him.

II. THE UNIVERSAL OBLIGATION OF SELF-DENIAL.

A. A Wrong Concept of the Obligation of Self-Denial.

Too many, unwilling to take Christ's easy yoke upon them, in order to evade the force of the Gospel precepts would pretend that all the commands concerning self-denial and the renunciation of self and the world belonged to our Lord's first and immediate followers and not to us and our children. Such persons greatly err, not knowing the Scriptures nor the power of godliness in their life.

B. The True Concept of the Obligation of Self-Denial.

The teaching of Christ, like Himself, never changes. All the commands which we have in the epistles about mortifying our members which are upon the earth, of setting our affection on things above, and of not being conformed to this world; these are but so many incontestable proofs that the same holiness, heavenly mindedness, and deadness to the world is as necessary for us as for our Lord's immediate followers.

III. THE REASONABLENESS OF SELF-DENIAL.

A. Illustrated in the Old Testament.

Naaman's servants said, when he refused to wash in the Jordan, "If the prophet had bid thee do some great thing, wouldst thou not have done it? How much rather then, when he saith to thee, wash and be clean?" If Christ had bid you do some difficult thing, would you not do it? Much more should you do it when He only bids you to deny what is harmful.

B. Illustrated in the New Testament.

When Peter was released from prison, had he hugged his chains and begged to have them replaced around his hands, would that not have revealed his love for slavery? Does not the person who refuses to deny himself act inconsistently? If we do not gird up the loins of our mind and follow Christ, are we not still in love with bondage?

IV. THE ENCOURAGEMENTS FOR THE PRACTICE OF SELF-DENIAL.

A. The Life of Christ.

Follow Christ from His cradle to the cross and see what a self-denying life He led! Do you think that He suffered everything in order to have us excused and exempted from sufferings? Far be it from any Christian to judge after this manner. Peter tells us, "He suffered for us, leaving us an example, that we should follow His steps."

B. The Lives of Godly Men.

Think often on the lives of the apostles, prophets, and martyrs who lived holy, self-denying, blameless lives. If self-denial was necessary for them, why not for us also? Are we not men of like passion with them? Do we not live in the same wicked world as they did? Have we not the same Spirit to assist, support, and purify us as they did?

C. The Pains of Hell.

Think often on the pains of hell. Consider whether it is not better to cut off a right hand or foot and pluck out a right eye if they cause us to sin "rather than to be cast into hell, where the worm dieth not, and the fire is not quenched." Think how many thousands are now reserved with lost spirits unto the day of judgment. This must be our case shortly unless we deny ourselves and follow Jesus.

D. The Joys of Heaven.

Meditate on the joys of heaven. Think with what unspeakable glory those happy souls are now encircled who on earth were called to deny themselves as well as we, and were not disobedient to that call. Lift up your hearts frequently toward the mansions of eternal bliss and with an eye of faith see the Son of Man with His retinue of departed saints solacing themselves in eternal joys.

CONCLUSION

Let us believe on the Lord Jesus Christ and deny ourselves! By this alone, every saint that ever lived ascended into the joy of the Lord. We also shall soon be lifted up into the same blissful regions, there to enjoy eternal rest with the people of God singing doxologies and songs of praise to the adorable Trinity.

George Whitefield

THE MOST NEEDFUL THING

> _But one thing is needful._
> —LUKE 10:42

IT WAS a characteristic of our blessed Redeemer to go about doing good. This motive brought Him to the house of His friend Lazarus at Bethany. Mary, the sister of Lazarus, seated at the feet of Jesus in a posture of a disciple. Martha, "cumbered with much serving," complained about Mary to Jesus. He answered her with these words, "Martha, Martha, thou art careful and troubled about many things, but one thing is needful; and Mary has chosen that good part, which shall not be taken away from her."

I. THE IMPORT OF THE WORDS OF THE TEXT.

A. The Meaning Stated.

Now, in a few words, the one thing needful is the care of the soul, opposed as you see in the text to the excessive care of body, about which Martha was gently admonished by our Lord. This is a general answer and it comprehends a variety of important particulars which is the business of our ministry often to open to you at large.

B. The Implications Suggested.

1. The care of the soul implies a readiness to hear the words of Christ, to receive both the law and the Gospel from His mouth.

2. It supposes that we learn from this Divine Teacher the worth of our souls, their danger, and the remedy.

3. It assumes the sincere dedication of ourselves to the service of God and a faithful adherence to it, notwithstanding all oppositions arising from inward corruptions or outward temptations.

C. The Scriptural Terms Enumerated.

This one thing needful is represented in various Scriptures by various names. Sometimes it is called "regeneration" or "the new creature," because it is the blessed work of God's efficacious grace. Sometimes it is termed the "fear of God" and sometimes "His love, and the keeping of His commandments"; and very frequently in the New Testament it is called "faith" or "receiving Christ and believing in Him," which therefore is represented as the "great work of God."

II. THE INTENTION OF THE WORDS OF THE TEXT.

A. To Show That It Is of Universal Concern.

Our Lord, you see, speaks of this "one thing" as needful in the general sense. He says not, for this or that particular person or for those of such an age, station, or circumstance in life, but needful for all. And indeed, when discoursing on such a subject, one might properly introduce it with these solemn words of the Psalmist, "Give ear, all ye people, hear, all ye inhabitants of the earth, both high and low, rich and poor together" (Psalm 49:1–2).

B. To Show That It Is of Highest Consequence.

As Solomon says of wisdom, that it "is more precious than rubies: and all the things thou canst desire are not to be compared unto her" (Proverbs 3:15), so I may properly say of this great and most important branch of wisdom, namely soul care. Whatever can be laid in the balance with it will be found lighter than vanity. This is strongly implied when it is said in the text, "one thing is needful"; one thing, and one thing alone is so.

C. To Show That It Is of a Comprehensive Nature.

The care of the soul is of so comprehensive a nature that everything truly worthy of our concern may be considered as included in it or subservient to it. As David observes that "the commandment of God is exceeding broad" (Psalm 119:96), so we may say of this one thing needful. Solomon also, very justly and emphatically expresses it, "to fear God and to keep His commandments is the whole duty of man" (Ecclesiastes 12:13).

III. THE IMPORTANCE OF THE WORDS OF THE TEXT.

A. The Testimony of the Godhead.

In the Proverbs God speaks of those who neglect Him and their souls as fools, while the godly alone are designated as wise. If we enquire what our Lord judged to be needed most, the words of the text contain as full an answer as can be imagined; and the sense is repeated in Matthew 26:26.

B. The Testimony of Men.

The wisest and best men of all ages have agreed in this point, that this has been the unanimous judgment, this the common and most solicitous care, of those characters who are most valuable, to secure the salvation of their own souls and to promote the salvation of others.

C. The Testimony of the Evident Reason of the Case.

1. The care of the soul is the one thing needful because without it you cannot secure peace of mind nor avoid the upbraiding of conscience.

2. It is necessary because happiness depends upon it.

3. It is needful in order to avoid a state of eternal misery.

IV. THE IMPRESSIONS FROM THE WORDS OF THE TEXT.

A. Reason to Lament Man's Folly of Neglect.

Since the care of the soul is true wisdom, then surely we have reason to say with Solomon that madness is in men's hearts (Ecclesiastes 9:3). Look on the conduct of mankind in general and you will imagine that they consider it the one thing needless, the vainest dream, and the most idle amusement of the mind. Can we, my Christian brethren, behold such a scene with indifference? The Lord awaken our compassion, our prayers, and our endeavors to bring them to Christ.

B. Necessity for Serious Inquiry.

Let me entreat you to remember your own concern in it and enquire: Have I thought seriously of it? Have I seen the importance of it? Has it lain with an abiding weight on my mind? Has it brought me to Christ, that I might lay the stress of these eternal interests on Him? Am I willing to give up other things, my interests, my pleasures, my desires, to this? Am I conversing with God and with man as one who believes these things?

CONCLUSION

May this care be awakened in those by whom it has been neglected! May it be revived in each of our minds. In order that you may be encouraged to pursue it with greater cheerfulness, let me conclude with this comfortable thought: in proportion to the necessity of the case through the merits of Jesus Christ is the provision which grace has made for our assistance. If you are disposed to sit down at Christ's feet, He will teach you by His Word and Spirit.

George Whitefield

THE PHARISEE AND THE PUBLICAN

I tell you, this man went down to his house justified rather than the other: For everyone that exalteth himself, shall be abased; and he that humbleth himself, shall be exalted.

—LUKE 18:14

IN ALMOST all of our Lord's discourses He preached the Gospel to poor sinners and denounced terrible woes against proud self-justifiers. The parable to which the words of the text belong (read the entire parable, Luke 18:10–14) includes both. The evangelist informs us that our Lord "spoke it into certain ones who trusted in themselves, that they were righteous, and despised others." It is a parable worthy of your most serious attention.

I. THE TWO MEN IN THE PARABLE.

A. They Differ in Reputation.

1. The Pharisee was a respected hypocrite. The Pharisees were very zealous for the traditions of the fathers and for the observation of the rites and ceremonies of Judaism. For these reasons they were highly venerated by the people. They had such a reputation for piety among the Jews that it was said if there were but two men saved, one of them must be a Pharisee.

2. The publican was a hated sinner. The publicans were gatherers of the Roman taxes and amassed much wealth by falsely wronging men. They were so universally infamous that our Lord tells His disciples that the excommunicated man should be to them as a publican. The Pharisees thought it a sufficient impeachment of our Lord's character that He was their friend and ate with them.

B. They Agree in the Duty of Public Worship.

1. The evidence of the agreement. They both came up to the temple. We have very early notice of men's sacrificing to and calling upon the Lord's name in the Old Testament. And it is nowhere contradicted in the New Testament. Our Lord and His apostles went to the temple, and we are commanded by the apostle: "not to forsake the assembling of ourselves together, as the manner of some is."

2. The importance of public worship. Although our devotions begin in our closets, they must not end there. If people do not enter into public devotions, I must suspect that they have little or none at home. The two men of the parable came to the temple, says our Lord, to pray. Thither should the children of God go up, to walk with and pour out their hearts before the mighty God of Jacob.

II. THE TWO PRAYERS OF THE PARABLE.

A. The Pharisee's Prayer.

1. It was a relating of his works. The Pharisee came to the temple to boast rather than to pray. He makes no confession of guilt or request for pardon of past sins or for grace to help assist him for the time to come. He only recounts his performances to God. This no one can justly do, that is, glory in His presence.

2. It was a revealing of his self-righteousness. If all of his boasted righteousness were true, he still could be a child of the devil. There is no mention made of his loving the Lord his God with all of his heart or a single syllable of inward religion. It is only an outward piety at the best; inwardly he is full of pride, self-justification, and great uncharitableness.

B. The Publican's Prayer.

1. It was a prayer of confession. God be merciful to me a sinner by birth, a sinner in thought, word, and deed; a sinner as to my person, a sinner as to all of my performances; a sinner in whom is no health, in whom dwelleth no good thing; a sinner full of wounds and bruises and putrifying sores from the crown of the head to the sole of the feet.

2. It revealed his self-abasement. Methinks I see him standing afar off, pensive, oppressed, and even overwhelmed with sorrow. And to show that his heart was full of self-resentment and that he sorrowed after a godly sort, he smote upon his breast. The word in the original implies that he struck hard upon his breast. He will lay the blame upon none but his own wicked heart.

III. THE TWO RESULTS IN THE PARABLE.

A. In Relation to the Two Men.

1. The Pharisee was not justified. Let Pharisees take heed that they do not pervert this text: for when it is said, "This man went down to his house justified rather than the other," our Lord does not mean that both were justified, and that the publican had more justification than the Pharisee. That the Pharisee was not justified is certain, for God resisteth the proud.

2. The publican was justified. A broken and a contrite heart God will not despise. I tell you, says our Lord, I who am God and therefore know all things, I who can neither deceive nor be deceived, whose judgment is according to right; I tell you this publican, this despised, sinful, but broken-hearted man, went down to his house justified (acquitted and looked upon as righteous in the sight of God) rather than the other.

B. In Relation to Its Teaching.

1. The self-righteous will be abased. Everyone without exception, young or old, high or low, rich or poor, who exalts himself; everyone who trusts in himself and rests in his duties, or thinks to join them with the righteousness of Christ for justification in God's sight; he shall be abased in the sight of all good men, angels, and God Himself. He shall be abased to live with demons in hell forever more.

2. The self-abased will be exalted. He that humbles himself through grace, whatever he be, shall be exalted. He shall be exalted in a spiritual sense. He shall be freely justified from all of his sins through the blood of Christ. He shall have peace with God and joy in believing. He shall be indwelt by Christ.

He shall drink of the divine pleasures as out of a river. He shall be brought into the presence of God.

CONCLUSION

One act of true faith in Christ justifies you forever. He is able to exalt you. God has exalted and given Him a name above every name, that at the name of Jesus every knee shall bow; nay, God has exalted Him to be not only a Prince, but a Savior. May He be a Savior to you.

George Whitefield

SERMON NINETEEN

THE CONVERSION OF ZACCHEUS

And Jesus said unto him, "This day is salvation come to this house, forasmuch as he also is a son of Abraham. For the Son of Man is come to seek and to save that which was lost."
—LUKE 19:9–10

SALVATION, throughout Scripture, is said to be a free gift of God through Jesus Christ our Lord. Not only free because God is a sovereign agent and therefore may withhold it from or confer it upon whom He pleases, but free because there is nothing to be found in man that can in any way induce God to be merciful unto him. The righteousness of Jesus Christ is the sole cause of our finding favor in God's sight. (Read Luke 19:1–10.)

I. THE OBSTACLES TO ZACCHEUS'S CONVERSION (Verse 2).

A. He Was a Tax Gatherer.

Surely, no one will say that there was any fitness in Zaccheus for salvation. He was a publican and therefore, in all probability, a sinner. Publicans were gatherers of the Roman taxes and were infamous for their abominable extortion. Zaccheus being chief among the publicans consequently was chief among the sinners.

B. He Was Rich.

One inspired apostle has told us that "not many mighty, not many noble are called" (I Corinthians 1:26). Another says, "God hath chosen the poor of this world rich in faith" (James 2:5). The Lord Jesus assures us that "it is easier for a camel to go through a needle's eye than for a rich man to enter into the kingdom of God" (Luke 18:25).

II. THE DETERMINATION OF ZACCHEUS (Verses 3–4).

A. To See Jesus.

Rich as he was, we are told that "he sought to see Jesus." Our Lord's fame was now spread abroad throughout all Jerusalem and all the country round about. Some said that He was a good man and others, a deceiver. Therefore, curiosity drew out this rich publican to see who this person was of whom he had heard such conflicting accounts.

B. To Overcome the Hindrances to Seeing Jesus.

Zaccheus, finding that he could not see Christ because of the crowd and the littleness of his stature, did not smite on his breast and depart saying, "It is in vain to seek after a sight of Him any longer, I can never attain to it." No, finding he could not see Christ if he continued in the midst of the crowd, he ran before the multitude and climbed up a sycamore tree to see Him.

III. THE LORD JESUS' INVITATION TO ZACCHEUS (Verse 5).

A. The Friendliness of the Invitation.

Christ calls Zaccheus by name, as though He were well acquainted with him. Indeed, well might He so think; for the tax gatherer's name was written in the book of life. He was one of those whom the Father had given to Him from all eternity. "For whom He did predestinate, them He also called" (Romans 8:30).

B. The Substance of the Invitation.

Amazing love! Well might Luke usher in the account with "behold." It is worthy of our admiration. When Zaccheus thought of no such thing, nay, thought Christ did not know him; behold the Lord Jesus does what we never hear He did before or after, I mean, invite Himself to Zaccheus' house. It was not, "Pray let Me abide," but: "I must abide this day at thy house."

IV. THE RESPONSE OF ZACCHEUS TO JESUS' INVITATION (Verses 6–8).

A. He Received Christ.

With this outward call there went an efficacious power from God which overruled Zaccheus' natural will. Therefore, "He made haste, and came down, and received Him joyfully" (verse 6); not only into his house but also into his heart. Thus it is that the great God brings home His children. He calls them by name, by His Word or providence. He speaks to them also by His Spirit.

B. He Confessed Christ.

Zaccheus, having believed on Jesus in his heart, now makes confession of Him with his mouth. He "stood forth" (verse 8). He was not ashamed before his fellow publicans. True faith casts out all sinful fear of man. Again, he said, "Behold Lord" (verse 8). It is remarkable how readily people in Scripture have owned the deity of Christ immediately upon conversion.

V. THE FRUITS OF ZACCHEUS'S SALVATION (Verse 8).

A. Charity.

"Behold the half of my goods I give to the poor." Not some small amount, but the half. Of what? My goods; things that were valuable. I give; not, I will give when I die, but I give them now. To whom would he give? Not to the rich, but to the poor, the maimed, the halt, the blind.

B. Restitution.

However, knowing that he must be just before he could be charitable, and conscious that in his public administrations he had wronged many persons, he adds, "If I have taken anything from any man by false accusation, I restore him fourfold." I suppose, before his conversion, he thought it no harm to cheat; but now he is grieved for it at his heart.

VI. THE ASSURANCE OF SALVATION GIVEN TO ZACCHEUS (Verses 9–10).

A. Christ's Statement That Salvation Has Come to Zaccheus's House.

B. Christ's Statement That Zaccheus Is Now a True Son of Abraham.

He is a true son of Abraham not so much by a natural, as by a spiritual birth. He was made partaker of like precious faith with Abraham. Like Abraham he believed on the Lord and it was accounted to Him for righteousness. His faith, like Abraham's, worked by love; and I doubt not that he has been long since sitting in Abraham's harbor.

CONCLUSION

"For the Son of Man is come to seek and to save that which was lost" (verse 10). These words were spoken by our Savior in answer to some self-righteous Pharisees, who, instead of rejoicing with the angels in heaven at the conversion of such a sinner as Zaccheus, murmured "that He was gone to be guest with a man that is a sinner" (verse 7). To vindicate His conduct, He tells them that this was an act agreeable to the design of His coming.

George Whitefield

SERMON TWENTY

THE MARRIAGE AT CANA

This beginning of miracles did Jesus in Cana of Galilee, and manifested forth His glory; and His disciples believed on Him.
—JOHN 2:11

THE CHIEF end that the apostle John had in view when He wrote the Gospel was to prove the deity of Jesus Christ against those arch heretics, the Ebionites and Cerinthians, whose pernicious principles too many follow in these last days. For this reason John is more particular than any other evangelist in relating our Lord's divine discourses and also the glorious miracles which He wrought, not by the power derived from another, but from a power inherent in Himself.

I. THE CIRCUMSTANCES OF THE MIRACLE.

A. It Was a Feast.

By our Lord's being at a feast we may learn that feasting upon solemn occasions is not unlawful. The Son of Man, we know, "came eating and drinking." If a Pharisee asked Him to come to his house our Lord went and sat down with him. Then, we find, His conversation was always such as tended toward edification. We may then, no doubt, go and do likewise.

B. It Was a Marriage Feast.

1. Christ's presence sanctions marriage. Our Lord graced a marriage feast with His first public miracle. It was an institution of God Himself, even in paradise; and therefore lawful for all Christians, even for those who are made perfect in holiness through the faith of Jesus Christ.

2. Christ should be consulted in every marriage. We may learn the reason why we have so many unhappy marriages in the world. It is because the parties concerned do not call Jesus Christ by prayer. Christ and the Scriptures are the last things that are consulted.

C. It Was an Unusual Marriage Feast.

1. Mary's request. The persons who called our Lord and His disciples to the marriage feast seem not to have been rich. They had an insufficient quantity of wine. It was Mary who said to the Lord, "They have no wine." Herein she set an example to rich and poor. The rich should be willing to go into the cottages of the poor and consider their needs. The poor who are disabled from helping can pray for one another.

2. Jesus' response. The Lord's answer to Mary gives us reason to think that there was something which was not right. He said to her, "Woman, what have I to do with thee?" (verse 4). Will the Lord Jesus entirely disregard His mother's request? No; He intimates that He will do at the proper time the thing she desired of Him. "Mine hour is not yet come." As though He said, "When they are come to an extremity and sensible of the need of My assistance, then I will show forth My glory."

II. THE PURPOSES OF THE MIRACLE.

A. To Prove the Deity of Christ.

One of the purposes of this miracle the evangelist mentions in the text, "to show forth His glory," or to give a proof of His eternal power and godhead. This was the chief design of our Lord's turning water into wine. However, there are more which our Lord may be supposed to have had in view, some of which I shall proceed to mention.

B. To Reward the Host.

He might do this to reward the host for calling Him and His disciples to the marriage. Those who honor the Lord He will honor. A cup of cold water given in the name of a disciple shall in no wise lose its reward. Although those who abound in alms deeds out of a true faith in and a love for

Jesus Christ may seem, as it were, to throw their bread upon the waters, yet they shall find it again after many days.

C. To Signify the Outpouring of the Holy Spirit.

Our Lord's turning the water, which was poured out so plentifully, into wine is a sign of the pouring out of His Spirit into the hearts of believers. The Holy Spirit is in Scripture compared to wine. Therefore the prophet calls us to buy wine (Isaiah 55:1), that is, the Spirit of love who fills and gladdens the soul as it were with new wine. The apostle alludes to this when he bids the Ephesians "not to be drunk with wine, wherein is excess, but be filled with the Spirit" (5:18).

D. To Reveal the Glory of the Latter Days.

1. The work of God during past and present time. Great things God has done already. Great things God is doing now. Many righteous men have desired to see the things which we see and have not seen them.

2. The greater work of God in the future. Glorious things are spoken of the times when "the earth shall be full of the knowledge of the Lord as the waters cover the sea" (Isaiah 11:9). All the former glory shall be nothing in comparison of that glory which shall excel.

E. To Show the Happiness of the Heavenly State.

1. Present blessings. The rewards which Christ confers on His faithful servants and the comforts of His love wherewith He comforts them while pilgrims on the earth are often so exceeding great that, if it were not promised, it would be almost presumption to hope for any reward hereafter. Nevertheless, my brethren, all the manifestations of God that we can possibly be favored with here, when compared with the glory that is to be revealed in us, are no more than a drop of water when compared with the ocean.

2. Future glory. This corruptible is to put on incorruption; this mortal is to put on immortality. When God shall cause all His glory to pass before us then we shall cry out, "Lord, Thou hast kept Thy good wine until now. We have drunk deeply of Thy Spirit; we have heard glorious things of Thy city, O God! But now we find that not half, not the thousandth part has been told us."

CONCLUSION

I have spoken of the miracle for the same purpose for which He at first performed it, that is, "to show forth His glory," that you also may be brought to believe in Him. "Behold the Lamb of God who taketh away the sins of the world" (John 1:29). Look unto Him and be saved. May God give to all of you a hearing ear and an obedient heart.

SEARCHING THE SCRIPTURE

Search the Scriptures.
—JOHN 5:39

WHEN the Sadducees came to our Lord and put to Him the question of whose wife that woman should be in the next life, who had seven husbands in this; He told them that they erred, not knowing the Scriptures. If we would know whence all the errors that have overspread the church of Christ first arose, we should find that in a great measure they flowed from the same fountain, ignorance of God's Word. Our Lord, although He was the eternal God, yet as man, He made the Scriptures His constant rule and guide.

I. THE DUTY TO SEARCH THE SCRIPTURES.

A. Because They Reveal How All Mankind Died in Adam.

By the Scriptures, I understand all the books which have been accounted canonical and which make up that volume commonly called the Bible. Had man continued in a state of innocence he would not have needed an outward revelation because the law of God was written in his heart. Among other things, the Scriptures show us our misery, our fall, or in a word, after what manner we died in Adam.

B. Because They Reveal How All Men May Be Made Alive in Christ.

The Scriptures show us not only our fall in Adam, but also the necessity of the new birth in Christ Jesus. Hence then arises the need of searching the Scriptures. Because they are nothing else but the grand charter of our salvation, the revelation of a covenant made by God with men in Christ, and a light to guide us in the way of peace; it follows that all are charged to read and search them, because all are equally fallen from God, all equally stand in need of being informed how they must be restored to and united with Him.

II. THE DIRECTIONS FOR SEARCHING THE SCRIPTURES.

A. Remember the Chief End of the Scriptures.

Have always in view the end for which the Scriptures were written, namely, to show us the way of salvation by Jesus Christ. "Search the Scriptures," says our blessed Lord, "for they are they that testify of Me." Look, therefore, always for Christ in the Scriptures. In the Old Testament you will find Him under prophecies, types, sacrifices, and shadows; in the New He is manifested in the flesh to become a propitiation for our sins as a priest, and as a prophet to reveal the whole will of His heavenly Father. Have Christ always in view when you read God's Word.

B. Search the Scriptures with a Humble Disposition.

Whosoever does not read the Scriptures with a humble childlike disposition shall in no wise enter into a knowledge of the things contained in them. God hides the sense of them from those that are wise and prudent in their own eyes; He reveals them only to babes in Christ, who think they know nothing yet as they ought to know; who hunger and thirst after righteousness and humbly desire to be fed with the sincere milk of the Word in order that they might grow thereby. Be as willing to learn what God shall teach you as Samuel was when he said, "Speak, Lord, for Thy servant heareth."

C. Search the Scriptures with a Sincere Intention to Obey Them.

Search the Scriptures with a sincere intention to put into practice what you read. A desire to do the will of God is the only way to know it. If any man will do God's will, says Christ, "he shall know of the doctrine, whether it be of God, or whether I speak of Myself." Again, speaking to His disciples, He says, "to you (who are willing to practice the Word) it is given to know the mysteries of the kingdom of God, but those who are without (who do not practice the Word) all these things are spoken in parables" that they may not see nor understand.

D. Apply the Scriptures to Yourself.

In order to search the Scriptures still more effectively, make an application of everything you read to your own lives. Whatever was written in the Book of God was written for our learning. What Christ said unto those aforetime, we must look upon as spoken to us also. Since the Holy Scriptures are nothing but a revelation from God, how fallen man is to be restored by Jesus Christ, all the precepts, threats, and promises belong to us and to our children, as well as to those to whom they were immediately made known.

E. Seek the Direction of the Holy Spirit.

The natural man does not discern the words of the Spirit of God because they are spiritually discerned. The words which Christ has spoken, they are spirit and they are life. They can be no more understood as to the true sense and meaning of them by the mere natural man than a person who never had learned a language can understand another speaking in it. It was the lack of the assistance of the Holy Spirit that made Nicodemus, a teacher of Israel, so utterly ignorant concerning the doctrine of regeneration.

F. Pray Immediately before Searching the Scriptures.

Let me advise you to pray before you read the Scriptures. Intersperse short ejaculatory prayers while you are engaged in reading. Pray over every word and verse, if possible, and when you close the Book most earnestly beseech God that the words which you have read may be engrafted into your hearts and bring forth in you the fruits of a good life. It will cause the Scriptures to enlighten, quicken, and enflame your soul.

G. Constantly Search the Scriptures.

"Search the Scriptures," that is, dig in them as for hidden treasure. Here is a manifest allusion to those who dig in mines; and our Savior would thereby teach us that we must take as much pains in constantly reading His Word, if we would grow wise thereby, as those who dig for silver or gold. Search the Scriptures daily.

CONCLUSION

Taste and see how good the Word of God is, and then you will never leave it to feed on the dry husks, those trifling sinful compositions in which men of false taste delight themselves. You will then disdain such poor entertainment and blush that you once were fond of it. The Word of God will then be sweeter to you than honey and the honeycomb, and dearer than gold and silver. Your souls, by reading it, will be filled, as it were, with marrow and fatness.

THE KILLING SIN— THE REJECTION OF CHRIST

And ye will not come to Me, that ye may have life.
—JOHN 5:40

OUR LORD says to the religious teachers of Israel, "Ye will not come to Me, that ye may have life"—I am now present with you, I am now come to explain the Scriptures and fulfill them, I am now come to proclaim to you that life, that eternal life, which the Scriptures declare was to be proclaimed by Me, yet "Ye will not come." God knows this is the treatment Jesus Christ meets with even today.

I. THE IMPLICATION OF THE CONDITION OF THE SINNER.

A. He Is Legally Dead.

The text supposes that we are all dead in sin, for if we are not, why do we need to come to have life? Sin is transgression of the law. Every transgression of the law incurs damnation. Have we eaten of the forbidden fruit? We must die. We are legally dead. We have broken God's law. We are liable to eternal condemnation. We are therefore legally dead, every one of us without distinction or exception.

B. He Is Spiritually Dead.

Besides legal death, there is spiritual death. By the latter is meant that the sinner is deprived of that life of God in which he originally stood. The consequence of this is eternal death. If a man dies physically when he is in the state of spiritual death he must die forever, by which is meant that he must live eternally banished from God.

II. THE REVELATION OF THE PROVISION FOR THE SINNER.

A. Legal Life.

"Ye will not come to Me, that ye may have life." What life is this? If ever a sinner possesses life he must be acquitted, he must be pronounced not guilty. His conscience says guilty, but Jesus Christ came that he might have legal life, that he might be acquitted from all that condemnation which he is under because of the breaking of God's law.

B. Spiritual Life.

Because man through sin has lost the divine image which was his original dignity, he will never reach glory without the restoration of that image. Spiritual life in the heart comes from Jesus Christ and this is the life of God in the soul of man. This is not something metaphorical, but it is a real thing. Death came through Adam, but life comes through Jesus Christ.

III. THE IMPLICATION OF THE MANNER OF THE SALVATION OF THE SINNER.

A. What It Is.

The only way to get this life is to come to Jesus Christ. Our text says, "Ye will not come unto Me, that ye may have life"; implying that without coming to Him man cannot have life. "There is no other name under heaven given among men whereby we must be saved" (Acts 4:12). "I am the way, the truth, and the life" (John 14:6). In order to have this life we must come to Christ for it.

B. What It Does Not Mean.

1. It does not mean coming to see His person. It can never mean this. Our Lord talks of coming to Him when He Himself was the preacher and they were all around Him. Although so many were around Him, yet there was only one who touched Him.

2. *It does not mean coming to the ordinances and church services.* Thousands come to the ordinances and do not see the God of the ordinances in them. Thousands go to church and do not come to Christ.

C. What It Does Mean.

We must come to Christ to be acquitted, to be pardoned. We must believe in Him not only with a speculative belief, but we must have His blood applied and brought home to the soul. We must come to Him as the author and finisher of our faith. We must come to Jesus Christ and believe in Him for life eternal.

IV. THE EXPLANATION FOR THE REJECTION OF SALVATION BY THE SINNER.

A. Because He Does Not Think He Is Dead.

Why will not people come to Christ to have life? Because they do not think that they are dead and therefore they do not want salvation. They do not see themselves as fallen creatures. Remember when you say you are "rich and increased in goods" that you know not, says Christ, that "you are poor and miserable and blind and naked" (Revelation 3:17).

B. Because He Is Self-Righteous.

Men do not choose to come to Christ because they do not chose to have Him as a free gift. They do not like to come to Him as poor and needy. The lawyers and other Jews thought they were righteous and therefore they would not come to Jesus Christ. Our Lord spoke of the Pharisees who trusted in themselves that they were righteous and would not come to Him that they might have life.

C. Because He Loves the World.

You will not come to Him because you love the world. "If any man love the world, the love of the Father is not in Him" (I John 2:15). When I talk of loving the world, I mean an inordinate love. I may live in the world and live up on it; yet my heart may be toward God. The love of the world is to be renounced and therefore men will not come to the Lord Jesus, they think, until they are going out of the world.

D. Because He Hates Christ.

If you are one of those who hate Christ, why you are the man that will not come to Him. "Why," you say, "does anybody hate Christ?" Every one of us by nature hates Him. We hate Christ because He is despised, we hate Him because of the appearance of the people that are His followers, we hate Him because of the narrowness of the way we are to pass into Him, we hate Him because we must part from our lusts.

CONCLUSION

As the Lord lives, in whose name I speak, if you will not come to Christ to have life you must come to His bar to hear Him pronounce you damned to all eternity. If you come to Him that you may have life, "Come ye blessed" will be the gracious welcome; but if you refuse, "Depart ye cursed" will be your sentence from the Lord. "For yet a little while, and He that shall come will come, and will not tarry" (Hebrews 10:37).

George Whitefield

SERMON TWENTY-THREE

THE INDWELLING OF THE HOLY SPIRIT

In the last day, that great day of the feast, Jesus stood, and cried, saying, "If any man thirst, let him come unto Me and drink. He that believeth on Me, as the Scripture hath said, out of his belly shall flow rivers of living water." But this spoke He of the Spirit, which they that believe in Him should receive.

—JOHN 7:37–39

OUR LORD attended the temple service in general and the Jewish festivals in particular. The festival at which He was now present was that of the Feast of Tabernacles, which the Jews observed according to God's appointment in commemoration of their living in tents. At the last day of this feast it was customary for many pious people to fetch water from a certain place and bring it on their heads singing the anthem, "And with joy shall ye draw water out of the wells of salvation" (Isaiah 12:3). Our Lord observing this cries out the words found in the text. The inspired evangelist adds the explanatory words (verse 39a) which are the basis of the present discourse.

I. THE PERSON OF THE SPIRIT.

A. He Is the Holy Spirit.

By the Spirit is evidently to be understood the Holy Spirit.

B. He Is Deity.

He is the third person in the ever-blessed Trinity, consubstantial and coeternal with the Father and the Son, proceeding from, yet equal to them both. Our Lord, when He gave His apostles the commission to go and teach all nations, commanded them to baptize in the name of the Holy Spirit, as well as the Father and the Son. Peter in Acts 5:3 said to Ananias, "Why hath Satan filled thine heart to lie unto the Holy Ghost?" and in verse 4 he says, "Thou hast not lied unto men, but unto God." From these passages it is plain that the Holy Spirit is truly and properly God.

II. THE POSSESSION OF THE SPIRIT.

A. The Persons Possessing the Spirit.

Unless men have eyes which see not and ears that hear not, how can they read the latter part of the text and not confess that the Holy Spirit is the common privilege of all believers, even to the end of the world? "This spake He of the Spirit, which they that believe in Him should receive." Observe, He does not say, they that believe in Him during one or two ages, but they that believe in Him at all times and in all places. So we must believe that even we also shall receive the Holy Spirit if we believe in the Lord Jesus with our whole hearts.

B. The Significance of Possessing the Spirit.

Our Lord, just before His bitter passion, prayed that all of His true followers might be united to Him by His Holy Spirit, by as real, vital, and mystical an union as there was between Jesus Christ and the Father (John 17:21–23). I say all of His true followers; for it is evident from our Lord's own words that He had us and all true believers in view when He prayed this prayer (John 17:20). Unless we treat our Lord as the high priests did, and count Him a blasphemer, we must confess that all who believe in Jesus Christ through the Word or ministration of His servants are to be joined to Jesus Christ by being made partakers of the Holy Spirit.

III. THE REASONABLENESS OF THE DOCTRINE OF THE INDWELLING OF THE SPIRIT.

A. Man's Natural Condition.

However this doctrine of the indwelling Spirit may seem foolishness to the natural man, yet to those who have tasted the good Word of life and have felt the power of the world to come, it will appear to be founded on the highest reason; and is capable to those who have eyes to see, of a demonstration—because it stands on this self-evident truth that we are fallen creatures. Do we not find that by nature we are prone to pride? Do we not find in ourselves the seeds of malice, revenge and all uncharitableness? Do we not by nature follow and suffer ourselves to be led by our natural appetites? We are no better than those whom Jude calls brute beasts (verse 10).

B. Man's Need in Order to Dwell with God and to Enjoy Him.

Because it is true that we are all by nature, since the fall, a mixture of brute and devil, it is evident that we all must receive the Holy Spirit before we can dwell with and enjoy God. We, as well as the apostles, must receive the Spirit of God. For the great work of sanctification, or making us holy, is particularly referred to the Holy Spirit; therefore, our Lord said, "Except a man be born . . . of the Spirit, he cannot enter into the kingdom of God" (John 3:5). However often we have told God we believe in the Holy Spirit, yet, if we have not believed in Him, so as to be united to Jesus Christ by Him, we have no more concord with the Lord Jesus than Belial himself.

CONCLUSION

Notwithstanding you are sunk into the nature of the beast and devil, yet, if you truly believe in Jesus Christ you shall receive the quickening promised in the text and be restored to the glorious liberty of the sons of God. "For by grace are ye saved through faith; and that not of yourselves: it is the gift of God: not of works, lest any man should boast" (Ephesians 2:8–9). Come then, my guilty brethren, come and believe in the Lord that bought you with His precious blood; look up by faith and see Him whom ye pierced. Behold Him with arms stretched out to receive you; cry unto Him as did the penitent thief. He will be to you wisdom, righteousness, sanctification, and eternal redemption.

George Whitefield

SERMON TWENTY-FOUR

THE GOOD SHEPHERD

My sheep hear My voice, and I know them, and they follow Me:
and I give unto them eternal life; and they shall never perish,
neither shall any man pluck them out of My hand.
—JOHN 10:27–28

WE ARE TOLD that our Lord was at Jerusalem at the Feast of Dedication and it was winter. This feast was held in commemoration of the restoration of the temple and altar after its profanation by Antiochus Epiphanes. "He walked in the temple in Solomon's porch." The Jews surround Him and endeavor to catch Him by a question. After aswering the question He speaks the words of the text.

I. THE GOOD SHEPHERD'S SHEEP.

A. Their Description.

1. They love to be together. There are only two kinds of people mentioned in Scripture. Christ divides the whole world into two classes: sheep and goats. Believers are always compared to something good and profitable and unbelievers are always described by something that is bad. Sheep generally love to be together. We speak of a flock of sheep, we do not say a herd of sheep.

2. They are small, harmless, and quiet. Sheep are little creatures, and Christ's people may be called sheep because they are small in the eyes of the world and they are even less in their own eyes. Sheep are looked upon as the most harmless and quiet creatures that God has made. May God give us to know that we are his sheep by having this blessed temper infused into our hearts by the Holy Spirit.

3. *They easily stray and are lost.* Of all creatures, sheep are the most apt to stray and be lost. Christ's people may in this respect be compared to sheep. Turn out a horse or a dog and they will find their way home, but a sheep wanders about. Thus Christ's sheep are too apt to wander from the fold; having their eyes off the great Shepherd they go into this field and that field, over this ledge and that ledge.

4. *They are useful.* Sheep are the most useful creatures in the world. They clothe our bodies with wool, and there is not the least part of a sheep but is useful to man. May God grant that you and I may, in this respect, answer the character of sheep. We should labor with our hands that we may have to give to all those in need.

B. Their Ownership.

1. *They are given to the Shepherd.* Believers consider Christ's property in them; He says, "My sheep." Oh, blessed be God for that little, yet great word "My." We are His by eternal election: "the sheep which Thou hast given Me," says Christ. They were given by God the Father to Christ Jesus in the covenant made between the Father and the Son from all eternity.

2. *They were purchased by the Shepherd.* I want to lead you to Calvary, there to see at what expense of blood Christ purchased those whom He calls His own. He redeemed them with His own blood, so that they are not only His by eternal election, but also by actual redemption in time. They were given to him by the Father upon condition that He should redeem them by his heart's blood.

3. *They voluntarily surrender to the Shepherd.* They are His because they are enabled in a day of God's power voluntarily to give themselves up unto Him. Christ says of these sheep especially that they hear His voice and that they follow Him. Here is an allusion to a shepherd. In the eastern nations the shepherds generally went before, they held up their crook, and they had a particular call that the sheep understood.

II. THE GOOD SHEPHERD'S ASSURANCE TO HIS SHEEP.

A. *He Knows His Sheep.*

1. He knows their number and name. If you belong to Jesus Christ, He is speaking of you when He says, "I know My sheep." What does this mean? Why, He knows their number, He knows their names, He knows every one for whom He died; and if there were to be one missing for whom Christ died, God the Father would send Him down again from heaven to fetch Him. "Of all (saith He) that Thou hast given Me I have lost none."

2. He knows all about them. Christ knows His sheep. He not only knows their number and name, but the words speak the peculiar knowledge and notice He takes of them. He takes as much care of them as if there were only one single sheep in the world. He knows His saints. He is acquainted with all of their sorrows, trials, and temptations. He bottles up their tears. He knows their inward corruptions. He knows all their wanderings and He takes care to bring them back again.

B. *He Keeps His Sheep.*

1. They shall never perish. Christ says, I have brought them out of the world to Myself and do you think that I will let them go to hell after that? "I give to them eternal life"; pray, mind that: not I will, but I do. Some speak of being justified at the day of judgment. That is nonsense. If we are not justified here, we shall not be justified there. He gives them eternal life, that is, assurance of it; the indwelling of the Spirit of God here is the earnest of the glory hereafter.

2. They shall never be plucked out of the Shepherd's hand. He holds them by His power, none shall pluck them thence. There is always something plucking at Christ's sheep. The devil, the lusts of the flesh, the lusts of the eye, and the pride of life, all try to pluck them out of Christ's hand. We help all three to pluck themselves out of Jesus' hand; but "none shall pluck them out of My hand," says Christ. Upon that text I can leave all of Christ's sheep to the protection of His love.

CONCLUSION

If you never were among Christ's sheep before, may He bring you now. Come, see what it is to have eternal life. Do not refuse it. May the great, good Shepherd draw your souls. If you have never heard His voice before, God grant you may hear it now. And you, dear Christian, who are already in His hands, may God keep you from wandering and keep you near Christ's feet.

THE CONVICTING WORK
OF THE HOLY SPIRIT

And when He is come, He will reprove the world of sin,
and of righteousness, and of judgment.
—JOHN 16:8

THESE words contain part of a gracious promise which the Lord Jesus made to His sorrowing disciples. The person referred to in the words of the text is plainly the Holy Spirit. The promise was first made to our Lord's apostles and fulfilled on the day of Pentecost. Nevertheless, as the apostles were the representatives of the whole body of believers, we must infer that this promise must be looked upon as spoken to us and to as many as the Lord our God shall call.

I. THE HOLY SPIRIT CONVICTS THE WORLD OF SIN.

The word which we translate reprove ought to be rendered convincing. In the original it implies a conviction by way of argumentation and coming with a power upon the mind equal to a demonstration.

A. He Convicts the Sinner of Sin in the Life.

The Holy Spirit generally convinces of some enormous sin, the worst perhaps of which the convicted person was ever guilty. Thus our Lord dealt with the persecutor Saul. He convinced him first of the horrid sin of persecution. Such a sense of all his other sins probably at the one time revived in his mind that he immediately died to all his false confidences.

B. He Convicts the Sinner of Sin in the Nature.

When the Holy Spirit accosts a sinner and convinces him of sin, all carnal reasoning against original sin is immediately thrown down; and he is made to cry out, "Who shall deliver me from the body of this death?" Now he does not so much bewail his actual sins as the inward perverseness of his heart which he finds to be in direct enmity against God.

C. He Convicts the Sinner of the Sin of Legal Righteousness.

We are by nature legalists, thinking to be justified by the works of the Law. When somewhat awakened by the terrors of the Lord, we immediately go about to establish our own righteousness by works and think thereby to find acceptance with God. The Comforter convinces the soul of these false notions and makes the sinner to see that all his righteousnesses are as filthy rags.

D. He Convicts the Sinner of the Sin of Unbelief.

There is a fourth sin of which the Comforter convinces the soul and which alone our Lord mentions (verse 9), as though it were the only sin worth mentioning. Indeed it is the root of all other sins. It is the reigning as well as the condemning sin of the world. It is the cursed sin of unbelief.

II. THE HOLY SPIRIT CONVICTS THE WORLD OF RIGHTEOUSNESS.

A. The Meaning of Righteousness.

By the word righteousness, in some places of Scripture, we are to understand that common justice which we ought to practice between man and man. However, in our text (as in a multitude of other places in Holy Writ) it refers to the active and passive obedience of our Lord; it is that perfect, personal, all-sufficient righteousness which He has wrought out for the world of which the Spirit is to convince.

B. An Evidence of the Righteousness of Christ.

"Of righteousness," says our Lord, "because I go to the Father, and ye see Me no more" (verse 10). This is one argument which the Holy Spirit uses to prove Christ's righteousness: because He is gone to the Father and we see Him no more. Had He not wrought out a sufficient righteousness, the Father would have sent Him back as not having done what He undertook.

C. The Importance of the Holy Spirit's Work of Convicting of Righteousness.

Whoever knows himself and God must acknowledge that Jesus Christ is the end of the Law for righteousness to every one that believes and that we are to be made the righteousness of God in Him. Whatever other scheme of salvation men may lay, I acknowledge I can see no other foundation whereon to build my hopes of salvation but the rock of Christ's personal righteousness imputed to my soul.

D. The Reason for the Holy Spirit's Work of Convicting of Righteousness.

Many, I believe, have a rational conviction that salvation depends on the imputation of Christ's personal righteousness to the soul; but rational convictions, if rested in, avail but little. It must be a spiritual, experimental conviction of saving truth. Therefore our Lord says that when the Holy Spirit comes He convinces of that righteousness; of its reality, completeness, and sufficiency to save a poor sinner.

III. THE HOLY SPIRIT CONVICTS THE WORLD OF JUDGMENT.

A. The Explanation of Judgment.

The next thing of which the Comforter, when He comes, convinces the soul is judgment. By the word judgment I understand that well-grounded peace, that settled judgment, which the soul forms of itself when it is enabled by the Spirit of God to lay hold on Christ's righteousness, which I believe it always does when convinced of righteousness.

B. The Significance of the Conviction of Judgment.

The soul being enabled to hold on Christ's perfect righteousness by a living faith has a conviction wrought in it by the Holy Spirit that the Prince of this world is judged. The soul now being justified by faith has peace with God through our Lord Jesus Christ. The strong man armed is now cast out;

my soul has true peace; the Prince of this world will come and accuse, but he has now no share in me.

C. The Confidence of the Conviction of Judgment.

The blessed Spirit which I have received and whereby I am enabled to apply Christ's righteousness to my poor soul, powerfully convinces me of this: Why should I fear or of what shall I be afraid, because He, the Spirit of God, witnesses with my spirit that I am a child of God? Such a one can triumphantly say, "It is Christ that justifies me, who is he that condemns?"

CONCLUSION

Thank God for His gift of the Holy Spirit. You would never have been thus highly favored had not He who first spoke darkness into light loved you with an everlasting love and enlightened you by His Holy Spirit, and that too, not on account of any good thing foreseen in you, but for His own name's sake. Be humble and extol free grace. Walk as it becomes the children of light. And, oh, that the Holy Spirit would come and convince the Christless of sin, righteousness, and judgment.

George Whitefield

SERMON TWENTY-SIX

CONVERSION

*Repent ye, therefore, and be converted, that your sins
may be blotted out, when the times of refreshing shall
come from the presence of the Lord.*

—ACTS 3:19

PETER charged his audience with the sin of murdering the Son of God. No doubt the charge entered deep into their conscience and that faithful monitor began to give them a proper sense of themselves. Then the apostle informed them that great as was their sin, it was not unpardonable; that although they had been connected with the crime of murdering the Lord and thereby incurred the penalty of eternal death, yet there was mercy for them as pointed out in the text.

I. MEN'S CONCEPTS OF CONVERSION.

I shall endeavor to show you what conversion is not. I believe there are thousands that think themselves converted, and yet at the same time, if you come and examine them, they know not so much as speculatively what real conversion is.

A. Some Think Conversion Is Only a Change from One Religious System to Another.

There is a notion that a person's change from one church or denomination to another is conversion. This may take place while no thought is given to Jesus Christ. This is conversion only from one persuasion to another persuasion.

B. Some Think Conversion Is Only a Change from one Doctrinal Position to Another.

Possibly a person may go further and be converted from one set of principles or doctrines to another. Neither is this real or Scriptural conversion, that is, conversion that will bring a soul to heaven.

C. Some Think Conversion Is Only Reformation.

Some think they are converted because they are reformed; but reformation is not renovation. A man may be turned from profanity to a regard for morality, and because he does not swear nor attend the theater nor play cards he considers himself converted; yet he may still be unsaved. I speak not against reformation or being good. This is right in its place; but this conversion, or the two previously mentioned, you may have and yet never be truly converted.

II. SCRIPTURAL VIEW OF CONVERSION.

A. Its Meaning.

A man must be a new creature and be converted from his own righteousness to the righteousness of the Lord Jesus Christ. As a child when born has all the several parts of a man, so when a person is converted to God there are all the features of the new creature and growth until he become mature in grace and is taken to glory. Anything short of this is but the shadow instead of the substance. Conversion means a person turned from hell to heaven, from the world to God.

B. Its Evidence.

They that are really converted to Jesus and are justified by faith in the Son of God, such will take care to evidence their conversion by grace diffusing itself through every faculty of the soul and making a universal change in them. He that is "in Christ is a new creature: old things (not will be, but) are passed away; behold, all things (not only will, but) are become new" (II Corinthians 5:17).

C. Its Author.

The author of this conversion is the Holy Spirit. It is not man's free will; it is not moral persuasion; nothing short of the influence of the Spirit of the living God can effect this change in our lives. We are said to be born of the Spirit (John 3:5). "That which is born of the flesh is flesh; and that which is born of the Spirit is spirit" (John 3:6).

III. MOTIVES FOR CONVERSION.

A. Conversion Is Necessary for Soul Rest.

Permit me to say that you ought to repent and be converted, for until then you never can, never will, never shall find true rest for your souls.

B. Conversion Is Necessary for Eternal Happiness.

Unless you are converted you can never be happy hereafter. You must be converted if you will go to heaven. The unconverted man would not enjoy heaven, if he could enter, which, of course, he cannot.

C. Conversion Is Necessary for Deliverance from Condemnation.

I mention one more thing, which is, that you must be converted or be damned. This is plain English, but not plainer than my Master made use of when He said, "He that believeth not shall be damned" (Mark 16:16).

IV. ANSWERS TO OBJECTIONS AGAINST CONVERSION.

A. There Is Still Sufficient Time to Be Converted.

The common saying is, "I do not care to be converted yet; I think there is time enough to be converted." You may think to put it off until the morning, but before morning you may be damned. If you were in prison and you would be permitted to leave, you would choose to go immediately. Why will you not do for your soul what you would do for your body?

B. People Will Laugh.

I would be converted but people will laugh at me. Suppose you were promised $50,000, but you must be laughed at all your lifetime. Would you accept the offer? There is none but would say, "Give me the $50,000." If you loved God and your souls you would say, "Give me God and call me what you will." Is the Gospel the glory of our country and are you ashamed of the Gospel?

C. It Is Not the Right Time.

Is it time for the poor prisoners to be converted, who are to be hanged tomorrow morning? If it is time for them, it is time for you, for you may be dead before them. There was a poor woman who a few days ago was cursing most shockingly; now she is a dead corpse. God grant that may not be the case with you; but the only way to prevent it is to remember that "now is the accepted time; now is the day of salvation" (II Corinthians 6:2).

CONCLUSION

Young people, I charge you to consider. God help you to repent and be converted. You middle-aged people, oh, that you would repent and be converted! You old, gray-headed people, the Lord make you repent and be converted that you may thereby prove that your sins are blotted out. I could preach until I preached myself dead. I would be glad to preach myself dead if God would convert you. May God bless His work on you that you may blossom and bring forth fruits unto Him.

SERMON TWENTY-SEVEN

THE ALMOST CHRISTIAN

Almost thou persuadest me to be a Christian.
—ACTS 26:28

THE CHAPTER out of which the text is taken contains an account of Saint Paul's conversion to Christianity which he gave before governor Festus and King Agrippa. The king accuses the apostle of madness to which he replies in the negative and confronts the ruler with the words, "believest thou the prophets? I know that thou believest them." The text is Agrippa's confession.

I. THE IDENTIFICATION OF THE ALMOST CHRISTIAN.

A. He Wavers between Christ and the World.

An almost Christian, if we consider him in his duty toward God, is one that halts between two opinions; that wavers between Christ and the world; that would reconcile God and mammon, light and darkness, Christ and Belial. He is one who depends much upon outward form and therefore considers himself righteous, despising others; but at the same time he is a stranger to the divine life.

B. He Is Just to All.

If you consider him in respect to his neighbor, he is one who is strictly just to all. This does not proceed from any love to God or regard to man, but only through a principle of self-love. He knows dishonesty will spoil his reputation and consequently hinder his thriving in the world.

C. He Depends on Negative Goodness.

He is one who depends upon being negatively good and contents himself with the consciousness of having done no one any harm; even though he reads in the Gospel that "the unprofitable servant was cast into outer darkness" (Matthew 25:30) and the barren fig tree was cursed and dried up from the roots, not for bearing bad fruit, but because it bore no fruit (Matthew 21:19).

D. He Is Publicly Charitable.

He is no enemy to charitable contributions, if not approached too frequently; but he is unaquainted with the ministry of visiting the sick and imprisoned, clothing the naked, and relieving the hungry in a private manner. He thinks that those things belong only to the clergy, yet his own false heart tells him that nothing but pride keeps him from exercising these acts of humility.

E. He Practices Sobriety.

As he is strictly honest to his neighbor, so he is likewise strictly sober in himself. Both his honesty and sobriety proceed from the same principle of self-love. It is true, he does not run into the same excesses of riot with other men, but it is not out of obedience to God, but because he is naturally temperate or is fearful of forfeiting his reputation or unfitting him for business.

II. THE REASONS FOR BEING AN ALMOST CHRISTIAN.

A. False Ideals of Christianity.

Many who live in a Christian country do not know what Christianity is. Some consider that it is found in this or that communion, others think it is morality, many more hold it to be a round of performance of duties. Only a few acknowledge it to be what it is in reality, a divine life, a union of a soul with God.

B. Fear of Man.

A second reason that so many are only almost Christians is a servile fear of man. There are many who have been awakened to a sense of the divine life, yet out of a sinful fear of being considered peculiar they have allowed all of these good impressions to wear off. They love man's praise more than the honor which God gives.

C. Love of Money.

This was the pitiable case of the young man in the Gospel who inquired of our Lord what to do to inherit salvation, but went away sorrowful because he refused to part with his wealth (Luke 18:18–23). Thus many today when they find that they must forsake all to follow Christ say, "The Lord pardon us in this thing! We pray Thee have us excused."

D. Love of Pleasure.

Neither is the love of pleasure a less uncommon or less fatal cause why so many are no more than almost Christians. They have too great a love for pleasures. Tell them to "mortify their members" (Colossians 3:5) and they consider it as difficult as to cut off a right hand or to pluck out a right eye. They cannot think our Lord requires so much.

E. Instability of Character.

Many a minister and sincere Christian has wept over promising converts who seemingly began in the Spirit, but after a while fell away and ended in the flesh through an instability and fickleness of character. Christianity was to them a novelty, something which pleased them for a short time, but after their curiosity was satisfied they laid it aside.

III. THE FOLLY OF BEING AN ALMOST CHRISTIAN

A. It Is Not Salvation.

The first proof I shall give of the folly of being an almost Christian is that it is ineffectual to salvation. It is true that such men are almost good; but almost to hit the mark is really to miss it. God requires us to love Him with all our hearts, with all our souls, and with all our strength (Matthew 22:37). He loves us too well to admit any rival.

B. It Is Detrimental to Others.

An almost Christian is one of the most harmful creatures in the world. He is a wolf in sheep's clothing. He is one of those false prophets our

Lord bids us beware, who would persuade men the way to heaven is broader than it really is and thereby "enter not into the kingdom of God themselves; and those who are entering in, they hinder."

C. It Is Ingratitude toward Christ.

It is the greatest instance of ingratitude that we can express toward our Lord and Master Jesus Christ. Did He not come down from heaven and shed His precious blood to purchase these lives of ours and shall we only give Him half of them? How can we say we love Him when our hearts are not wholly with Him?

CONCLUSION

Let us scorn all base and treacherous treatment of our King and Savior, of our God and Creator. Let us not take some care to go to heaven and yet be lost at last. Let us give God our whole hearts and no longer halt between two opinions. If the world is god, let us serve that; if pleasure is a god, let us serve that: but if the Lord is God, let us serve Him alone.

THE BELIEVER'S BLESSINGS IN CHRIST

But of Him are ye in Christ Jesus, who of God is made unto us, wisdom, righteousness, sanctification, and redemption.
—I CORINTHIANS 1:30

OF ALL the verses in the Book of God, this which constitutes our text is, I believe, one of the most comprehensive. What glad tidings it brings to believers! What precious privileges are believers herein invested! Without referring you to the context I shall from these words point out to you the fountain from which these blessings flow and then consider what these blessings are wisdom, righteousness, sanctification, and redemption.

I. THE FOUNTAIN OF THE BELIEVER'S BLESSINGS

A. It Is God the Father.

First, I point out to you the fountain of the blessings that the children of God partake of in Jesus, "who of God is made unto us": the Father, He it is who is spoken of here.

B. It Is the Father's Covenant with His Son.

There was an eternal contract between the Father and the Son: "I have made a covenant with My chosen, and I have sworn unto David My servant" (Psalm 89:3). David was a type of Christ with whom the Father also made a covenant that if He would obey, suffer, and make Himself a sacrifice for sin He "shall see His seed, He shall prolong His days and the pleasure of the Lord shall prosper in His hands" (Isaiah 3:10).

C. It Is the Father's Love.

The apostle when here speaking of the Christian's blessings, lest they should sacrifice to their own worth or think that their salvation was owing to their own faithfulness or improvement of their own free will, reminds them to look back on the everlasting love of God the Father—"who of God is made unto us."

II. THE EXPLANATION OF THE BELIEVER'S BLESSINGS.

A. Christ the Believer's Wisdom.

1. The meaning of true wisdom negatively stated. (a) It is not indulging the desires of the flesh: eat, drink, and be merry. This is only the wisdom of brutes. (b) It is not the gaining of things: for riches often take wings and fly away. "A man's life consisteth not in the abundance of the things which he possesseth" (Luke12:15). (c) It is not the gaining of knowledge. It is possible for you to tell numbers of the stars and call them all by their names and yet be mere fools. Learned men are not always wise.

2. The meaning of true wisdom positively stated. (a) It is to know oneself. One of the wise men of Greece said, "Know thyself." This is certainly true wisdom. It is the wisdom spoken of in the text. We are made to know ourselves so as not to think more highly than we ought to think. (b) It is to know what we are by nature. Once we were in darkness, fallen creatures, dead in trespasses in the sins, sons, and heirs of hell and children of wrath. (c) It is to know what we are by grace. Now we are light in the Lord and know He is the only Savior and have received Him as our all in all.

B. Christ the Believer's Righteousness.

1. This means the imputation of Christ's righteousness to the believer. Christ's whole personal righteousness is made over to and accounted to the believer. God the Father blots out our transgressions as with a thick cloud; our sins and iniquities He remembers no more. We are made the righteousness of God in Christ Jesus, who is the end of Law for righteousness to every one who believeth (Romans 10:4).

2. This means the believer's deliverance from the guilt of sin. The believer is actually acquainted. Hence it is that the apostle, under a sense of this blessed privilege, breaks out in this triumphant language, "It is Christ that justifies, who is he that condemns?" (Romans 8:33–34). Does sin condemn? Christ's righteousness delivers believers from the guilt of it. Christ is their Savior and the propitiation for their sins. Who shall lay anything to their charge?

C. Christ the Believer's Sanctification.

1. Sanctification is the renovation of the whole man. By sanctification I do not mean a hypocritical attendance on outward ordinances nor a mere outward reformation. By sanctification I mean a total renovation of the whole man. By the righteousness of Christ believers become legally alive, by sanctification they are made spiritually alive. By the one they are entitled to glory, by the other they are made ready for glory. They are sanctified therefore in spirit, soul, and body.

2. Sanctification is the effect and evidence of justification. Although sanctification is not the cause, yet it is the effect of our acceptance with God—"who of God is made unto us righteousness and sanctification." He therefore who is really in Christ is a new creation. To look into our lives and see that they are changed and renewed gives to us a comfortable and well-grounded assurance of the safety of our states. By our fruits we must judge whether we have or do not have the Holy Spirit.

D. Christ the Believer's Redemption.

1. Redemption's end. It is the believer's glorification. Our text sufficiently proves the final perseverance of all true believers. God never justified a man whom He did not sanctify, nor sanctify one whom He did not completely redeem and glorify. As for God, His way and work is perfect. He always carries on and finishes the work He begins. Those whom God has justified, He has in effect glorified.

2. Redemption's area. By the word redemption we are to understand not only a complete deliverance from all evil, but also a full enjoyment of all good both in body and soul. (a) Christ's resurrection was an earnest of our resurrection. As in Adam all die so all in Christ shall be made alive. (b) The complete redemption of our souls will be in heaven when the very being of sin will be destroyed and an eternal stop will be put to inbred, indwelling corruption.

CONCLUSION

You see, brethren, partakers of the heavenly calling, what great blessings are treasured up for you in Jesus Christ and what you are entitled to by believing in His name. Take heed, therefore, that ye walk worthy of the vocation wherewith you are called. Think often how highly you are favored; and remember, you have not chosen Christ, but He has chosen you.

George Whitefield

SERMON TWENTY-NINE

A WORTHY RESOLUTION

I determined not to know anything among you,
save Jesus Christ, and Him crucified.
—I CORINTHIANS 2:2

THE PERSONS to whom these words were written were the members of the Corinthian Church. They were not only divided into different sects, by one saying, "I am of Paul," and another, "I am of Apollos," but also had many amongst them who were so full of this world's wisdom and so wise in their own eyes that they set at naught the simplicity of the Gospel, and accounted the apostle's preaching foolishness. What was the sum of Paul's wisdom? He tells them in the words of the text, which is a resolution worthy of the great apostle Paul and no less worthy for every minister and every disciple of Christ.

I. THE CONTENT OF THE RESOLUTION.

A. A Determination to Know.

1. Not just historical knowledge. By the word "know" we are not to understand a bare historical knowledge; for to know only historically that Christ was crucified by His enemies at Jesusalem will do us no more good than to know that Caesar was slain by his friends at Rome.

2. But to approve. The word "know" means to know so as to approve; as when Christ said, "I know you not," that is, I know you not so as to approve you. It implies experimental knowledge.

B. A Determination to Know Jesus Christ Crucified.

By Jesus Christ we are to understand the eternal Son of God. He is called Jesus, Savior, because He saves us from the guilt and power of our sins. He is called Christ, which signifies anointed, because He was anointed by the Holy Spirit to be a prophet to instruct, a priest to make atonement, and a king to govern. He was crucified upon the cross that He might become a curse for us; for it is written, "Cursed is every man that hangeth upon a tree" (Galatians 3:13). This knowledge so gripped the apostle that he was determined not to know anything else. He resolved to make this the governing principle of his life.

II. THE REASONS FOR THE RESOLUTION.

A. Without Christ Crucified Our Persons Will Not Be Acceptable to God.

Christ is the way, the truth, and the life, and no one comes to the Father but through Him (John 14:6). He is the Lamb slain from the foundation of the world (Revelation 13:8). None ever were or ever will be received up into glory but by an experimental application of His merits to their hearts. We might as well think to rebuild the tower of Babel or reach heaven with our hands as to imagine we could enter therein by any other door than that of the knowledge of Jesus Christ. Other knowledge may make you wise in your own eyes and puff you up; but this alone edifies and makes wise unto salvation.

B. Without Christ Crucified Our Deeds Will Not Be Acceptable to God.

"Through faith," that is, through a living faith in a Mediator to come, "Abel offered a more acceptable sacrifice than Cain" (Hebrews 11:4). It is through a like faith, an experimental knowledge of the same divine Mediator, that our sacrifices of prayer, praise, and thanksgivings come up as an incense before the throne of grace. As our devotions to God will not, so neither, without this knowledge of Jesus Christ will our acts of charity to men be accepted by Him. If we gave all our goods to feed the poor and yet were destitute of this knowledge, it would profit us nothing.

C. Without Christ Crucified Our Morality Will Not Be Acceptable to God.

While we grant that morality is a substantial part of Christianity and that Christ came not to destroy or take away moral law as a rule of action, but to explain and so fulfil it; yet we affirm that our moral actions are not acceptable in the sight of God the Father unless they proceed from the principle of a new nature or a vital faith in the Son of God. Whether we eat or drink or do anything for man, it must all be done out of a love for and knowledge of Him who died and rose again. This is necessary to render our works, even our most ordinary deeds, acceptable in the sight of God.

III. THE PRACTICE OF THE RESOLUTION.

A. The Essential Thing in the Practice of the Resolution.

May I exhort you to put the apostle's resolution into practice and beseech you, with him, to determine "not to know anything, save Jesus Christ, and Him crucified." I say, determine, for unless you sit down first and count the cost and from a well-grounded conviction of the excellency of this above all other knowledge whatsoever, resolve to make this your chief study, your only end, your one thing needful, every frivolous temptation will draw you aside from the pursuit after it. The more your enemies persuade you to know other things, the more should you determine not to know anything but Christ crucified.

B. The Importance of the Practice of the Resolution.

Riches shall fail, pomp shall cease, vanities shall fade away; but the knowledge of Jesus Christ and Him crucified abides forever. Of whatever, therefore, you are ignorant, do not be ignorant of this. If you know Christ and Him crucified you know enough to make you happy, although you know nothing else; without this all of your other knowledge cannot keep you from being everlastingly miserable. Do not value the contempt of friends with which you must necessarily meet upon your open profession to act according to this determination. Your Master, whose you are, was despised before you.

CONCLUSION

Let us not be content with following Christ afar off, for then we shall, as Peter did, soon deny Him. Let our speech and all of our actions declare to the world whose disciples we are and that we have indeed determined not to know anything save Jesus Christ and Him crucified. Then it will be well with us and we shall be unspeakably happy here; and, what is infinitely better, when others that despised us shall be calling upon the mountains to be falling upon them, we shall be exalted to sit down on the right hand of God and shine as the sun in the firmament, in the kingdom of our Redeemer.

George Whitefield

TEMPLES OF THE LIVING GOD

Ye are the temples of the living God.
—II CORINTHIANS 6:16

IF I MISTAKE not, the end proposed by the apostle Paul in the words of the text is to encourage believers to use all diligence to walk worthy of Him who called them. The expression, "Ye are the temple of the living God," undoubtedly is metaphorical, but under the metaphor something real and of infinite importance is to be understood. There seems to be an allusion not only to temples or churches in general, but to the Jewish temple in particular.

I. DEDICATION TO GOD.

A. In Relation to the Jewish Temple.

I trust but few, if any, need be informed that the preparations for the Jewish edifice were exceedingly grand, that is, it was modeled and built by a divine order and when completed it was separated from common uses and dedicated to the service of Jehovah with the utmost solemnity.

B. In Relation to Christians.

1. The requirement. Christians are the temple of the living God. Loved from eternity, effectually called in time, they are chosen out of the world and voluntarily devote themselves soul and body to the service of God. This is the Christian's reasonable service. It implies no less than the total renunciation of the world; in short, it turns the Christian's entire life into one continued sacrifice of love to God; so that, whether he eats or drinks, he does all to God's glory.

2. Its signification. I would not insinuate that obedience to the words of the text requires us to become hermits. Christians are said to be the salt of the earth and the lights of the world and are commanded to "let their light shine before men." How can this be done if we shut ourselves up? True renunciation of the world is to be in the world but yet not of it; to have our hands employed on earth and our hearts at the same time fixed on things above.

II. DEVOTION TO GOD.

A. In Relation to the Jewish Temple.

The Jewish temple was a house of prayer. For this end was it built and adorned with such furniture. Solomon, in that admirable prayer which he offered to God at the dedication of the temple, said, "Hearken therefore unto the supplication of Thy servant, and of Thy people Israel which they shall make toward this place." What was said of the first, our Lord applies to the second temple, "My house shall be called a house of prayer."

B. In Relation to Christians.

1. Its expression. When believers are wholly dedicated to God their hearts become the seats of prayer from whence, as so many living altars, a perpetual sacrifice of prayer and praise is continually ascending up to the Father of mercies, the God of all consolations. Such, and such only, who thus worship God in the temple of their hearts, can truly be said to be made priests unto God or be styled a royal priesthood; such only can be styled "the temple of the living God." Devotion is expressed through prayer and praise.

2. Its nature. Let no one say that such a devotion is impracticable or practicable only to a few and those few being such as have nothing to do with the common affairs of life; for this is the common duty and privilege of all true Christians. To "pray without ceasing" and to "rejoice in the Lord always" are precepts equally obligatory on all who name the name of Christ.

Such devotion, as expressed through prayer and praise should be habitual and universal among the children of God.

III. DWELLING OF GOD.

A. In Relation to the Jewish Temple.

The Jewish temple was also a place where the great Jehovah was pleased to reside. Hence, He is said to place and record His name there and to sit or dwell between the cherubims. When Solomon first dedicated it, we are told, "the house was filled with a cloud, so that the priests could not stand to minister by reason of the cloud, for the glory of the Lord had filled the house."

B. In Relation to Christians.

Wherefore all this manifestation of the divine glory in the Jewish temple? To show how the high and lofty One makes His abode in all those who tremble at His Word.

1. The testimony of the inspired apostle Paul. To this the apostle more particularly alludes in the words immediately following our text; for having called the Corinthians "the temple of the living God," he adds, "as God hath said, I will dwell in them, and I will walk in them, and I will be their God, and they shall be My people." Strange and strong expressions are these words! Strange and strong as they are, they must be experienced by all who are indeed "the temple of the living God."

2. The testimony of Christ. The testimony of the apostle Paul declares nothing more or less than the prayer of our Lord which He prayed for His people a short time before His bitter passion, "that they may be one, even as we are one: I in them, and Thou in Me, that they may be made perfect in one." The truth of this glorious passage is not only for the apostles, but for all of God's children. The time would fail to mention all the Scriptures that speak of this blessing.

3. The testimony of the church universal. In asserting this doctrine we do not give utterance to the fancies of a disordered brain and uncontrolled imagination; neither do we broach any new doctrines or set up the peculiar opinions of any particular sect or denomination of Christians; but we speak the words of truth, we show you the right and good way, even that

401

which all the articles of all the protestant churches and all sincere Christians, however differing in other aspects, do universally agree.

CONCLUSION

When Jehovah filled the temple with His glory, King Solomon burst forth into the pathetic exclamation, "Will God dwell with men on the earth?" With greater astonishment we ought to say, "Will the high and lofty One who inhabits eternity dwell in us?" Are you not ready to say, "Not unto us, but unto Thy free, unmerited, sovereign, distinguishing love and mercy, O Lord, be all the glory." We have nothing but what is freely given us from above.

George Whitefield

THE POWER OF CHRIST'S RESURRECTION

That I may know Him, and the power of His resurrection.
—PHILIPPIANS 3:10

THE APOSTLE in the context cautions the Philippians to beware of the Judaizing teachers. And that they might not think he spoke out of prejudice or ignorance he acquaints them of his life as a Pharisee. However, when it pleased God to reveal His Son in him, the privileges he had formerly boasted in he counted loss for Christ." He shows the sincerity of this conversion from Pharisaism when he says, "I count them but dung, so that I may win Christ, that I may know Him and the power of His resurrection."

I. THE FACT OF CHRIST'S RESURRECTION.

A. _The Precautions to Prevent Dishonesty._

He was buried in a sepulcher hewn out of a rock, so that it could not be said that any digged under and conveyed Him away. It was a sepulcher wherein never man before was laid, so that if anybody did rise from thence, it must be the body of Jesus of Nazareth. Besides, the sepulcher was sealed; a great stone rolled over the mouth of it; and a band of soldiers (consisting not of friends, but of His professed enemies) was set to guard it.

B. _The Postresurrection Appearances of Christ._

Our blessed Lord's postresurrection appearances at different times and various ways to His disciples, as when they were assembled together, when they were walking to Emmaus, when they were fishing; nay, and condescending to show them His hands and feet, and His appearing to over five hundred brethren at once, put the truth of His resurrection out of all dispute.

C. The Qualification of the Writers of the Gospel Records.

They were eyewitnesses of what they related; they ate and drank with Him after His resurrection. They were plain men, therefore less suspected of telling a lie, particularly since they laid down their lives for a testimony of the truth of it. The wonderful success God gave to their ministry when three thousand were converted by one sermon, and twelve poor fishermen in a very short time enabled to be more than conquerors over all the opposition of men or demons was a plain demonstration that Christ was risen.

II. THE NECESSITY FOR CHRIST'S RESURRECTION.

A. In Order to Fulfill Christ's Teaching.

Christ had often appealed to His resurrection as the most convincing proof He would give them that He was the true Messiah (Matthew 12:39–40). He also said, "Destroy this temple of My body, and in three days I will build it up" (John 2:19–21). These words His enemies remembered and urged as an argument to induce Pilate to grant them a guard to prevent His being stolen from the grave (Matthew 27:63). Had He not risen again they might have justly said, "We know that this man was an imposter."

B. In Order to Give Believers Assurance of Salvation.

It had pleased the Father to wound His only Son for our transgressions and to confine Him in the grave as our surety for our guilt. Had Christ continued in the grave, we could have had no more assurance of salvation than any debtor can have of his creditor's satisfaction while his surety is kept confined. But by Christ being released from the power of death, we are thereby assured that with His sacrifice God was well pleased and that our atonement was finished upon the cross.

C. In Order to Give Assurance of the Resurrection of Our Bodies.

It was necessary that our Lord should rise again from the dead to assure us of the certainty of the resurrection of our bodies. The doctrine of the resurrection of the body was set at naught by the Gentiles, as appears from the Athenians' mockingly calling Paul a babbler and a setter forth of strange doctrines when he preached to them Jesus and the resurrection (Acts 17:18). Although it was believed by most of the Jews, nevertheless, the whole sect of the Sadducees denied it. But the resurrection of Jesus Christ put it out of dispute.

III. THE IMPORTANCE OF THE POWER OF CHRIST'S RESURRECTION.

A. The Explanation of the Power of the Resurrection.

It is to be raised from the death of sin to a life of righteousness and true holiness by the operation of the Holy Spirit. The resurrection of Christ's body Paul was satisfied would avail him nothing unless he experienced its power in raising his dead soul. One of the chief ends of our Lord's rising from the dead was to enter heaven as our representative and to send down the Holy Spirit to apply that redemption He had finished on the cross to our hearts by working an entire change in them.

B. The Appropriation of the Power of the Resurrection.

"He that liveth and believeth in Me shall live" (John 11:25). "By grace are ye saved through faith" (Ephesians 2:8). Believe and you shall live in Christ and Christ in you. By this faith we are not to understand a dead speculative faith, an intellectual faith only; but a living principle wrought in the heart by the powerful operation of the Holy Spirit, a faith that will enable us to overcome the world and forsake all in affection for Jesus Christ.

C. The Results of the Power of the Resurrection in the Life of the Believer.

Says the apostle, "being made conformable to His death" (verse 11); thereby implying that we cannot know the power of Christ's resurrection unless we are made conformable to Him in His death. If we can reconcile light and darkness, heaven and hell, then we may hope to know the power of Christ's resurrection without dying to ourselves and the world. There is such an opposition between the spirit of this world and the Spirit of Christ that he who will be at friendship with the one must be at enmity with the other.

CONCLUSION

Oh, the depth of the riches and excellency of Christianity! Well might the great apostle Paul count all things but dung and dross for the excellency of the knowledge of it. Well might he desire so ardently to know Jesus and the power of His resurrection. For even on this side of eternity it raises us above the world and makes us to sit in heavenly places in Christ Jesus. Oh, that we were all like-minded; that we felt the power of Christ's resurrection as the great company of worthies in Hebrews 11.

George Whitefield

SERMON THIRTY-TWO

INTERCESSION, THE DUTY OF EVERY CHRISTIAN

Brethren, pray for us.
—I THESSALONIANS 5:25

IF WE ENQUIRE why there is so little love amongst Christians, we shall find our answer largely in the neglect or superficial performance of intercessory prayer—imploring the divine grace and mercy in the behalf of others. Some neglect this duty because they seldom pray for themselves or are so selfish in their prayers that they do not enlarge their petitions for the welfare of their fellow Christians and others as they ought.

I. THE CHRISTIAN'S RESPONSIBILITY IN RELATION TO INTERCESSORY PRAYER.

A. The Universality of Prayer.

1. It is present among all mankind. Prayer is a duty founded upon natural religion; the heathen never neglect it, although many Christian heathen amongst us do.

2. It is an essential part of Christianity. It is so essential to Christianity that you might as reasonably expect to find a living man without breath as a true Christian without the spirit of prayer and supplication. In the heart of every true believer there is a heavenly tendency which draws him to converse with God.

B. The Reasons for Prayer.

1. Personal. A sense of their own weakness and of Christ's fulness will not let them rest from crying day and night to their Almighty Redeemer. Thus earnest and importunate are all sincere Christians in praying for themselves.

2. Intercession. Whereas, were the love of God shed abroad in our hearts and we loved our neighbor in the same manner that Christ loves us, we would be as importunate for their spiritual and temporal welfare as for our own.

II. THE SUBJECTS OF THE INTERCESSORY PRAYER.

A. All Men.

"I exhort therefore," says the apostle, "that first of all, supplications, prayers, intercessions, and giving of thanks be made for all men" (I Timothy 2:1). For as God's mercy is over all His works, as Christ died to redeem a people out of all nations; so we should pray that "all men may come to a knowledge of the truth, and be saved" (I Timothy 2:4).

B. Rulers of Nations.

Next to praying for all men we should pray for rulers, in order that we may lead quiet lives in all godliness and honesty (I Timothy 2:2). If we consider the heavy burden of government and how much the welfare of any people depends on the zeal and godly conduct of the rulers, the difficulties and temptations to which they are exposed, we shall not only pity but pray for them.

C. The Ministers of the Gospel.

You ought especially to pray for those whom "the Holy Spirit has made overseers over you." This is what the apostle Paul begs again and again of the churches to whom he writes. He says in the text, "Brethren, pray for us"; and again, in his epistle to the Ephesians, "praying always with all prayer and supplication for me, that I may open my mouth boldly, to make known the mystery of the Gospel" (Ephesians 4:18–19).

D. Our Friends.

Our friends claim a place in our intercessions. We should not be content with praying in general terms for them, but we should suit our prayers to their particular circumstances. We have many instances in Scripture of the success of such intercessory prayer; but none more remarkable than that of Abraham's servant who prayed in a most particular manner in behalf of Isaac, and his intercession was answered (Genesis 24).

E. Our Enemies.

As we ought to intercede for our friends, so in like manner must we also pray for our enemies. "Bless them that curse you, and pray for them which despitefully use you, and persecute you" (Matthew 5:44). These commands of the Lord Jesus were enforced in the strongest manner by His own example, as for instance, His prayer on the cross, "Father, forgive them, for they know not what they do" (Luke 23:34).

F. The Afflicted.

We should intercede for all who are afflicted in mind or body, for all who desire and stand in need of our prayers and for all who do not pray for themselves. And oh! That all believers would set apart some time every day for the due performance of this most necessary duty.

III. THE INCENTIVES TO INTERCESSORY PRAYER.

A. It Will Increase Our Love to One Another.

He who daily intercedes at the throne of grace for all mankind will in a short time be filled with love and charity to all. Envy, malice, and such like hellish tempers can never long harbor in a gracious intercessor's breast; but he will be filled with joy, peace, meekness, long-suffering and all of the other graces of the Holy Spirit. He will rejoice with those who do rejoice and weep with those who weep.

B. It Is Efficacious.

Consider the many instances in Holy Scripture of the power and efficacy of intercessory prayer. It has stopped plagues, it has opened and shut heaven, and it has frequently turned away God's fury from His people. Abraham's intercession freed Abimelech's house of the disease which God had sent amongst them. When Daniel interceded for the Lord's inheritance, how quickly was an angel dispatched to tell him that his prayer was heard.

C. It Is Probably the Frequent Employment of Glorified Saints.

Although the glorified saints are delivered from the burden of the flesh and restored to the glorious liberty of the sons of God, yet their happiness cannot be perfectly consummated until the resurrection. Therefore we cannot but think they are often importunate in beseeching our Heavenly Father shortly to accomplish the number of His elect and to hasten His kingdom. Shall not also we who are on earth be often exercised in this divine employ?

D. It Is the Unceasing Employment of the Glorified Christ.

To provoke you to this great work and labor of love, remember that it is the never ceasing employment of the holy and highly exalted Christ who sits at God's right hand to make continual intercession for us. So that he who is constantly employed in interceding for others is doing that on earth which the eternal Son of God is always doing in heaven.

CONCLUSION

And now brethren, what shall I say more, since you are taught of Jesus Christ to abound in love and in this good work of praying one for another. Although ever so humble and as poor as Lazarus, you will then become benefactors to all mankind; thousands and twenty times ten thousands will then be blessed for your sakes.

George Whitefield

SERMON THIRTY-THREE

PERSECUTION, EVERY CHRISTIAN'S LOT

Yea, and all that will live godly in Christ Jesus,
shall suffer persecution.
—II TIMOTHY 3:12

WHEN our Lord Jesus was pleased to take upon Himself the form of a servant and go about preaching the kingdom of God, He took all opportunities to forewarn His disciples of the many distresses, afflictions, and persecutions they must expect to endure for His name's sake. The apostle Paul, the author of the epistle, following the steps of His Master, takes particular care to warn young Timothy of the difficulties he must expect to meet within the course of his ministry.

I. THE MEANING OF LIVING GODLY IN CHRIST JESUS.

A. Such Persons Must Experience the New Birth.

To live godly in Christ Jesus supposes that we are made the righteousness of God in Christ, that we are born again and are made one with Christ by a living faith and a vital union even as Christ and the Father are one. They that are in Christ are new creatures; old things are passed away and all things are become new in their hearts. Their life is hid with Christ in God; their souls daily feed on the invisible realities of another world.

411

B. Such Persons Must Submit to God's Will

To live godly in Christ is to make the divine the sole principle of all our thoughts, words, and actions. Those who live godly in Christ may not so much be said to live as Christ to live in them. They are led by His Spirit and are willing to follow the Lamb whithersoever He leads them. They hear, know, and obey His voice. They habitually live to God and daily walk with God.

II. THE CLASSIFICATIONS OF PERSECUTION TO WHICH THE GODLY ARE EXPOSED.

A. The Persecution of the Heart.

The Pharisees hated and persecuted our Lord long before they laid hold of Him: and He mentions being inwardly hated of men as one kind of persecution which His disciples were to undergo. This heart enmity is the root of all other kinds of persecution and is in some degree or other to be found in the soul of every unregenerate man. Many are guilty of this persecution who never have it in their power to persecute in any other way.

B. The Persecution of the Tongue.

Many, I suppose, think it no harm to shoot out arrows, even bitter words, against the disciples of the Lord. However they may esteem it, in God's account evil speaking is a high degree of persecution. Thus Ishmael's mocking Isaac in the Old Testament is termed persecuting him in the New Testament. It is a breach of the sixth commandment to slander anyone; but to slander the disciples of Christ because they are His disciples must be highly provoking in God's sight.

C. The Persecution of Deeds.

The third and last kind of persecution is that which expresses itself in actions; as when wicked men separate the children of God from their company, or expose them to church censures, or threaten and prohibit them from making an open profession of Christianity, or interdict ministers for preaching the Word; or when they call them into courts; or when they fine, imprison, or punish them by confiscation of goods, scouring, or death.

III. THE REASON WHY THE GODLY MUST EXPECT PERSECUTION.

A. Because Our Lord Taught It.

Our Lord says, "Blessed are they which are persecuted for righteousness's sake: for theirs is the kingdom of heaven" (Matthew 5:10). We are not blessed with an interest in the kingdom of heaven unless we are or have been persecuted for righteousness's sake. Our Lord employs three verses in this beatitude and only one in each of the others; not only to show that men are unwilling to believe it, but also the necessary consequence of it upon our being Christians.

B. Because Our Lord Experienced It.

Follow Him from the manger to the cross and see whether any persecution was like that which the Son of God underwent while here on earth. How was he hated by wicked men! How was He reviled, counted, and called a blasphemer, a wine bibber, a Samaritan, a devil! How was He stoned, thrust out of the synagogues, arraigned a deceiver of the people, a seditious and pestilent fellow, an enemy of Caesar and as such scourged, spit upon, condemned, and nailed to an accursed tree!

C. Because the Saints of All Ages Experience It.

How soon was Abel made a martyr for his religion and Isaac mocked by the son of the bond woman! Read the Acts of the Apostles and see how the Christians were threatened, stoned, imprisoned, scourged, and martyred! Examine church history in after ages and the experiences of saints now living and I am persuaded that everyone will concur with the apostles' statement, that "all who will live godly in Christ Jesus, shall suffer persecution."

D. Because of the Sinners' Enmity Against God.

Wicked men hate God and therefore cannot but hate those who are like Him. They hate to be reformed and therefore they must hate and persecute those who by a contrary behavior testify against them that their lives are evil. Pride of heart leads men to persecute Christ's servants. They dare not imitate, therefore they persecute. Christians are not of the world, but Christ has chosen them out of the world, therefore the world hates them.

413

E. Because the Godly Need It.

If we have not all manner of evil spoken of us, how can we know whether we love contempt and seek only that honor which comes from above? If we have not persecution, how can our passive graces be kept in exercise? How can many Christian precepts be put into practice? How can we love, pray for, and do good to those who despitefully use us? How can we overcome evil with good? How can we love God better than life itself?

CONCLUSION

Not all are persecuted in a like degree, yet all Christians will find by their own experience that whether they act in a private or public capacity they must in some degree or other suffer persecution.

Not all who are persecuted are real Christians; for many sometimes suffer and are persecuted on other accounts than for righteousness's sake. The great question is, whether you are ever presecuted for living godly. If not, let the text sound an alarm in your ears and sink deep into your hearts.

George Whitefield

SOUL PROSPERITY

Beloved, I wish above all things that thou mayest prosper,
and be in health, even as thy soul prospereth.
—III JOHN 2

I AM SURE that there are some that if it were put to their choice had rather know that their soul prospers than to have $50,000 bequeathed to them. The great question is how shall I know that my soul prospers. Therefore, it will not be unprofitable to lay down some marks whereby we may know whether our souls are prospering or not.

I. PRAYER IS A MARK OF SOUL PROSPERITY.

A. Its Necessity.

1. The testimony of godly men. John Bunyan said, if we are prayerless, we are Christless. None of God's people come into the world stillborn. The commentator Burket agrees: "Come into the world stillborn! What language is that in a preacher's mouth?"

2. The testimony of Scripture. "I will pour out a Spirit of grace and supplication," says the Lord; and I will venture to say, if the Spirit of grace resides in the heart, the Spirit of supplication will not be wanting.

B. Its Nature.

1. It is voluntary. Persons under their first love dare not go without God; they go to God, not as the formalist does, not for fear of going to hell or being condemned. A person that has just been brought to a liberty of the sons of God goes freely to his heavenly Father.

2. It is constrained by love. Did not you hearken unto God like a fond mother if her beloved child made but the least noise? You could no more keep from the presence of God than the loving mother from the presence of her dear child. If your soul prospers, this connection between you and God will be kept up.

C. Its Outcome.

1. Faithfulness to the means of grace. If our souls prosper we will conscientiously attend on the means of grace. It is a most dreadful mark when persons think they are so high in grace that they thank God that they have no need of them. The various means of grace are intended for the nourishing of all God's children.

2. Love for the messengers of grace. If our soul prospers we shall be glad for a good plain country dish, as well as a fine garnished desert. If our souls prosper we shall be fond of the messengers as well as the message. We shall admire as much to hear a good ram's horn as a fine silver trumpet.

II. A GROWING KNOWLEDGE OF ONESELF IS A MARK OF SOUL PROSPERITY.

A. It Makes One More Sensible of His State.

1. His outward state. The knowledge of ourselves is the first thing God implants. "Lord let me know myself," was a prayer which one of the Church Fathers prayed. If you have high thoughts of yourselves you forget what poor silly creatures you are. Our first battle is with the outward man.

2. His inward state. As our souls prosper we shall be more and more sensible, not only of the outside, but of the inside. As we advance in the Christian life we have nearer views of the chambers of imagery that are in our hearts; and one day after another we find more and more abomination there.

B. It Makes One More Sensible of Christ's Glory.

1. The glory of the One who is our deliverer. Day by day we see more of the glory of Jesus Christ, the wonders of that Immanuel who daily delivers us from this body of sin and death.

2. The glory of the One who is our righteousness. I never knew a person in my life that diligently used the Bible and other means but as they improved in grace saw more and more of the necessity of depending upon a better righteousness than their own. If we grow in grace the Spirit of God leads us out of self and causes us to flee more and more to that glorious and complete righteousness that Jesus Christ wrought out.

C. It Makes One More Sensible to God's Grace.

The more your souls prosper, the more you will see of the freeness and distinguishing nature of God's grace, that all is of grace. We all naturally depend on ourselves. Therefore young Christians often say, "We have found the Messiah," whereas later, the believer learns that the Messiah had found him.

III. A VICTORIOUS LIFE IS A MARK OF SOUL PROSPERITY.

A. This Includes Good Works.

1. Good works do not constitute a basis for salvation. Perhaps some stranger will say, "I thought you were against good works." I tell you the truth, I am against good works; but do not run away before I finish my sentence; I am against good works being put in the room of Christ as the ground of our acceptance.

2. Good works are the result of salvation. An idle person tempts the devil to tempt him. In the state of paradise, Adam and Eve were to dress the garden and not to be idle there. After the fall they were to till the ground. A Christian should work hard that he may have to give to them who are in need.

B. This Includes a Growing Love.

1. The failure to love. There are some good souls, but very narrow souls, who are afraid of loving people who differ from them. Party spirits creep in among Christians. Whereas it was formerly said, "See how these Christians love one another!" now it may be said, "See how these Christians hate one another." People may boast of their wildfire zeal for God, until they cannot bear the sight of a person who differs from them.

2. The commendation of love. The apostle commends Gaius for his love. That was a glorious saying of a good Scottish woman, "Come in, ye blessed of the Lord, I have a house that will hold a hundred and a heart that will hold ten thousand." God give us such a heart. "He that dwelleth in love, dwelleth in God."

CONCLUSION

When I think of what God has done for me and how little I have done for Him, it makes me weep and cry, "Oh, my leanness." This makes me long to be in earnest for my Lord. What do you say? Have all of you the same desire?

George Whitefield

A FAITHFUL MINISTER'S PARTING BLESSING

The grace of our Lord Jesus Christ be with you all. Amen.
—REVELATION 22:21

IT IS very remarkable that the Old Testament ends with the word curse, whereby we are taught that the law made nothing perfect; but the New Testament ends otherwise, even with a precious blessing, that glorious grace put into the heart and dropped by the pen of the disciple whom Jesus loved. I can wish nothing better than that the words of our text may be fulfilled in our hearts.

I. THE INTERPRETATION OF GRACE.

A. It Is in General God's Favor to the World.

Perhaps there is not a word in the Bible that has a greater variety of interpretations than the word "grace." I do not intend to give you all of them. It will be enough in general to observe that the word signifies favor or may imply the general kindness that God bears to the world.

B. It Is Specifically the Work of the Holy Spirit in the Lives of God's People.

It signifies here the special grace of God communicated to His people; not only His favor displayed to us outwardly, but the work of God's Spirit imparted and conveyed inwardly and most powerfully to our souls. Grace takes in all that the Spirit of God does for a sinner from the moment he first draws his breath and brings him to Jesus Christ until He is pleased to call him by death.

II. THE DESCRIPTION OF GRACE.

A. It Is the Grace of Jesus Christ because He Procured It.

It is called "the grace of our Lord Jesus Christ" because He purchased it for us. If the Lord Jesus had not bought us with a price, even the price of His own blood, you and I would never have the grace of God manifested to our souls.

B. It Is the Grace of Jesus Christ because He Conveys It.

Moreover, this grace may be called "the grace of our Lord Jesus Christ" because it is conveyed into our hearts through Him. The Federal Head of His glorious body is a head of influence to those for whom He shed His blood. Thus His disciples said He was full of grace and truth and out of His fulness we receive grace upon grace.

III. THE CLASSIFICATION OF GRACE.

A. Restraining Grace.

If it were not for restraining grace God's people would be just as weak and wicked as other folks. The Son of God is always acting in a restraining way to His people; if it were not so, by the blindness of their understandings, the corruptions of their hearts and affections, together with the perverseness of their will; there is not a Christian that would not run away every day if Christ did not restrain him.

B. Convicting Grace.

There is convicting grace which acts every day and hour. It is a blessed thing to be under the Redeemer's convicting grace. I am not speaking of convicting grace that wounds before conversion and gives us a sense of sin and misery; I mean convicting grace that follows the believer from time to time.

C. Converting Grace.

We can no more turn our hearts than we can turn the world upside down. (1) It is the Redeemer by His Spirit that takes away the heart of stone and gives us a heart of flesh. (2) In the divine life, not to go forward is to go backward and it is one part of the work of the Holy Spirit to convert the soul from something that is wrong to something that is right.

D. Establishing Grace.

Many people have some religion, but they are not established; hence they are mere weather vanes turned about by every wind of doctrine. As believers grow in grace and in the knowledge of Christ they will be more settled, more confirmed, more manly, more firm, more steady.

E. Comforting Grace.

"In the multitude of my thoughts within me," says the Psalmist, "Thy comforts have refreshed my soul" (Psalm 94:19). We shall never be content or cheerful under sufferings but through the assistance of the Redeemer. In respect of parting from one another, what can comfort friends when separated but the Spirit of God? There are so many afflictions and trials that if it were not for the Lord Jesus Christ's comfortings no flesh could bear them.

F. Quickening Grace.

"The winter is past, the rain is over and gone, the flowers appear on the earth, the time of the singing of birds is come and the voice of the turtle is heard in our land, the fig tree putteth forth her green figs, and the vines with the tender grapes give a good smell" (Song of Solomon 2:12). What is all this but God's quickening grace, restoring the believer to his blessed joy?

IV. THE MINISTRATIONS OF GRACE.

A. In Prayer.

The grace of our Lord Jesus Christ is with His people in prayer. Who can pray without grace?

B. Bible Reading.

What profit will it be to us to read the Scriptures without the grace of God? Jesus Christ must open our minds to understand the Word of God, and the Spirit of God must take the things of Christ and show them to us.

C. In Providence.

The people of God see Him in His providence; the very hairs of their heads are all numbered and the grace of God is with them in every affair of life.

D. In Everyday Life.

The grace of God is with His people in the common business of life. We preach that the grace of God may attend men in their businesses and professions, and woe be to those persons who do not take the grace of God with them.

E. In Sickness and Death.

The grace of our Lord Jesus Christ is with His people when sick and dying. O my dear souls, what shall we do when death comes? What a mercy it is that we have a good Master to take us through that time. As another has said, "Do not fear, Jesus Christ will carry you safely through the dark valley of the shadow of death."

CONCLUSION

May the grace of God be with every unconverted soul. What will you do with the favor of man if you have not the grace of God? If you have the grace of God the Lord grant you more grace. Grace, mercy, and peace be multiplied to all of you.